ACCOUNTING INFORMATION DISCLOSURE AND COLLECTIVE BARGAINING

Accounting Information Disclosure and Collective Bargaining

B. J. FOLEY

Lecturer in Economics
University of Hull

and

K.T. MAUNDERS

Professor of Business Finance and Accounting
University of Leeds

HOLMES & MEIER PUBLISHERS, INC.
IMPORT DIVISION
30 Irving Place, New York, N.Y. 10003

© B. J. Foley and K. T. Maunders 1977

First edition 1977
Reprinted 1979

Published by
THE MACMILLAN PRESS LTD
London and Basingstoke
Associated companies in Delhi
Dublin Hong Kong Johannesburg Lagos Melbourne
New York Singapore Tokyo

ISBN 0 333 16693 0

Printed in Great Britain by
UNWIN BROTHERS LTD
Woking and London

Contents

Preface

As indicated by its title, this book is concerned with the impact of accounting information on collective bargaining. We take accounting to be 'the process of identifying, measuring and communicating economic information to permit informed judgements and decisions by users of the information' [1, p. 1]. It follows that 'accounting information' is all information which may be relevant to economic decision making. Whilst this may clearly encompass quantitative financial information of the type commonly associated with accounting reports such as balance sheets and profit and loss accounts, it also covers information of a non-financial nature insofar as this may be relevant to decision making.

The identification of what information is indeed relevant in a particular decision-making context has been the subject of much recent accounting research, especially in relation to the needs of investors [2], [3]. It was, in fact, a consciousness of the relative neglect of the needs of other users of accounting information which first prompted the present authors to begin the research which led to this book. Unlike investment decision making, however, which already had strong links with accounting as a teaching and research field, the present subject matter required an integration of two disciplines which have had little academic or professional interface in the past – accounting and industrial relations.

We expect, therefore, that, like each of the authors initially, most readers will be unfamiliar with at least one of the underlying disciplines involved. Nevertheless, readers with prior accounting experience and/or education should find the material of the book relatively self-contained, at least as far as Chapter 6. For a full appreciation of Chapter 6 some comparative knowledge of modern accounting theory is probably desirable. Because of its specific relevance, we recommend Revsine [3] for this purpose.

For those readers who are not accounting specialists a plethora of books exist on 'accounting for the non-accountant', a dip into any one of which should be sufficient to decipher the accounting terminology used as far as Chapter 6. For Chapter 6, we again recommend the book by Revsine [3] which includes a good introduction to and critique of the methodology of modern accounting theory.

This book then is intended to serve a variety of readerships, although we should expect the material to be of particular interest to students on degree level courses in accounting or industrial relations/labour economics, practitioners in the same fields (both management and union based), and fellow academics.

Chapter 1 describes the legislative background to information disclosure in collective bargaining and compares this as between the U.K., the U.S.A. and certain European countries.

Chapter 2 examines the arguments which have been put forward for and against the disclosure of information *in general*.

Chapter 3 then looks at a particular issue raised in Chapter 2 – the possible macro-economic relationship between the financial results of employers and wage and earnings levels. Particular attention is focused on the question of whether there is empirical support for the thesis that the declaration of increased profits may lead to increased labour costs and cost led inflation.

Chapter 4 surveys the literature of labour economics and industrial relations for collective bargaining models from which predictions can be made about the effects of information disclosure on bargaining outcomes. The results of some empirical research into the effects of information on particular bargaining outcomes are also examined.

Chapter 5 discusses the practical background to the use of information by both sides in company level bargaining. Properties of information actually used are examined, together with arguments for and against the disclosure of *specific* types of information.

Chapter 6 offers some preliminary analysis on a range of issues which the disclosure of information in collective bargaining raises for accounting theory and practice.

Chapter 7 is also concerned with identifying and making general comments on some possible problem areas – in this case the implications of a prediction of substantially increased disclosure in the future for certain interested groups.

As a result of legislation, in both the U.K. and U.S.A. union bargainers now constitute an *effective* demand for company accounting information. In view of this, the objectives of this book can be categorised as:

(1) summarising the current 'state of the art' with respect to the problem of identifying what union representatives' needs *are*; and

(2) bringing together practical and theoretical material which may be useful in taking decisions on what *should be* disclosed.

A root and branch approach to the identification of what *should be* disclosed requires the assistance of a logically sound, empirically verified model of the bargaining process by means of which the relationship between information inputs and bargaining actions could be predicted. With such a model the expected costs and benefits of disclosure could be quantified and disclosure decisions 'optimised'. Unfortunately, as will be seen herein, no such model yet exists. A third objective therefore is:

(3) to draw the attention of potential researchers to the many gaps in knowledge which need to be filled if disclosure decisions are to be more nearly 'optimised'.

It needs to be made clear, however, that the material of this book does not form a complete analytical structure for evaluating disclosure decisions. We do not ourselves propose any new model of the bargaining process herein – our research is at a stage where we feel this would be presumptuous.

Instead, recognising the need for people to take decisions *now* on what should be disclosed, we have brought together material which we feel represents the best assistance which can be offered at this stage. Thus the book will, we hope, at least enable decision makers to identify more easily the sources and nature of costs and benefits associated with information disclosure. The relative importance of these will still need evaluating in terms of the specific circumstances which apply. We do however, offer certain fairly definite conclusions about the nature of the necessary evaluation process (see Chapters 4 and 7).

We should like to thank the Nuffield Foundation for financing our early work with trade unions – the results of which contributed substantially to Chapter 5.

Thanks also, for the gargantuan task of deciphering and typing, must go to Mrs V. Wilson, Mr J. E. Price and the secretarial staff at Hull.

Our colleagues at Hull and Lancaster have, wittingly and unwittingly, contributed towards any academic merit the finished product may have. We alone are responsible for the defects.

Finally, for the fact that the book was completed at all we owe a great debt to the ever-persistent pressure (encouragement?) from our wives, Julie and Pauline. The fact that it was delayed, on the other hand, owes something to the activities of Millie and Timothy James.

K. T. Maunders
University of Lancaster
B. J. Foley
University of Hull

February 1976

REFERENCES

1 American Accounting Association, *A Statement of Basic Accounting Theory* (Evanston, Ill.. author, 1966).
2 N. J. Gonedes, *Accounting for Common Stockholders: An Eclectic Decision Making and Motivational Foundation* (Austin, Texas: University of Texas, 1971).
3 L. Revsine, *Replacement Cost Accounting* (Englewood Cliffs, N.J. Prentice-Hall, 1973).

1 The Legislative Background: Some International Comparisons

Unlike their counterparts in other developed economies, trade unions and employers in the United Kingdom have traditionally concentrated upon and developed collective bargaining at a national level. In such circumstances, i.e. where industry-wide negotiations have been either the rule or the ultimate objective, interest in the fortunes of any single company is obviously fairly limited. As a consequence of this historical bias, pressure from the *official* union movement for a general policy of company disclosure has only really built up strongly in the last decade. This pressure is, in turn, partly attributable to the emergence of shop-floor, plant or domestic bargaining which has been a growing feature of U.K. industrial relations over the past 25 years. Other countries with different systems of industrial relations, e.g. those where company bargaining has been prevalent, or those which have established formal structures at company or plant level, have in contrast been dealing with the disclosure issue for a much longer period.

The purpose of this chapter is twofold: first we shall look at some international experience in the practice of disclosure – this is important insofar as such practice may influence policy by example, as has certainly been true of American labour law in the case of the U.K.,[1] or even directly, where European developments may affect the legislation of member states of the E.E.C.; secondly, we shall review critically recently proposed or enacted statutes which deal with disclosure of company information to trade unions and/or employees as they relate specifically to the United Kingdom.

(A) THE U.S.A.

Collective bargaining in the United States has generally been regarded as relatively decentralised, operating primarily at company, rather than industry level.[2] Unions have traditionally tended to employ so-called 'whipsaw' tactics whereby they extract the best terms and conditions of employment possible in the more affluent companies; they then attempt, via parity arguments, to generalise the agreement throughout the industry [14, pp. 136–7]. European unions, on the other hand, appear more concerned to protect the least efficient employer by striking a bargain at industry level which will not endanger employment, and thereafter use less formal bargaining at plant level to supplement the industry agreement.[3] The tendency to concentrate on company agreements seems to have led American labour to be more conscious of ability to pay in bargaining tactics and, therefore, to request financial and economic data from companies[4] [1], [2]. Requests for information of this nature have, in fact, been made since the mid-1930s and, within the context of American legislation, have been relatively successful.

Industrial relations in the U.S.A. have been regulated for the past 40 years by two major Acts of Congress: the National Labor Relations Act 1935 (the so-called Wagner Act) and the Labor-Management Relations Act 1947 (the Taft-Hartley Act). Broadly speaking, the first Act extended the rights of trade unions and the scope of collective bargaining. The second Act, which subsumed much of the first within it, was slightly more restrictive of union activity attempting, in a sense, 'to restore the balance in collective bargaining' [15].

A third Act of Congress, the Landrum-Griffin Act, was passed in 1959, but this deals mainly with the internal affairs of unions and relations between union officers and the rank and file.[5] The administration and interpretation of these statutes is carried out, in the first instance, by the National Labor Relations Board (the N.L.R.B.).[6] Rulings by this body do not themselves carry the force of law and can be appealed against in the courts. In general, and particularly in the case of information disclosure however, the courts have tended to uphold decisions of the Board.

The right of trade union officials to obtain certain information from management is nowhere specifically stated in the above Acts. Rather, such rights have been inferred by the N.L.R.B. from a more general provision of the Acts: that it is an unfair labour practice for an employer to refuse to bargain *in good faith* about wages, hours and other conditions of employment.[7]

The procedure has thus been for unions who have been refused access to information in bargaining situations to file unfair labour practice charges against the relevant employer and obtain a ruling on the case from the N.L.R.B. This ruling might then, if not immediately accepted, be taken to the courts for testing. Decisions on such issues have in fact been made by the N.L.R.B. since 1936.[8] In this first case the Board took the view that the president of the company 'did no more than take refuge in the assertion that the respondent's financial condition was poor; he refused either to prove the statement or to permit independent verification. *This is not collective bargaining*'[9] [Italics added].

Since this early decision a number of cases have been dealt with involving issues of information disclosure. Three broad situations or categories may be distinguished:

(1) where a company refuses to provide data on business operations likely to affect the pay and status of employees;
(2) where a company refuses to supply wage data to unions for the purpose of negotiation;
(3) where a company refuses to support a contention of inability to pay the costs of a union's demands [16].

In general the N.L.R.B.'s decisions have been in favour of the unions in each of these types of situation. With regard to wage data, specific information on individual wage rates, incentive earnings, hours worked, job evaluation criteria, etc. has been ruled to be obtainable by the unions on request. Qualifications appear to extend only insofar as the union request is not shown to be motivated solely by a desire to harass management and that the employer does not need to go to unreasonable lengths to comply with the union's request. Thus, 'it would appear, at least in the light of the Board's interpretation of the limits on the duty of the employer to furnish wage data — as stated in the *Whitin Machine Works* case — that a union's request for wage data must not be used as an instrument of harassment against the employer; that the union's request must still evidence its "good faith" in the same; and, further, that arrangements for the compilation of the requested data must be reasonable, with apparent reference to volume, extent, time elements, and other factors relating to the procurement of such data' [16, p. 44].

On the subject of financial information the N.L.R.B., and subsequently the U.S. Court of Appeals, have ruled that an employer is guilty of 'lack of good faith in bargaining' if he argues inability to pay and then refuses to supply information to the union to substantiate his claims about the company's financial status. Trial examiners have recommended that firms be required to disclose such items as a breakdown of manufacturing costs including wages, raw materials, salaries for officials, depreciation, overheads and finally incoming and outgoing orders.[10]

The generally liberal interpretations of an employer's duty to provide information evident in earlier judgements were, however, somewhat restricted by decisions taken in the 1950s when it was indicated in two cases 'that the duty to inform trade unions need not extend to opening the books to inspection or changing established accounting practices'. The company merely had to 'substantiate' its counter-claims. As was pointed out in the *McLean* case, 'Either side may take a bargaining position regardless of the actual worth of a business and the success of its current operations . . . there is no right *per se* to review company books every time a claim of financial inability to meet economic demands is made, the requirements of collective bargaining may properly be met, in particular cases, by furnishing relevant information, data, financial reports or, perhaps, inspection of records depending on the circumstances.'[11]

This statement reinforced an earlier comment by the Court of Appeals when supporting an order by the N.L.R.B.: 'The Board's order does not require the respondent to produce any specific business books and records but information to "substantiate" its position in "bargaining with the union". As we interpret this, the requirement of disclosure will be met if the respondent produces whatever relevant information it has to indicate whether it can or cannot afford to comply with the union's demands.'[12]

Secondly, if an employer refused to provide a specific financial statement, such as a quarterly or half-yearly report, then this need not be interpreted as an example of bad faith, i.e. if the company did not normally prepare such statements then it would not be obliged to change its normal accounting practices to accede to a union's request.[13]

Although the limits on disclosure have thus been drawn somewhat more tightly, there has been considerable antagonism to the N.L.R.B.'s general posture on disclosure: 'Most American employers object strongly, on the grounds that it allows unions to pry into an employer's internal affairs, thus giving unions an unfair bargaining advantage, and makes available to a union which bargains with many employers information that might adversely affect the competitive position of one or more of the companies with which the union deals' [13, p. 92].

The American attitude founded as it is on case law and precedent is obviously very flexible in that decisions made by one court may be overturned, reinterpreted or limited by a later decision of the same or other courts. One would, therefore, quite naturally expect the line on information disclosure to be shifted back and forth according to the details of specific cases.

Given the prevailing philosophy of business unionism in the United

States, the issue of disclosure is regarded, fairly strictly, as a problem in collective bargaining; it is to trade union negotiators that such disclosure applies and not to works councils, joint consultative bodies or other non-union employee representatives. In Europe, on the other hand, the picture is considerably more confused, partly because of the overlapping nature of employee representation and partly because of continuing discussions about the most effective means of producing greater industrial democracy.

(B) EUROPEAN ATTITUDES

The European approach to the question of disclosure of company information is to see it as part of the development of industrial democracy and worker participation. Most continental European countries have, in fact, for many years accepted the general philosophy of worker participation in management and have established, via legislation, a set of formal institutions through which this process may be implemented.

Unlike the U.K. and the U.S.A. where trade union organisations and, therefore, collective bargaining have been strongly entrenched, for the past half century trade unions in Europe have relied more on the intervention of the State and legal pressures to advance employee interests. The balance of industrial relations, therefore, tends to be more heavily weighted toward formal workshop organisation in the guise of works councils.[14] It is argued by some authorities[15] that this approach is particularly suitable where unionism is weak, underdeveloped or badly divided; in such conditions unions may not have the leverage to represent employees adequately. Thus, for example, they may not be able to obtain recognition and bargaining rights and, therefore, supplementary institutions may be set up by statute.

The European model has been regarded with some suspicion by British trade unions as it is seen as a possible way in which employers may undermine the status and authority of the union, by-passing it by establishing direct relations with works councils composed of employees who may, or may not, be union members or representatives. Similar suspicions have, of course, been entertained by certain European unions: 'Plant egoism describes a heightened feeling of solidarity between council and management which unions fear may ultimately lead to the formation of "yellow" or "company" unions (or in any case may weaken the cohesion and combativeness of the union)' [22, p. 159].

There is, thus, a major division between those who see the interests of employees as operating only through the trade union and those who are against exclusive reliance on this particular channel of representation. That there is room for compromise, however, is indicated by attitudes toward the question of information disclosure. Thus, for example, in Belgium works councils were recently granted legal right to an extensive range of company level information; partly as a result of this, the socialist Fédération Générale du Travail Belgique (F.G.T.B.), which consistently opposed worker participation via 'co-determination, co-decision, or any other form of integration' now favours 'the continuation of the works council system, largely because of the company information they receive through this channel' [4, p. 87]. Similarly, when one looks at the German system, although only 30 % of the labour force are members of unions federated to the D.G.B. (the equivalent of the T.U.C.), 'the present level of union membership among works councillors is estimated to be about 80 %' [4, p. 27]. In industries characterised by a high level of unionisation works councils may quite often be composed almost entirely of union members. In these circumstances, therefore, certain legal rights enjoyed by works councils such as, for example, the right to a considerable range of company information, would *de facto* become available to trade unions also.

We shall be looking at the German and Belgian cases further below. Meanwhile, these two examples serve to show that the conflicting views on worker representation may be reconciled because the works council system can sometimes further the purposes of trade unions by acting as a vehicle for obtaining company information.

Access to more information on a company's operations may be gained by unions and/or other employee representatives within the E.E.C. if certain proposals put forward by the Economic Commission are adopted throughout the Community. These proposals are embodied in:

(a) the statute on the European company;
(b) the draft Fifth Directive on Company Law.

The first of these was put to the Council of Ministers in June 1970 and constituted a set of proposals which would, if adopted by member countries, provide a legal framework for companies which have plants or enterprises operating trans-nationally throughout the Community. The aim of the statute is therefore to transcend the different company laws which apply in member states. The proposal is by no means operational yet and will remain the subject of continuing discussion, but it is hoped that in the long term as firms develop Community-wide interests they will find it advantageous to register as Euro-companies and not merely be subject to registration in each of the individual countries where they operate. The ability to opt for Euro-company status may thus facilitate mergers, joint holding companies and joint subsidiaries.

Company information would become available to employee representatives in this new type of supra-national organisation via two channels:

(i) the supervisory board;

(ii) the works council or equivalent structure.

The statute envisages the establishment of a two-tier board structure. Day to day management would be the responsibility of a management board, but overall control would be vested in a supervisory board. This board would comprise both shareholders and employee representatives. The latter would constitute at least one third of total membership and they would be elected by nationally-based employee representative bodies.

The controlling function of the board extends in three directions: first, it has the right to appoint the management board and to choose the chairman; second, it can authorise or refuse permission for important changes in the organisation, namely, mergers, 'substantial' closures or extensions, and 'substantial' structural alterations within the company; third, the supervisory board has certain rights to information about the undertaking. These information rights are comprehensive as to subject area: as a matter of routine the board will receive quarterly progress reports, draft accounts and communications on 'all matters of importance' from the management; perhaps more significantly, however, special reports and documentation of any kind will be available on request. Although employee representatives would apparently have unlimited access to company information, they may be restricted in their right to communicate certain types of 'confidential' information to their constituents as such data is not to be passed outside the board. Thus, '*all* members of the supervisory board will be required "to have regard for the interests of the company and of its personnel and to exercise discretion in respect to confidential information concerning the company or its dependent companies" '[23, p. 44]. The definition of what is or is not confidential will clearly be crucial here.

The second channel through which more company information would become available under the statute is the European Works Council. It was originally envisaged that each separate establishment of the company would have its own works council set up under respective national laws. These would, in turn, elect in proportion to their size, employee representatives to the European Works Council.[16] This body would then enjoy three rights or powers: consent, consultation and information.

The management board would have to seek the *consent* of the council when deciding the criteria which will govern recruitment, dismissal and promotion, safety and health regulations and the introduction of vocational training. Certain wage issues also require consent, e.g. overall principles and methods of payment, normal working hours and the timing of holidays. *Consultation* with the works council is prescribed for decisions regarding the operation of the payment system and job evaluation schemes, while the supervisory board must similarly consult the council before deciding upon the major issues within its competence. Finally, the information rights of the council are, as usual, not specific but include regular access to the management board for 'discussions', the right to obtain a quarterly report on the company and data on future developments and investment.

It is important to note that, technically, the information obtained by employee representatives on the supervisory board and that received by the E.W.C. is not to be used in the process of negotiations. It is extremely difficult to see this restriction being effective in practice as the council and the board are likely to contain union members, or even lay-officials (i.e. shop stewards in the case of the U.K.), who could pass on to their negotiating colleagues, or use themselves, in the negotiating process, information gained in these other capacities. Thus in Germany, where the two-tier board structure already exists, the D.G.B. has claimed that the right to company information enjoyed by the supervisory board 'has been helpful in providing information for collective bargaining purposes' [23, p. 44].

The draft Fifth Directive on Company Law put before the Council of Ministers in September 1972 is similar to the Euro-company statute in providing for a two-tier board structure, but it may have much greater impact in that, if it were adopted, it would be mandatory on *all* public companies in the E.E.C. There are no provisions for the establishment of works councils and only in companies with more than 500 employees would there be a requirement for employee representation on the supervisory board. The Directive envisages appointment to the supervisory board as being decided by one of two general guidelines:

(a) Not less than one third of the members will be appointed by the workers, the remaining two thirds being appointees of the shareholders. Election to the supervisory board can be carried out by direct elections, with the electorate being all employees or simply employee representatives, but practices may differ in member states, e.g. works councils in Germany, recognised shop steward committees in the U.K.; or elections could even be conducted via the official union machinery.

(b) The second guideline (which has been called the Dutch system) allows for the co-option of the whole supervisory board including worker representatives. The general meeting of shareholders and employee representatives in the company retain the right to veto all the nominees to the board, either on grounds of lack of ability or on the question of 'balance of interest'. There is no specific ratio of employee/shareholder representatives. It is merely required that they should in some sense ensure a balance. Any objections raised would have to be sustained by an independent tribunal.

As yet, it remains unclear which employee representatives would in fact employ the power of the veto, but presumably this could again be left to the discretion of member countries.

The powers and rights of the supervisory board differ slightly from those laid down in the Euro-company statute: the Fifth Directive gives the board the right to appoint the personnel 'director' on the management board, but *not* to appoint the chairman. Perhaps more important from our point of view, however, is that the Directive would expand the board's information rights as it would allow only *one-third* of the supervisory board to 'obtain for itself, or a delegate member or expert, all information and relevant documents to undertake all necessary investigations' [4, p. 10]. Obviously this provision would considerably extend the ability of employee representatives, acting in concert, to ferret out and evaluate information in whatever area is thought desirable.

The implication of both these major proposals seems to be clear for the question of information disclosure: if the supervisory function of the top-level board or the consultative function of the E.W.C. are to work effectively, they will require data relating not only to the previous and current performance of the undertaking, but also to its plans and expectations. To expect this type of information to remain outside the realm of collective bargaining would appear extremely optimistic, particularly in the case of the U.K., and bearing in mind the comments made by the D.G.B. referred to earlier.

In this latter respect it may be instructive to investigate the German approach as:

(1) the E.E.C. proposals mirror the German system fairly closely;[17] and

(2) prior to the Works Constitution Act 1972, there had been criticism

of the type of information made available to worker representatives in Germany; as a result of these criticisms information rights of works councils have been extended.

(C) WEST GERMANY

The German system of *Mitbestimmung* or co-determination first came into being in 1951 in the coal and steel industries. This differed in two significant respects from the Works Constitution Act 1952, which otherwise generalised the notion of worker participation on supervisory boards and works councils.[18] The supervisory boards of coal and steel companies comprise an *equal* number of representatives and shareholders, with a 'neutral' member chosen by both sides. The workers' side is a mixture of employee and trade union representatives. Also one member of the management board is nominated or simply accepted by the trade union. He is usually the labour director and is responsible for industrial relations problems.

The 1952 Act extended worker representation into the internal management of the German corporation: under the Act, employees in companies with a labour force in excess of 500 could directly elect one third of the supervisory board on the basis of nominations made by the works council.[19] The representatives are elected by secret ballot and at least two of them must be employees of the company; any others may be non-employees including trade union officials.

The Works Constitution Act 1972 is a further addition to the lengthy history of legal intervention in German industrial relations. Although basically the structure remains fairly intact there have been certain extensions: wage earners and salaried employees are to be separately represented; a company council must be established in multi-plant enterprises; and if the company has over 100 employees it must form an economic committee of the works council to liaise with the management on economic affairs and to act as a channel through which management can pass economic information to the council.[20] Two further important provisions of the Act are that it is now possible to invite a trade union official on to the council, and the council's rights have been extended in the areas of co-determination, consultation and information. While the roles of union and works council are conceptually distinct there is evidence that the influence of the trade unions has been growing: as the T.U.C. points out, 'increasingly, the system has been dominated by trade union activity' [23, p. 15] and this is reflected in the high penetration of councils by union members and the fact that 'D.G.B.

nominees now effectively control 70 % of works councils' [23, p. 16].

There is an attempt not to trespass on the territory traditionally occupied by trade unions, insofar as: 'Works agreements shall not deal with remuneration and other conditions of employment that have been fixed by collective agreements',[21] except where the agreement has allowed for supplementary negotiations at plant level. In practice, however, there is a certain leeway which allows a form of plant bargaining to develop. Thus each enterprise has a wages committee consisting of equal numbers from management and the works council; this 'Lohn und Akkord Kommission' oversees the application of job evaluation systems, piece-work rates and overtime. It is possible to manipulate the job evaluation system to obtain a regrading of a particular group and in this way push up the wage level. The development of plant bargaining is limited by the simple fact that works councils cannot legally initiate strike action; their bargaining power, therefore, depends upon the degree of union support the council has at the outset.

The works council has traditionally been charged with four separate functions:
(1) general functions covering production, technical and financial information about the enterprise. Proposals arising out of such matters tended to be largely advisory;
(2) social functions dealing with welfare activities, training facilities, vacation schedules, accident prevention, employee housing, etc.;
(3) personnel functions: recruitment, transfer, job assignment, discipline and discharge;
(4) economic functions: work practices, plant layout, production programming and the introduction of new techniques.

Since the 1972 Works Constitution Act these functions of the council have been increased. Under 'economic' issues, for example, co-determination now extends to reduction or close-down of the company or subdivisions, transfer of the company or subdivisions thereof, mergers, important changes in organisation, business purposes or production facilities.[22]

The last three functions are strictly co-determinative in the sense that the permission of the works council is required before decisions on these matters take effect (in the absence of permission such issues require arbitration); the first is more in the nature of a co-operative, consultative function. Prior to the 1972 Act it was trenchantly criticised by one observer: 'The system has worked quite differently from the way the law prescribes . . . consultation on economic matters is often meaningless – that is, information is provided after the fact, and advice, when given, is disregarded' [21, p. 95].

In an effort to counter this type of criticism, the new Act proposes that the works council or the economic committee are informed on investment plans, personnel and manpower planning and a quarterly report on company affairs. In fact, to be more specific, information must be provided on stocks, production, planned changes in production and investment, plant-level changes in production objectives, planned cutbacks in production and any issues which could threaten the interests of employees. Further, to make these provisions more effective, if an employer does not provide adequate information within a satisfactory period of time, he may be reported to an arbitration tribunal which may impose a fine of 20,000 Deutschmarks.

Formally at least, employee representatives in West Germany have information rights considerably in advance of their British counterparts. This situation may not of course continue, given the dual combination of the Industry Act and the Employment Protection Act now in operation in the United Kingdom. The disclosure provisions of these statutes will be discussed further below [pp. 15–18] but at the time of writing it is too early to evaluate their practical impact. Despite access to more company information becoming more effective since the Works Constitution Act 1972, the situation is possibly less problematical for German employers: although the bargaining activities of works councils are evidently growing they certainly remain more limited than joint shop-steward committees which are their broad equivalents in the U.K.

There have of course been occasional difficulties in the German system as 'It has sometimes proved difficult to establish a demarcation line between a worker's activity as a member of the works council or staff council . . . and his function as the union shop steward, and there have even been occasional clashes in this connection' [18].

In a sense, the major advantage for German companies and the major difficulty for German trade unions is that legally, there is a gulf between the official movement operating at regional and national level and the works councils which are primarily responsible for workplace industrial relations. The councils, therefore, are outside the *direct* control of trade unions[23] and, furthermore, have very few industrial sanctions of their own with which to back up plant-level negotiations. It can be argued, therefore, that information given to works councils may result in 'responsibility without power', i.e. the council stands in danger of becoming identified with management policy and may not effectively represent employee interests. It has been suggested that 'Management generally considers that the works council is essential and conducive to effective management. There is very little feeling that management is hindered in its actions by the works council . . .' but, 'In order to use the works council for its own purposes management must meet some of its demands so that there is a trade-off in the situation as successes on the part of the works council strengthen its members at election times. Nevertheless the situation does give rise to difficulties because if the works council becomes increasingly integrated into the enterprise, then its policy is likely to be increasingly influenced by the policy of management' [4, p. 31].

It is precisely this type of situation which U.K. trade unions fear most in the works council structure, i.e. that employee representatives will become 'collaborationist' thus weakening union influence at plant level. German trade unions also strongly disapprove of this co-operative posture. In order to change the situation and to close the gulf between themselves and works councils, trade unions in Germany have been pushing to get more explicit union/council integration and co-operation written into the law. In this way they hope to establish control of wage negotiations down to company level. In the United Kingdom, as is well known, the power to negotiate at shop-floor level is taken for granted and, therefore, the giving of financial and economic information will not be passively accepted as a consultative procedure but is likely to produce a bargaining response, particularly if discussions of future plans and prospects are involved.

(D) THE UNITED KINGDOM

There have been several important legislative developments in the U.K. in recent years which relate to the disclosure of financial and economic information by companies. In fact, there are currently six Acts of Parliament requiring provision of information of one sort or another. Not all of these are concerned with employee or trade union needs and, therefore, we mention them very briefly for the sake of completeness. In addition, a number of White Papers and Bills have explored various proposals, and these, without necessarily becoming law, may have influenced the eventual legislation.

Until very recently, company disclosure was governed solely by the Companies Acts of 1948 and 1967 and the Contracts of Employment Act of 1963. The Companies Acts are obviously geared much more closely to the interests of shareholders and creditors rather than any other party. Nevertheless, a considerable volume of information is given about the performance of the undertaking in the annual report and accounts required by the legislation. Such information may, however, be of only limited use to trade unions and perhaps even less use to employees. Possibly the most significant criticism from the view point of unions and employees concerns the degree of aggregation and the fact that the information is invariably historical.

Beside the Companies Acts there are obligations imposed on the employer under the Contracts of Employment Act mentioned above. This requires the company to indicate to employees the terms and conditions of their employment, including such things as the rate or level of pay, hours of work, holiday entitlement and pay, the minimum length of notice to quit, sick schemes, pension arrangements (where they exist) and the nature of grievance procedures. This information will normally be given in writing to each individual and this will either detail the items mentioned or refer the employee to documentation relating to specific items. This statute seems necessary as a means of clarifying the nature of the employment relationship and giving employees certain minimum protections. It is of course precisely within the competence of trade unions to change these conditions via bargaining, or they may be unilaterally changed by management. Whichever occurs, such changes must be notified to employees. Extending this the 1970 Finance Act made approval of pension schemes for tax purposes conditional on every employee receiving written particulars of the scheme. Then, too, the Social Security Pensions Act passed in 1975 requires both employees and unions to be informed, and recognized trade unions to be consulted, if an employer elects to contract out of the Act.

The Health and Safety at Work Act 1974 makes it obligatory on employers to give full information about their safety and health policies and programmes, and it also places a duty on inspectors to pass on information about safety and health conditions at premises to which the Act applies.

The legislation so far discussed, while indicative of increasing pressure on companies to become 'open societies', is not necessarily central to our interest: instead, two further recent statutes, the Employment Protection Act 1975 [7] and the Industry Act 1975 [11] are of much greater concern as they directly relate to disclosure of company information which may be important to employees or trade unions for the purposes of collective bargaining.

THE EMPLOYMENT PROTECTION ACT

The clauses dealing with disclosure in this Act have their roots in the Labour Government's Industrial Relations Bill of 1970 and the Conservative Government's Industrial Relations Act 1971. *In Place of Strife* [12], the White Paper which preceded the Bill, gave a commitment to ensure a greater flow of information for bargaining purposes:

> If employee representatives are to participate with management on equal terms in the extension of collective bargaining and consultation at company or plant level, they will need adequate information to allow them to form an independent judgement on management proposals, policies and decisions . . .
>
> The Government proposes to go beyond the recommendations of the Royal Commission by including in the Industrial Relations Bill a provision to enable trade unions to obtain from employers certain sorts of information that are needed for negotiations. It will have detailed consultations on this proposal and will give full consideration to the safeguards needed to protect firm's 'commercial interests' [12, Clauses 47 and 48].

Although this Bill did not eventually reach the statute book, the commitment to provide information for bargaining purposes was carried over into the highly controversial Industrial Relations Act 1971 in virtually the same terms. Furthermore the authors of the Employment Protection Act seem simply to have taken the disclosure provisions of the Industrial Relations Act (see Sections 56 and 57), which themselves were extracted from the Industrial Relations Bill, and slotted them into the new statute. This comment applies to both the general duty to disclose and the qualifications to this.

Essentially, the Act obliges the employer to disclose to trade unions:
(a) 'information without which the trade union representatives would to a material extent be impeded in carrying out . .. collective bargaining;
(b) information which it would be in accordance with good industrial relations practice that he should disclose to them for the purposes of collective bargaining' [sec. 17].

The exceptions to these general provisions constitute the following:
(a) 'any information, the disclosure of which would be against the interests of national security, or

(b) any information which he could not disclose without contravening a prohibition imposed by or under an enactment, or

(c) any information which has been communicated to the employer in confidence, or which the employer has otherwise obtained in consequence of the confidence reposed in him by another person, or

(d) any information relating specifically to an individual, unless he has consented to its being disclosed, or

(e) any information, the disclosure of which would cause substantial injury to the employer's undertaking for reasons other than its effect on collective bargaining, or

(f) information obtained by the employer for the purpose of bringing, prosecuting or defending any legal proceedings.'

Finally there are two further points of interest which appear to limit the general duty to disclose: an employer shall not be required

(a) 'to produce, or allow inspection of, any document (other than a document prepared for the purpose of conveying or confirming the information) or make a copy of, or extracts from any document, or

(b) to compile or assemble any information where the compilation or assembly would involve an amount of work or expenditure out of reasonable proportion to the value of the information in the conduct of collective bargaining.'

With respect to the last two points, they appear to be very close to current American practice, and the emphasis on 'materiality' and 'good industrial relations practice' are similar criteria to those used by the N.L.R.B. in the United States.

In the context of the Industrial Relations Act, the question of what precisely constituted 'good industrial relations practice' in the matter of disclosure was passed over to the former Commission on Industrial Relations for definition. The report of this body emerged in 1972 and met with very little enthusiasm on either side of industry [3], [8]. The interpretation of the 1971 Act would ultimately have been the responsibility of the National Industrial Relations Court and the question of what is meant by 'material impedence' to collective bargaining and the application of the exceptions would have resided with the Court. The repeal of the Industrial Relations Act in 1973, however, swept away the legal structures through which the disclosure provisions were to operate. Thanks also to the intransigent opposition to the whole Act by the trade union movement we do not have the benefit of even one test case as a precedent.

The Employment Protection Act, therefore, while retaining almost exactly the same clauses, established a slightly different set of procedures for their implementation. Thus, for example, a new body, the Advisory, Conciliation and Arbitration Service on whose council both employers and unions are represented, has issued a draft code of practice on disclosure which is to be taken into account in deciding what information should be made available [24]. The types of information which the code lists as presumptively relevant to collective bargaining are similar to the C.I.R.'s recommendations [3]. The A.C.A.S. list is, however, more extensive insofar as it includes reference to productivity data, work schedules, orders, market share and, perhaps more importantly in the area of finance, relevant cost structures, transfer prices, government financial assistance, intra-group loans and interest charged.

The procedure envisaged in the Act for dealing with an employer's refusal to disclose information again seems to be little different from that set out in the Industrial Relations Act: in the latter case, a refusal to disclose could be taken by a registered trade union to the National Industrial Relations Court. The Court could then make one or more of three orders:

(1) determining the rights of the union or the employer in the matter;
(2) directing the employer to discharge his duty by disclosing the information;
(3) authorising the presentation of a claim by the union to the Industrial Arbitration Board.

The latter body could then make an award which would be an implied term in the contract of employment of the employers concerned. This award could also be back-dated to the time when the employer was in breach of the disclosure provisions.

In the new Act the union may complain to the Central Arbitration Committee in the event of an employer refusing or failing to disclose. The complaint would then be referred to conciliation to be undertaken by the A.C.A.S. If conciliation fails the Central Arbitration Committee is to decide on the complaint and will make a declaration specifying:

(a) 'the information in respect of which the Committee finds the complaint is well-founded;
(b) the date on which the employer refused or failed to disclose . . . any of the information specified under (a);
(c) a period within which the employer ought to disclose [7, sec. 19(6)].

A further refusal at this stage may result in the trade union submitting a written claim that the information be included as part of the terms and conditions of employment for the group concerned. After a further meeting the C.A.C can direct that these terms and conditions, or others that it considers appropriate, shall have effect as part of the contract of employment.

It is clear that problems of conflict over disclosure are to be resolved primarily via moral suasion and conciliation.

Given the approach to disclosure adopted by the Employment Protection Act, there are two major points of criticism worth making:

(1) Many critics of the Industrial Relations Act felt that the list of exceptions contained in section 158 (1) were sufficiently widely drawn for any determined employer to refuse to disclose anything. Precisely the same criticism can be levelled at the present statute. In particular, three aspects of the Act might effectively emasculate the disclosure provisions:

    (a) the list of exceptions to the general duty; (sec. 18 (1))

    (b) the fact that the union will be unable to inspect *any* original documentation; (sec. 18 (2) (a)) and

    (c) the question of what amount of work or expenditure is reasonable in proportion to the value of the information (sec. 18 (2) (b)).

These appear to constitute effective channels for any employer to get around the legislation. This is particularly true of section 18 (2) (b), insofar as it is extremely difficult to define *ex ante* what the value of the information in collective bargaining will be.

(2) The second major point of criticism relates to the rather cumbersome and lengthy appeals procedure. Unless disputes are dealt with expeditiously they tend to produce frustration, particularly if the data or information sought is out of date when a declaration is finally made.

THE INDUSTRY ACT 1975

The Industry Act received the Royal Assent on 12 December 1975. Its provisions cover five major areas:

(a) the setting up of a National Enterprise Board with a set of miscellaneous rights, including the right to buy into or take over established, profitable companies in the private sector, to establish new manufacturing concerns, to give financial and managerial advice and to extend grants and loans to industry where necessary;

(b) it gives the Government powers to stop undesirable foreign takeovers of U.K. manufacturing companies;

(c) it expands the powers of the Industry Act 1972;

(d) it sets out the arrangements for voluntary 'planning agreements' to be concluded between the Government and major manufacturing companies;

(e) finally, it gives power to ministers to compel firms, whether or not they are entering into planning agreements, to disclose certain types of economic/financial information to the Government and to trade union representatives where thought desirable.

Our discussion will be confined to those aspects of the Act dealing with disclosure. We shall first discuss the Planning Agreements as these will apply to a relatively small range of companies, i.e. larger concerns in key sectors.

(A) PLANNING AGREEMENTS

The Act envisages a series of ongoing discussions between Government and major companies taking place on an annual basis and concluding with a signed agreement about strategic plans. The agreements are strictly voluntary and there are no sanctions or powers envisaged to induce reluctant companies to enter into the arrangements. In the event of an agreement being established, however, any promises of assistance will be binding upon the Government and not subject to change with shifts in overall economic policy. Theoretically the exercise is an attempt to reconcile macro-economic decision-making with micro-economic planning, so that each level benefits from knowledge of how the other operates, or plans to operate. The Government, therefore, will look for certain types of information from companies in return for certain *quid pro quos*, i.e. the State will provide help via grants and loans, support export programmes and find skilled workers where necessary. It will also provide information about its own short- and medium-term forecasts of inflation, G.D.P. and sectoral movements and an assessment of world trade and prospects in the major industrial countries. The information to be provided by the companies covers:

(1) overall strategy and longer-term objectives, but including 'quantification of the important changes in the envisaged balance of the company activities in the longer term and the broad implications for investment, productivity, employment, exports, and product and process development' [5, p. 9];

(2) specific aspects of company plans with details of U.K. sales, exports, investment, productivity, employment and training.[24] The way the planning agreement will tackle each of these items may be exemplified in the following:

A. With respect to U.K. sales the company is expected to divulge:
 (i) sales for each main product;
 (ii) market share;
 (iii) the basis of company forecasts and how they fit in to N.E.D.O. or trade association forecasts;
 (iv) the effect of government policy;
 (v) in the appropriate cases, the prospects for import substitution or saving.

B. Where investment is concerned, Government departments will concentrate on:
 (i) the level of investment, identifying major projects and the total investment by company division and major plants;
 (ii) investment in assisted areas;
 (iii) export-related or import-saving investment;
 (iv) data on investment per employee and any investment constraints.

The underlying emphasis throughout is on company plans, expectations and decision-making criteria.

The agreements, therefore, will obviously require considerable discussion of factors which, heretofore, have been regarded as within the confines of the company's management. This may at first sight seem a radical departure until one realises that these sorts of discussion were undertaken under the Industry Act 1972: section 4 of this Act says that companies requesting Government aid may have to submit to conditions imposed by the Industry Secretary: these may include examining the company's books. The major difference with the new Act is simply that these procedures are formalised into a Planning Agreement and any levels of aid agreed will be guaranteed and not arbitrarily cut off as Government policy might require.

Originally it was also envisaged that unions would be heavily involved in the system, e.g.:

19. Employees and their representatives will have a major interest in the issues covered by the Planning Agreements. The Government intend that the plans to be covered by an Agreement will be drawn up by management *in close consultation with trade union representatives from the firm*. The framing and updating of Agreements will thus involve a continuing discussion between the management and unions, and will constitute an important advance in the part to be played by industrial democracy in the planning of company strategy. The Government envisages that union representatives from companies, while not formally parties to Planning Agreements, would also take

part where they so wished, in consultations . . . with the Government.

20. If consultation is to be effective, *union representatives must be provided with all the necessary information relevant to the contents of Planning Agreements.* The Government will, therefore, require employers to disclose information of this kind, except where disclosure could seriously prejudice the company's commercial interests or would be contrary to the interests of national security [17, p. 5] [Italics added].

This initial view, with its emphasis on 'union representatives' having access to 'all the information' has, however, been considerably toned down and made nebulous. In its discussion document, the Government now simply states: 'Workers have a right to be informed and concerned in decisions affecting wider areas than pay and conditions, and the Government is convinced that the new climate which it is the aim of Planning Agreements to create will contribute to a greater spirit of co-operation between both sides of industry in the major areas of common interest' [5, p. 4]. Obviously this reduction in the role of union representatives will be regarded by management with relief, as it apparently restricts union access to sensitive or confidential data in the event of a company opting to involve itself in an Agreement. Holding union representatives at arm's length in this way, however, may forfeit one potential advantage which could otherwise have resulted: a Planning Agreement obviously has to take into account the future development of wages and salaries. By involving the unions in discussions prior to the signing it may have been possible to induce them to discuss their own wage strategy. If successful this would fix an important element in future uncertainty for the company and, ultimately, could have led to the emergence of longer-term wage agreements in the relevant firms. As the Planning Agreements are not compulsory there has been relatively little controversy regarding that particular aspect of the statute. The same cannot be said for those provisions which deal explicitly with disclosure of information to be required of manufacturing companies (secs. 27—31).

(B) DISCLOSURE

It would appear that companies making a 'significant contribution' to the U.K. manufacturing industry (i.e. those described in Orders III to XIX in the Standard Industrial Classification) may be required to divulge information to the Industry or Agriculture Minister and then to trade unions. The information may relate to the past or, more importantly, to some future period. Information or forecasts may be required on the following items: persons employed, capital expenditure, capital assets used, intended disposals and acquisitions, output and productivity, sales, capacity utilisation, R. & D. expenditure, etc. (sec. 29 (2) (5) (6)). Confidential information must nevertheless be given to the relevant Minister, but there are restrictions on passing on this type of information to unions and other Government departments. Thus, information or forecasts are not to be passed on if in the Minister's view it:

(1) is against the national interest;
(2) contravenes an existing statute;
(3) is given in confidence;
(4) would cause substantial injury to the company;
(5) would cause substantial injury to a substantial number of employees (sec. 30 (3) & (4)).

The Act also includes a set of penal sanctions to enforce disclosure to the Ministers or to union representatives. Similarly, prosecution and a fine may follow if a person makes a statement knowing it to be false or reckless in a material particular. Finally, in an attempt to ensure confidentiality, it is an indictable offence liable to a possible term of two years imprisonment, to disclose information of a confidential nature without consent.

Thus there are four remarkable features in Part IV of the Industry Act:

(1) the extremely wide discretion given to the relevant Minister to decide the type of information he requires, the companies to which an order may apply and whether or not to give the information to union representatives;
(2) the information may relate to the immediate past, but more problematically, it may relate to forecasts of a short- or long-term nature. The problem for most businessmen is simply the notorious difficulties involved in forecasting beyond the short run;
(3) the third aspect of this part of the Act is that the confidentiality strictures do not apply to information once given to trade unions: thus, businessmen fear that competitively sensitive information may be passed to competitors by union representatives – how far this fear is justifiable is discussed in Chapter 2;
(4) finally, the Act is not very specific about the purposes for which the information disclosed is to be used. Thus it may be used 'to form or

further national economic policies' and for 'consultations' between Government, employers and workers on the prospects for a particular sector or major companies in that sector (sec. 27 (1)).

Clearly, as in the case of the Planning Agreements, the data is to be used to clarify and reconcile macro- and micro-economic decision-making in an attempt to improve both. It may also be hoped that giving this information to union representatives will result in a better understanding of company problems and a willingness to become more deeply involved in solving them. It may well be of course that the fact that disclosure can be forced on companies under this part of the Act (and then be passed on to the unions) may make the Planning Agreements system more attractive, i.e. if one *has* to disclose anything, it might as well be in circumstances where Government financial assistance may be forthcoming, and 'consultation' with unions is the order of the day. The Planning Agreements, therefore, do not require back-up powers – in effect they will exist anyway.

This Act undoubtedly gives the Government power to 'open company books' much further than any previous legislation. It has been pointed out that this could damage a company's competitive position if civil servants, or more particularly, trade unions, pass on sensitive information. This argument is taken up at a more general level in the next chapter, but in the context of this Act a great deal will hinge on how the Minister interprets the 'substantial injury' clauses. It has also been argued that the Act will damage investment flows into the U.K. from abroad, e.g. 'Let us look at the effect on employment of companies which have investment to make in this country or elsewhere in Europe, because they want a base within the Common Market. Will they come here? Will they invest in this country? Will they invest in partnership schemes in Europe with British companies knowing that they have the choice between a non-British and a British partner, one of which carries with it total disclosure, and the other total confidentiality?' [10].

These questions are important, but they do rather overstate the case: we have already seen that some E.E.C. proposals and some European countries have in fact been in advance of the U.K. in certain disclosure areas. Thus, if we may briefly illustrate with yet a further example – Belgium: 'Under a Royal decree of November 1973 the nature and amount of financial and economic information that the employer is required to impart [to works councils] has been greatly extended, and is now among the most extensive in Europe' [4, p. 84].

The councils have the right to an enormous range of information, including such items as:

(iv) 'Competitive position . . . competitive possibilities; fundamental sales or purchasing agreements; government contracts; general information on the sales patterns, distribution channels and profit margins of the company's products; turnover; costs and selling prices by unit of production;

(v) productivity including production by number, volume and weight as well as value per man-hour and per head;

(vi) budget and calculation of costs, including sufficient information on the elements or structure of costs to make informed criticism of the evolution of costs, set out under cost-headings by products or group of products or department' [4, p. 172].

The list goes on to talk about 'the foreseeable evolution of sales, orders, the market, production, costs and cost prices, stocks, productivity and the numbers employed' [4, p. 172].

More information is available as of right, but this short list serves to show that the U.K. is by no means alone in expanding requirements for company disclosure. Some of the arguments for and against these developments will be examined in the next chapter.

NOTES

1 It can be argued that the Industrial Relations Act 1971 was to some extent modelled on American legislation – see Iserman [13].

2 For a discussion of recent American practice see Cullen [6].

3 Hence the emergence of the 'Earnings Gap'.

4 This particular style of bargaining may help to explain why 'profitability' shows up more strongly in econometric studies of wage determination in the U.S. compared to British studies – see Chapter 4.

5 A short but comprehensive review of U.S. labour law is provided by Gregory [9].

6 Charged with a role similar to the Industrial Relations Court under the former Industrial Relations Act 1971: the N.L.R.B. is not itself a Court.

7 Thus section 8 (d) of the Taft-Hartley Act defines the obligation to bargain collectively as follows: 'For the purposes of this section to bargain collectively is the performance of the mutual obligation of the employer and the representatives of the employees to meet at reasonable times and confer in good faith with respect to wages, hours, and other terms and conditions of employment, or the negotiation of an agreement, or any question thereunder . . .' 61 Stat. 142 (1947), 29 U.S.C. 158 (Supp. 1949).

8 Pioneer Pearl Button Co. (1 N.L.R.B. 837 1936) see Shanklin [19].

9 N.L.R.B. loc. cit.

10 Southern Saddlery Company (90 N.L.R.B. 1205, 1950) and The Jacobs Manufacturing Co. (94 N.L.R.B. 1214, 1951) enforced 196 F2d 680 (C.A.2 1952) cited in [20] and [19].

11 McLean-Arkansas Lumber Co. (109 N.L.R.B. 157, 1954) and Truitt Manufacturing Co. – F2d – (C.A.4 1955) den. enforcement to 110 N.L.R.B. no. 143, 1954.

12 Jacobs Manufacturing Co. cited in note 10.

13 McLean-Arkansas Lumber Co. cited in note 11.

14 A lucid discussion of the history of works councils with particular reference to France and Germany is provided by the same author in [21].

15 'Works councils were established in Germany and in other European nations when trade union organisation was weak and collective bargaining poorly developed' T.U.C. [23].

16 The accession of the U.K. has involved minor problems insofar as there are no legal requirements in this country to establish such councils, as in Germany, France, Italy Belgium and Holland. The nearest comparable institution is the joint consultative committee which is a voluntary body and has been in decline for some years. Nevertheless the statute covers this problem in allowing each country to decide its own system for electing councillors to the E.W.C. The T.U.C. has already suggested that these representatives and those elected to the supervisory board should be members of the relevant trade unions.

17 Doubtless this indicates the relative success of the German system of board structure and works councils. The fact that the U.K. entered the E.E.C. late meant that we could not bring our own brand of pragmatism and voluntarism to bear.

18 Works councils have been in existence in Germany for many years. See Sturmthal [22].

19 Under the Works Constitution Act 1972, Works Councils are to be established for industrial undertakings with as few as five employees; for agriculture and forestry concerns the limit is ten employees.

20 As this committee has no decision-making power it has been suggested that it is merely a means of limiting the number of people who obtain confidential information. Its membership is limited to between 4 and 7.

21 Works Constitution Act 1972 Section 77 (3).

22 A complete list is provided in [4].

23 The same can be argued for shop stewards and joint shop-steward committees in the U.K. but the latter do have considerably more bargaining leverage than seems to be the case where works councils are concerned.

24 These items will be required in the early phases. Certain other information may be required as general background in the first year, and then, may come further into the picture in later years, e.g. Finance, Industrial Relations, Consumer and Community interest, Product and Process development [5].

REFERENCES

1 A.F.L.-C.I.O., 'Financial Information in Collective Bargaining', *Collective Bargaining Report*, 3, no. 3 (Mar 1958).

2 O. Brubaker, L. Kirkland, W. Gomberg *et al.*, 'What Kind of Information Do Labor Unions Want in Financial Statements?', *Journal of Accountancy* (May 1949).

3 Commission on Industrial Relations, Report no. 31, *Disclosure of Information* (London: HMSO, 1972).

4 Commission on Industrial Relations, Study no. 4, *Worker Participation and Collective Bargaining in Europe* (London: HMSO, 1974).

5 *The Contents of a Planning Agreement*, A Discussion Document, Department of Industry (London, 1975).

6 D. E. Cullen, 'Recent Trends in Collective Bargaining in the United States', *International Labour Review*, 105, no. 6 (June 1972).

7 Employment Protection Act, 1975 (London: HMSO, 1975) ch. 71.

8 B. J. Foley and K. T. Maunders, 'The C.I.R. Report on Disclosure of Information: A Critique', *Industrial Relations Journal*, 4, no. 3 (Autumn 1973).

9 C. Gregory, 'Government Regulation or Control of Union Activities', in *Labor in a Changing America*, ed. William Haber (New York: Basic Books, 1966).

10 M. Heseltine, House of Commons Parliamentary Debates, *Weekly Hansard*, no. 989, 14–20 Feb 1975, col. 964 (London: HMSO, 1975).

11 The Industry Act 1975 London: HMSO, ch. 68.

12 *In Place of Strife: A Policy for Industrial Relations*, Cmnd. 3888 (London: HMSO, 1969).

13 T. R. Iserman, 'Labour Laws Anglo-American Style', *Management Today* (Mar 1972).

14 E. M. Kassalow, *Trade Unions and Industrial Relations: An International Comparison* (New York: Random House, 1969).

15 C. C. Killingsworth, *State Labor Relations Acts, A Study of Public Policy* (Chicago: University of Chicago Press, 1948).

16 M. J. Miller, 'Employers' Duty to Give Economic Data to Unions', *The Journal of Accountancy* (Jan 1956).

17 *The Regeneration of British Industry*, Department of Industry, Cmnd. 5710 (London: HMSO Aug 1974).

18 H. Reichel, 'Recent Trends in Collective Bargaining in the Federal Republic of Germany', *International Labour Review*, 104, no. 6 (Dec 1971).

19 J. E. Shanklin, 'The Employer's Duty to Supply Data for Collective Bargaining', *Monthly Labor Review* (Oct 1952).

20 H. L. Sherman jr., 'Employer's Obligation to Produce Data for Collective Bargaining', *Minnesota Law Review*, 35, no. 24 (1950).

21 A. F. Sturmthal, *Comparative Labor Movements* (Illinois: Wadsworth, 1972).

22 A. F. Sturmthal, *Workers Councils* (Cambridge, Mass.: Harvard University Press, 1964).

23 Trades Union Congress, *Industrial Democracy*, Interim Report by the T.U.C. General Council (London, 1973).

24 Advisory Conciliation and Arbitration Service, *Disclosure of Information to Trade Unions for Collective Bargaining*, Draft Code of Practice, (London, 1976).

2 The Disclosure Debate

We have seen in Chapter 1 that a considerable volume of legislation dealing with greater disclosure of company information has been proposed and enacted in most of the Western economies. In the U.K., for example, every major political party has accepted the principle of greater disclosure of financial and economic information to both employees and trade unions. [1] Sections of the business community have similarly displayed sufficient concern to suggest, as standard practice, certain disclosure proposals in advance of the law [23].

The main purpose of this chapter is to examine the arguments bearing upon the issue of disclosure as they have clearly been instrumental in producing the kind of behavioural and legislative changes referred to above. The chapter is, therefore, divided into two sections – in the first part we shall deal with the case *for* greater disclosure; in the second we shall take up some of the major objections.

(1) THE CASE FOR GREATER DISCLOSURE

Although those advocating disclosure do so from a number of different social and political standpoints their arguments can be organised round two distinct yet interrelated areas:
(a) those concerning disclosure directly to employees;
(b) those concerning disclosure to, in the first instance, officially recognised trade unions.
This distinction must be borne in mind throughout since there are considerable differences in the objectives of those favouring one or the other.

(A) DISCLOSURE TO EMPLOYEES

Four or five major arguments are adduced by those who advocate and support disclosure directly to employees. In the first place there are those individuals and groups, influenced to some extent by the 'human relations' approach to management, who view disclosure, in a rather utilitarian way, as a motivational phenomenon. On the basis of research findings by organisation theorists it is possible to argue that 'feedback of information' to employees will improve job performance via learning effects and also serve to increase motivation.[2]

The behavioural characteristics of control systems have constituted a highly controversial area in management accounting for some time [41] but one of the few clear-cut conclusions to emerge from related research concerns the influence of feedback: 'Harold J. Leavitt and R. A. H. Mueller, in a study of the effects of varying amounts of feedback found that performance improved as the quantity of feedback increased. They also observed that the absence of any feedback was accompanied by high hostility and low confidence' [18, pp. 89–90]. Similarly Herzberg, summarising the factors which produce a positive motivational response, included 'making periodic reports directly available to the worker' [30].

Whilst any efficient control system will provide some feedback of information to the individual about his immediate activities as a matter of standard practice, the arguments for doing this may be generalised to support the provision of further information as to the financial and economic performance of the department, the plant or the company since this may in turn produce some convergence, or rather congruence, of objectives between employees and the company as a whole.

There is no direct evidence to support this generalisation, although it is certainly plausible and accepted by large sections of management: the British Institute of Management in a survey of the objectives of providing financial information to employees conducted in 1957 found that almost 40 % of the 160 firms sampled gave as the major reason for disclosure 'identification of [employees'] interest with employer' [12].

One might well argue that the link between *company*-level information and the shop floor's effort is much too tenuous to produce greater motivation. A policy simply resulting in the employees receiving the annual accounts is unlikely to be a great deal of use in this respect unless it is supported by greater disaggregation and more interpretative material than is currently the case. It is conceivable that merely making the accounts available will, in fact, be counter-productive: it might, for example, lead to a concentration on absolute levels of profit rather than rates of return, or it may divert attention to extraordinary items which inflate profit abnormally. This is *not* an argument against disclosure, rather it serves to underline the point that financial reporting, as it is presently orientated, is primarily for shareholder purposes. Disclosure for employees or unions should be designed differently in order to minimise misunderstanding.

In the meantime, until conventions on reporting to employees are widely agreed and established, firms will, and on balance ought to, continue to offer information based on their annual accounts. This is a minimum commitment which may contribute to greater understanding of company affairs and help to eradicate rumours which may damage morale.

The second main argument put forward by some protagonists of greater disclosure concerns its role in worker participation in management. The latter has become extremely fashionable over the past decade or so and has been treated very seriously by a number of European governments of different political complexions [16].

Whatever the details regarding the institutional structure of worker participation there seems to be a fairly wide consensus that it will contribute to the *efficiency* of the company [56]. This, it is argued, will occur through a number of factors operating simultaneously, e.g. a greater readiness to accept technological change because such decisions are shared; better *two*-way communications will improve management knowledge of actual operating conditions; stronger possibilities of industrial peace; and, even more, nebulously 'the recognition of the human being's right to be treated as an intelligent human being desirous of controlling his own destiny, will increase efficiency by increasing employees' willingness to work and to contribute their best to the enterprise' [56, p. 16].

Whether or not such benefits do actually flow from worker participation is not at issue here;[3] the fact remains that many people predict such consequences. They, therefore, tend to favour greater disclosure of company information from two angles: first, as part of a strategy for moving toward the type of participation they regard as desirable; second, in situations where the institutions of participation exist, e.g. in the form of joint committees or works councils, greater disclosure is regarded as a necessary, even if insufficient, condition of real participation.

The characteristic feature of these first two arguments in favour of greater disclosure is their emphasis on it as a device for improving the efficiency and stability of the firm. The motive for its introduction into company industrial relations policy can, in these terms, be rationalised as highly practical and economic and, therefore, in conformity with traditional views of the function and nature of the business enterprise.[4]

The third argument favouring disclosure of financial and economic information derives *precisely* from our changing notion of the role of the firm in a modern society. Traditionally, private companies have been required by the law to act in the interest of shareholders only. As late as 1962, this essentially nineteenth-century view of company obligations was upheld in the case of Parke v. the *Daily News* and others.[5] In line with this approach, as mentioned earlier,[6] the purpose of financial reporting via annual accounts and statements has been seen primarily as a way of demonstrating to shareholders how the resources of the firm have been deployed and husbanded in the year in question. Disclosure of information to other interested parties, for example employees and trade unions, had not been regarded as of major importance until fairly recently.

The traditional, and in many ways, the classical view of the business enterprise which has conditioned the attitude of both company lawyers and management accountants originates very largely in economic theory.[7] Essentially the firm is analysed, in a highly mechanistic frame of reference, as a locus of decision making in which the manager/entrepreneur attempts to maximise profits subject to a well defined and known set of external, market and technological constraints. Combined with other restrictive assumptions, some of which are concerned with the nature of these external constraints, it is possible to demonstrate that the pursuit of maximum profit will simultaneously maximise the benefits to society as a whole.[8] This identity of interest, while subject to the most rigorous of theoretical assumptions became, and still remains, the basis of *laissez-faire* ideology. It offered a ready-made justification and rationale for businessmen to make profit the over-riding goal and to promote the interest of owner-shareholders while ignoring or even downgrading the interests of other parties in the productive process. This vision of the firm, combined with prevalent attitudes to the rights of ownership, has constituted the bedrock upon which company law and much management accounting practice is based.

Since the 1930s, however, research into both the empirical and the analytical dimensions of company behaviour has been continuously undermining the simple 'instrumental' version of the firm. The work of Berle and Means on patterns of share ownership [8] aided and abetted by the propagandising of James Burnham [15] has made it commonplace to discuss the divorce of 'ownership' from 'control' of the modern company, the increasing professionalisation of management and the wider possibilities of pursuing other business objectives than mere profit maximisation. There have also been a number of important developments in economic theory, each recognising that non-competitive environments afford the decision maker considerable discretion over his choice of goals. As a consequence numerous models of the firm now abound emphasising various possible objectives, e.g. sales maximisation [3], maximisation of managerial emoluments [57], or simply satisficing [49].

The notion of the 'socially responsible' business firm is only one step away from these empirical and theoretical contributions: to a large extent this conception of the company has emerged in a great deal of recent academic research. Thus, in his later work, Berle talks about the 'corporate conscience' which acts to restrain management from selfish or socially irresponsible behaviour, and the 'public consensus' to which managements are accountable [6], [7]. The concept of the 'soulful corporation' has similarly been used expressively to encapsulate the view that the private company is responsible to more than one constituency and that its activities transcend more than one interest group. Fogarty has been a consistent proponent of this 'organic' view of the company: 'The Company is the meeting place of a number of groups of individuals, each with his own purpose in view, who combine to set up a socio-technical system in order to achieve a common good . . . The set of purposes which the company pursues is thus a composite of the goals needed to attract its participants . . . including among others the goals of workers' [25, p. 1].

Many of these ideas have been around in academic circles for 30 to 40 years and have gradually percolated through to the business community at large; it is not at all uncommon to hear sentiments such as: '. . . any company which forgets that it has three *co-equal* interests to serve – those of its shareholders, its employees, and its customers – will be failing in its duty and could not achieve the maximum degree of success, and *it seems to me to be sterile to attempt to rank the claims of any one of those interests above those of the others*' [33, p. 49]. This could be supplemented by numerous statements from company chairmen and industrialists in many areas of business in both the U.K. and the U.S.A. The point is that these radical changes in the vision of the firms' responsibilities have made it quite legitimate to ask what should be the proper relationship of the firm to its employees. We shall try to deal with this issue below, at least in terms of the informational requirements of this relationship. At this juncture we merely wish to establish some of the reasons why management and government seem prepared to acknowledge the need for greater disclosure of financial and economic information to employees. The 'utilitarian' and 'ethical' reasons so far advanced certainly go some way to explaining why, from time to time, pressure has arisen *from within* the ranks of management for greater disclosure. As far back as 1949 the British Institute of Management sponsored a conference to sound out opinion on the desirability of disclosure and explanation of financial information as an important element in joint consultation [11]. Further, in 1957 the B.I.M. in conjunction with bodies such as the A.C.C.A. (now the Association of Certified Accountants), the I.C.W.A. (now the Institute of Cost and Management Accountants) and the I.P.M. (Institute of Personnel Management) published a booklet investigating the methods and reasons for disclosing information to employees [12]. This looked at current U.K. practice and that of some continental countries.

The salient fact about these two pioneering efforts is that disclosure is primarily seen as an adjunct to joint consultation and not collective bargaining. In other words it is seen as relating to areas of *common interest* to management and employees rather than areas of disputation and conflict. This tends to be a typical managerial orientation insofar as it arises from viewing the company and industrial relations within a *unitary* frame of reference where 'everyone is part of the same team', or 'we're all in the same boat' or 'we all ultimately share the same aspirations', are prevalent attitudes. [9] If this were really the case there would be no reason for management ever to refuse any information, yet among reasons for not doing so can be found the suggestions that this information will be used unscrupulously or that competitors will acquire it. [10]

The attitude of employees, given their experience with shop-floor bargaining in the post-war world, is likely to be very different. Financial and economic information for them will act primarily to clarify and then to *enlarge* the bargaining area. McCarthy's study of shop stewards carried out for the Donovan Commission pointed out the paradoxical nature of 'joint' consultation: 'it is assumed that management should only agree to share responsibility on controversial and conflicting subjects, like wages, on non-controversial and common interest subjects, like manning, it cannot do more than consult. So we reach a position where it is suggested that agreements are possible when the two sides are basically opposed; when they are really united there cannot be any question of an agreement' [37, p. 36]. Partly because of the 'unilateral' nature of joint consultation it has declined in importance in the U.K. since the Second World War. [11] A further decline could be expected particularly as stewards 'tend to believe that *any* subject which affects their members is a fit and proper matter for negotiation and agreement' [37, p. 36].

Given these contrasting attitudes there is clearly room for considerable disagreement between management and employees (through their immediate representatives) over the objectives, the timing and the content of the financial and economic information to be disclosed.

The arguments so far advanced for the greater disclosure of information to employees: that it is in the long-term interest of the company; that it recognises the fundamental change in the nature of the firm; and that it may be an important component of joint consultation, are all arguments which have recommended themselves at one time or another to management and to those of an essentially reformist mentality. Underlying this approach is a basic acceptance of the mixed economy, disclosure is viewed as a way of making that economy more efficient, more humane and more democratic.

There are two further arguments put forward in favour of disclosure to employees: arguments which derive from minority viewpoints outside the general consensus. The first of these is in the socialist tradition and, while the ultimate objective is a change in the basis of ownership and control of economic resources, it sees the extension of information to employees as *partially* serving this objective by helping to increase 'workers' control' and developing 'workers' self-management'.

The demand for management to 'open the books' has a very long history in socialist thought and reflects a deep-felt mistrust of the 'capitalist' economy, in which, it is thought, companies are able to manipulate their financial and economic operations at the expense of the workers. Thus, Hugh Scanlon, President of the A.U.E.W., has argued as follows:

> For the proper understanding of the functions and problems of any undertaking it is necessary, in the first instance, to have ready access to the relevant information. There seems to be an organised conspiracy to shut off the workers from effective knowledge of the firm's operations, financial dealings and plans . . . One of the key demands of industrial democracy is *open the books*. This does not mean as it has so much in the past, just the cooked up balance sheets that shop stewards are frequently saddled with in the negotiations they undertake. It means that workers have full and detailed information concerning costing, marketing and all other essential financial details [45, p. 6].

The proponents of workers' control reject joint consultation and most schemes of worker participation as potentially injurious to employee bargaining power by causing divisions among the rank and file and their representatives. They similarly question the bona fides of companies which voluntarily offer information: 'Fancy formulas for calculating bonuses or the "sharing" of "added value", combined with the selective doling out of misinformation adds to the possibility of confusion among workers and to the danger that some shop stewards may find themselves cosily incorporated into management's ethos and "mysteries" ' [54 p. 101]. The essence of the argument is that nothing less than 'an unambiguous, general and unrestricted access to all commercial secrets' is required, but in the meantime, offers of partial information should be taken up 'since appetite grows with the eating' [54].

The case for greater disclosure from this school of thought appears to be based on two fundamental principles:
(1) that it is a technique which helps employees to establish greater democratisation of decision making in industry;
(2) that it may usefully act as a check on those aspects of the market system which result in adverse external effects in the form of pollution and environmental degradation.

The question of democracy in industry is too broad a topic to detain us here,[12] suffice it to say that there remains considerable disagreement on such basic issues as what precisely it means, what institutional structures are necessary to achieve and maintain it and finally, given the nature of technology, whether it is even possible.[13]

What is not in dispute is that, whatever the ultimate shape of industrial democracy, relevant information is a *sine qua non* for a discerning and mature electorate. The issue then becomes, what constitutes relevant information for employees given that they are a significant part, if not the whole, of this electorate?

While the question of industrial democracy is highly controversial the second argument favouring greater disclosure is much less so. 'Externalities' or 'spillover' effects arise where a firm is imposing, as a result of its main activity, costs (or benefits) on individuals who themselves are not directly party to the activity. The problem of social costs (or benefits) thrown up by the market system has a fairly long history of analysis in conventional economic theorising,[14] but only in the last few years has it really begun to catch the attention and interest of accountants [27]. When one combines this interest with recent ideas on the theory of the firm, the greater emphasis on *social* accountability which has emerged over the past decade is largely explained. According to this view management is seen as the custodian of scarce resources and the misuse of these resources may damage not simply the firm but also the wider community. The efficiency of management, therefore, is to be evaluated in broader terms than conventional profitability and possibly from the standpoint of different interest groups [47]. As employees have inside knowledge of the firm's actions and potential they may be a key group in the development of social accountability since disclosure to them could become a useful and powerful instrument of social audit. To the extent that employees can act in this capacity advantages may accrue to the other parties: customers, government, the local community or even conceivably shareholders.

The final argument advanced in favour of greater disclosure derives from employers who see it as a possible way of breathing life into the concept of joint consultation as a means of avoiding unionisation. It must be emphasised that, while this is a minority view, it may well be significant. Anti-union feeling has certainly not disappeared in the U.K. as is evidenced by the concern for union recognition embedded in much recent industrial relations legislation. In a specific example studied by Coker and McCarthy it was noted that 'management had decided to wind up the consultative committee for manual workers because the stewards refused to stand for election to it; at the same time they created a new consultative committee for non-manual workers, *as part of a plan to discourage them from joining trade unions*'[37,p. 34] [Italics added]. It is this possibility which has led the Labour Party and large sections of the trade union movement to insist upon 'a single channel of representation' for employees. The fear that simple, direct involvement of firms with employees or non-union-accredited employee representatives will by-pass and weaken the trade union structure is a very real one. It goes a long way to explain why many unionists are lukewarm towards various schemes for worker participation and why they insist that disclosure should primarily be to trade union representatives who will in turn communicate with their members. Company policies which may help to set up a new focus of loyalty for employees, for example by identifying the worker with the interests of the firm, are potentially divisive of union membership[15] and are, for that reason, unlikely to be wholeheartedly endorsed. These comments are particularly apt in relation to white-collar workers: traditionally their loyalties were assumed to be direct to the company and, consequently, this has been an area where union recruitment and recognition proved both difficult and precarious until recent years.

The notion that voluntary disclosure may help to pre-empt the development of independent union organisations has particular appeal, therefore, to the more paternalistic employer sharing the 'unitary' view of industrial relations referred to earlier.

Given these arguments in favour of greater disclosure to employees, the question naturally arises as to *what* precisely should be disclosed? Two distinct strategies are possible:

(i) a blanket request or demand that comprehensive and detailed information be made available or accessible;

(ii) a rather more cautious approach which starts by identifying broad employee needs and then relates specific items to these needs.

The first of these strategies is perhaps exemplified by the lengthy, itemised list drawn up by the T.U.C. in 1970 [55, p. 462]. This was done by simply circulating member unions inviting them to add to the list, or offer comment, on the types of information they would like to receive. It must be noted that they were primarily concerned with information for collective bargaining rather than for employees but, nonetheless, the implications of this approach are that companies would have to divulge what they may regard as competitively sensitive information, for example, production schedules, cost-structures and performance indicators of various kinds. They may also have to collect data with which they would normally not bother: smaller and medium-sized firms may not carry such details as rates of turnover, sickness or absenteeism, and very few of any size have anything as sophisticated as a manpower plan, plans for recruitment, selection and training, all of which are included in the T.U.C. list. However, the assembling of this type of information and the construction of company plans may produce beneficial side effects as managerial supervision, control and, therefore, efficiency could be improved in areas previously ignored because of deficient or non-existent data.

Apart from the vexed question of competitive sensitivity which will be further examined below there is another, more substantial argument against a blanket approach to disclosure. Management may not gather certain types of data, not because of inefficiency, but rather because there are costs involved in the collection, analysis and dissemination of information: it requires both time and manpower which are scarce resources within the firm. It is important to recognise, therefore, that it may be quite legitimate to refuse to collect certain types of data where the costs significantly outweigh the potential benefits. In terms of conventional economic theory, information should be collected up to the point where marginal costs and benefits are equated. While this is self-evidently correct there are real problems in specific applications of the idea. It may be possible to calculate marginal costs but the calculation of potential benefits is very much more difficult.[16]

The resolution of this problem on practical grounds suggests the second way of approaching the disclosure issue. Instead of attempting to delineate *a priori* the *maximum* area over which disclosure will operate, we should initially identify broad areas of interest or need and look again, in each case, at disclosure of information as and when new needs arise. Information, to all but the purest of scientific investigators, is needed to solve certain problems, and the size of the problem normally dictates the effort required to produce a solution. In other words we should attempt to define the necessary information flow in terms of what it costs if the data is *not* available; We balance the cost of collection, analysis etc. against the advantage of overcoming a specific problem. This implies initially, a rather more pragmatic, circumspect indication of 'consumer' needs.

In the case of employees it is possible to argue that their needs in the first instance fall into four major categories:

(1) Job security

In spite of the existence of an extensive network of social security provisions, job security remains a question of crucial importance to most work- people. This has become increasingly the case in the atmosphere of rising unemployment and uncertain job prospects which has characterised the world economy in the last two years. Concern for security of employment has always been widely expressed, for example, in the hey-day of productivity bargaining in the U.K., i.e. 1964 to 1966 unemployment was not particularly high yet the majority of agreements included 'no redundancy' clauses or guarantees – indeed it is arguable that such guarantees were the most significant factor in getting deals accepted. [17]

Financial and economic information relating to job security will clearly have a high priority. This does not mean that employees should simply be informed of the company's or the group's overall profitability, it must include issues such as, how external economic changes affect company stability, how the firm obtains money to cover reported losses and the importance of an adequate flow of liquidity. The current state of the company's order book will also constitute a significant influence on the stability of both jobs and earnings. It may similarly be helpful to discuss the criteria which determine decisions on plant closure and redundancy.

These changes, which are hardly controversial, would mean that employees would be in a much better position to judge for themselves the need for such decisions. It would also increase the possibility of their framing and advancing constructive counter-proposals to obviate the threat of unemployment, a procedure presumably preferable to the technique of 'working-in' to which some groups have felt compelled to resort in the recent past.

(2) Working conditions

Hours of work, patterns of shift-working and stable earnings are clearly important factors for many employees. Where their social life is disrupted they obviously ought to be directly informed of the bases on which changes in shift-working patterns are decided, e.g. costing out of shift-working practices may demonstrate which of the systems is best in terms of capital utilisation and which is best in terms of least disruption. It is also possible to demonstrate to workers how overtime can be reduced or eliminated, while simultaneously earning levels can be maintained or expanded by more effective working during normal hours. Again this is not particularly novel since such changes were emphasised in most of the early and successful productivity bargains.

Some notion of what factors determine when equipment is to be replaced would make management decisions appear less arbitrary and more rational. It is quite common for employees to be antipathetic to new techniques, not only because they fear possible unemployment repercussions but also because they know 'there was nothing physically wrong with the previous machinery' since they may not be aware of the concept of 'economic life' or technical obsolescence.

(3) Achievement or performance indicators

These are very commonly used in industry particularly in connection with piece-work and other payment-by-results schemes. They tend to relate directly to the individual's immediate place of work, for example, output norms and spoilage rates, but it is also important to show how they may affect broader problems. The management may, for example, show how higher productivity can aid the competitive ability of the firm or why unit costs are reduced when output volumes increase. Employees require standards by which they can measure their own or their plant's performance. The usual managerial techniques of work measurement may be less important in setting these standards than inter- or intra-plant comparisons. Greater information on a disaggregated basis, e.g. sectionally or on a plant-by-plant basis would be useful in this latter respect and may make it easier for employees to identify their contribution to a company's overall performance.

(4) Equity

One of the most powerful influences operating on working people today concerns attitudes towards fairness in the distribution of economic reward. Equity is a concept which applies in a number of directions: between employees and shareholders, between workers and management and between workers themselves, i.e. *within* the wage structure.[18]

The overall division of company resources between workers and the rest is normally determined through the collective bargaining mechanism. It would nonetheless be attitudinally important for the company to produce more detailed information on the disposition of its revenues. Thus, for example, firms might explain why dividends should be maintained, what criteria influence the retention ratio and depreciation provisions and how loan finance affects profits.

It may be equally important to describe, explain and justify the company's wage structure and policy. This does not imply revealing every single worker's wage packet but it does mean a greater readiness to indicate more precisely the wage distribution so that rumours and grievances, real or imagined, can be dealt with. There is the continuous danger that only the extremes of the distribution will be noticed in the absence of information giving full details: 'Of course, all workers have some knowledge of the earnings of their workmates but, given all the complications of different hours of work, different tax codes and the like, this knowledge is likely to be *impressionistic and unreliable*' [14, p. 73] [Italics added]. It is interesting, and perhaps supportive of our earlier assertion,[19] to note that management itself is not always fully apprised of data on earnings: 'In most of the factories covered . . . management's own knowledge of earnings was very incomplete' [14, p. 75].

Whatever the nature of the relevant information it is important that disclosure should be a continuous process and not used simply as an *ad hoc* device when the company runs into difficulty. It is obvious that employees will eventually become suspicious of management which sees fit to 'open the books' only when the firm is in trouble.

(B) DISCLOSURE TO TRADE UNIONS

The arguments favouring greater disclosure of company information to trade unions resolve themselves into two major areas. First, there are those, inside and outside the trade union movement, who see it as a means of shifting bargaining power from management to union negotiators. They clearly see disclosure as a phenomenon which will increase the number of 'favourable' settlements to union members. The second argument is that *given* any particular distribution of settlements it is possible for disclosure to improve bargaining processes by making them more rational, reducing the possibility of break-down and developing other dimensions than that of distributive bargaining only.

The essence of the first argument seems to be that 'knowledge is power' and, where only one of the parties has access to it, the bargaining process is inherently unequal to the ultimate disadvantage of the ignorant party – in this case the trade union. Despite its initial plausibility, this view is not universally accepted and it has been suggested by several eminent academics that ignorance in bargaining situations is a powerful weapon because the uninformed can demand and receive favourable outcomes [46], [48]. At first sight this appears to contradict the orthodox view and implies that a trade union's negotiating position is weakened by disclosure. If this is true one is tempted to ask why employers have not learned the lesson in the real world. Why have they been so lukewarm in their attitudes to disclosure? These questions are answered in a later study which clearly shows that ignorance is strength *only when it is opposed by ignorance* [35]. In situations where a single bargainer is aware of the pay-off structure inherent in each potential agreement he can: 'neutralise [his] opponent's manipulative strategy by responding to it in kind, rather than by truckling to unreasonable demands' [35, p. 440].

The informed bargainer, i.e. the employer, would certainly appear to be better placed, as he can, in any single round of negotiations, readily accept claims which are, from his point of view, favourable while he can contend those which are not. As it is believed that such an arrangement consistently favours the employer, supporters of the trade union case wish to eliminate it by making the relevant information available – if necessary by enforced disclosure.

The second argument favouring disclosure for purposes of collective bargaining is less concerned with the distributional results of any one set of negotiations. Collective bargaining is seen as a continuing process whose scope need not be limited to the traditional areas such as wage negotiations or grievance procedures, instead it should be developed as a technique for arriving at mutually beneficial solutions to new problems. The sharing of company information is a necessary condition if integrative bargaining is to develop. Thus as McKersie and Hunter point out 'the more information the parties share, the better the problem-solving is apt to function. Some companies still feel reluctant to reveal the "inner-workings" of the enterprise. Such hesitation makes the definition of problems, the development of alternatives and the selection of solutions difficult to execute. Without basic data and the overture of trust that is involved in sharing sensitive information, problem solving cannot be effective and attitudes will remain frozen' [31, p. 173].

The emphasis here is on expanding and improving collective bargaining.[20] To the extent that such bargaining has become a plant or company level phenomenon carried out by shop stewards and other non-official worker representatives it could be argued that disclosure to the official union structure is misplaced: the full-time officers are generally concerned with the negotiation and application of national industrial settlements and *company* information may not be appropriate at that level. Nevertheless, trade unions are generally anxious to be the prime focus for disclosure,[21] first of all because direct disclosure to shop stewards confers recognition, status and authority which one day may constitute a challenge to the official union structure and secondly because they feel better equipped to deal with the type of data likely to be forthcoming. They are clearly better placed to process, analyse *and* question data where full-time research facilities are available.

Insofar as trade unions can assimilate shop stewards more closely into their formal structure the first objection is less acute. Also, where very large companies are concerned, the issue is less problematical because the firm may comprise a very high proportion of the industry's employment, in which case company information may quite naturally be relevant as part of national negotiations. Nevertheless, where it is common practice for employees in an industry to negotiate in-plant payments additional to the national award, disclosure of information, as a means of improving bargaining, may apply to their *immediate* representatives as well as to union officers. In what follows, therefore, although we may refer to information for bargaining purposes as relating *primarily* to the official union structure, the other levels at which 'unofficial' negotiations take place must be kept in mind.

Collective bargaining in the U.K. deals with many issues but the most important single item is that of remuneration. Whatever the level of negotiations – shop, section, plant, company or industry-level, one or more of the following criteria are used to support a claim for increased pay:[22]

(1) changes in the cost of living;
(2) comparability;
(3) productivity changes;
(4) ability to pay.

The emphasis shifts from one to the other according to the circumstances of the case but essentially these constitute the underlying arguments in nearly all wage claims. Ability to pay is rarely used by itself, or even as the most important factor, instead it tends to be used as a final supportive argument. Data on all four issues are normally deployed to decide, first of all, if there should be any increase in wages at all, i.e. as a way of re-opening negotiations, and then to help influence the size of the claim. In this sense cost of living and comparability arguments are usually 'defensive' as they are used in an attempt to maintain absolute real income and relative ranking in the pay hierarchy. Obviously the information used here is normally external to the company, from official and semi-official sources, but occasionally intra-company parity arguments do arise, in which case internal information may be necessary. Productivity and ability to pay arguments are more clearly related to plant or company performance and consequently rely almost entirely on internally generated data.

How far such financial and economic information does, in the last analysis, determine the precise size of the initial bid or the magnitude of the final settlement is difficult to decide and opinions are divided on the issue.[23] Some economists argue that the collection and use of information is mere 'window dressing' and that the union's stance is determined primarily by the exercise of 'raw power' or 'what it expects the employer to concede' [42]. Others argue that 'statistical facts are important primarily in providing a central area from which it is difficult to stray very far' [2].

As will be argued in Chapter 4 bargaining processes are highly complex and not simply a case of 'take it or leave it'. One or other of the parties may, by the introduction of new information, influence initial expectations so as to reduce expectational disparities, effect the possibility of equilibrium and increase the rate at which equilibrium solutions are reached. The basic argument for disclosure of company information to trade union negotiators is that it tends to make distributive bargaining more efficient and simultaneously offers the opportunity of developing mutual trust and confidence which is an essential component of integrative bargaining. Thus, for example, the Commission on Industrial Relations' report on disclosure pointed out that 'Trade unions claim certain advantages might result from improved disclosure of information – a speeding of the bargaining process because information is readily available, a greater likelihood of longer term wage deals and an increased chance of the employer obtaining greater co-operation from his employees' [21, para. 60, p. 13].

The fact that certain benefits may accrue from greater disclosure of company information to unions and employees must not blind us to some of the problems a more open policy could also induce. So far we have generally confined ourselves to a discussion of the arguments in favour of disclosure. There are, however, several objections of a more or less serious nature which also need to be considered. Some of these objections, on further analysis, may appear spurious or insubstantial but, nevertheless, as they may be quite widely held we shall deal with them in the following section.

(2) THE ANTI-ARGUMENTS – SOME OBJECTIONS TO DISCLOSURE

The first argument against a policy of greater disclosure relates to the fact that most union negotiators, particularly shop stewards, lack expertise and training in financial accounting. Revealing information in these circumstances may, therefore, result in misunderstanding, mistrust and damage to the bargaining process. This was mentioned as a major disadvantage of disclosure in the B.I.M. survey of 1957 [12] and comes up quite regularly as an objection. A N.E.D.O. (National Economic Development Office) study of the rubber industry indicated that management was reluctant to confide information to employees and shop stewards as 'they would not understand the complexity of the enterprise even if we told them the facts' [31, p. 209]. Even more recently it has been argued that 'unless negotiators are in a position to be able to understand fully the implications of any information which they may be given, it is unlikely that a policy of greater disclosure of information will have the desired effect of improving industrial bargaining' [36, p. 43].

The fact that shop stewards and other union negotiators are not trained in the fields of financial or management accounting cannot itself be an objection to disclosure: applying the same sort of reasoning to shareholders could result in the non-disclosure (or very limited publication) of the annual report and accounts as many members of the company are unable to understand the structure and meaning of a balance sheet or profit and loss account. This type of argument was effectively repudiated by Harold Rose more than ten years ago when, writing prior to the 1967 Companies Act, he pointed out that:

The contention that the provision of particular items of information would be wrongly construed is frequently made, especially in periods of difficult trading. Over the past year or so, for example, it is noticeable that a number of companies have ceased to publish figures for sales turnover on these grounds, and the general excuse that information might be misconstrued is the one commonly used to withhold half-yearly or quarterly reports. However it is difficult to imagine any single piece of information potentially more misleading than that which forms the foundation of present accounts, namely the annual profit figure, and *in general it is hard to understand why shareholders are likely to make a false assessment if they are presented with more information rather than with less* [43, pp. 18—19] [Italics added].

Inability to comprehend financial statements clearly implies a need for better trade union (and shareholder) education rather than a policy of non-disclosure.[24] In any case the process of making company data available to union negotiators may itself be highly educative: it is highly unlikely that management would simply present a list of figures and ratios without explanation or interpretation. The material will almost certainly be supported by verbal or written clarification. The difficult problem here then is not so much that union negotiators will necessarily misunderstand or misuse the data but that management itself will be tempted to bias data in its own favour. This tends to happen in any case as each party may well put its own construction on precisely the same information. The real danger is that if management were to manipulate the information deliberately and union negotiators become aware of this at a later date the atmosphere would be embittered for a long time thereafter.

The second argument against disclosure starts from the assumption that it will strengthen the bargaining position of shop stewards and trade unions: more aggressive bargaining and larger pay settlements may be expected as a result of this change especially in industries where industrial relations are already in poor condition — thus: 'Where employers thought unions resorted too readily to industrial action in support of their claims they were unwilling to disclose any information which might indicate changes in the strength or weakness of their bargaining position' [21, p. 14]. It is further argued that any such increase in militant behaviour is potentially damaging to the company and ultimately self-defeating. Even if larger settlements do not actually endanger the viability of the firm they certainly appropriate part of current resources; this, in turn reduces the 'investible surplus', inhibiting future development of the company which ultimately lowers the *growth* of earnings and jeopardises future job prospects. If the rate of return to capital is depressed it also becomes more difficult to raise investment funds in the capital market.

The extent to which this particular scenario is true is not at issue here:[25] the point is that if we take the argument on its merits then it clearly implies that union negotiators take the short-sighted view to the disadvantage of their members. On the other hand, to suggest that they take a longer view and reduce pay claims or accept lower settlements now, in the hope of higher future earnings, is implicitly asking for some form of investment on their part by foregoing current consumption in the expectation of larger real income in the future. It is reasonable to suppose that rational investors, including most company managements, when assessing their investment programmes, do so on the basis of the best current information as to likely returns. Presumably union negotiators and their members are no different in this respect, therefore, if one argues that they should accept lower settlements now, they should be informed of the reasons for expecting increased earnings later. This would necessarily involve the company in discussing ability to pay, investment policy, employment plans and the like. Paradoxically then an argument originally proposed to prevent or minimise disclosure may well be one of the stronger points in its favour.

The third objection to the more liberal provision of financial and economic information is indeed extremely important as it relates to the competitive position of the firm. It is a constant source of anxiety to businessmen that information of a sensitive nature, i.e. dealing with cost structures, efficiency indicators, pricing policy and future development plans once revealed to the union or the company's employees may become known to competitors.[26] The Confederation of British Industries, for example, argues that:

> The constraints which arise from competitive considerations are of absolutely vital importance. It is in the interests of everyone in a company that information should not be divulged if or at a time when to do so would have adverse consequences. Job security might well be jeopardised by inopportune or premature disclosure of information relating to mergers, takeovers or changes of location. Information about launching a new product or research and development should not be divulged if or when to do so would harm the company's prospects of sustaining or gaining a competitive edge [23].

Similar worries have been expressed by the Consultative Committee of Accountancy Bodies in its reaction to the disclosure provisions of the Industry Act:

We fear that having to carry on business in public in this way will inhibit management leading to a lack of initiative and enterprise rather than a regeneration of British industry. We have particular concern over disclosure of future plans and research and development information to employees, shareholders and others but it must be accepted that any requirement leading to possible premature disclosure of future plans may be a disincentive to enterprise [24, para 10].

In particular the Committee is very concerned at the possibility that *foreign* competitors may obtain significant competitive advantages over British firms because they may be in a better position to avoid the impact of the U.K. legislation: this is obviously true of foreign companies *without* a U.K. subsidiary, but the C.C.A.B. is also dubious about the law's application to foreign-owned subsidiaries: 'a Minister may be able to require a foreign parent company with a manufacturing subsidiary in this country to disclose information about the parent company's plans for the subsidiary: we doubt whether such a directive could be as effective as one served on a British parent company' [24, para. 9]. Whether such doubts will be borne out in fact we must wait and see, but, in the meantime, a further result of extending disclosure legislation in the United Kingdom may be to deter the flow of investment capital from abroad. The basic problem underlying these arguments about foreign competitors and investment is that we may be pushing back the borders of commercial secrecy considerably further than our external rivals[27] and the result may be costly as far as future employment and balance of payments prospects are concerned.

A different but related objection concerns the question of joint ventures undertaken by U.K. and foreign firms: quite obviously the fact that the British end of the operation may be subject to extra disclosure requirements may deter this type of co-operation. This type of difficulty may occur, for example, where consortia are being organised to deal with projects in other countries.

These anxieties about external competition and the future of certain types of foreign co-operation derive, primarily, from the disclosure provisions of the Industry Act insofar as these relate to company plans or forecasts.[28] As pointed out in Chapter 1 these clauses concern disclosure to the Minister and the relevant departments but there is provision for the data to be given later to trade union representatives. Safeguards do exist to prevent sensitive information being passed on to other parties but how effective these safeguards will be, must, at this stage, be a matter of guess-work.

Disclosure of company plans or forecasts constitutes a radical departure in the U.K. legislation and may itself bring up several further problems particularly in relation to budgetary information. Some companies may draw up perspective plans or long-range forecasts which do little more than delineate major objectives perhaps over a five- or ten-year time horizon. If such forecasts are prepared at all, management is unlikely to be too fearful about disclosing them as they are widely acknowledged to be highly uncertain and speculative. Where short-term planning or budgeted information is concerned, however, considerable difficulties are likely to occur. Planning, over however short a time period, is still extremely problematical: assumptions have to be made about availability of inputs, prospective costs, market reactions, the behaviour of major competitors etc. If any of these assumptions are mistaken the chosen course of action may be totally inappropriate. One very significant and almost inescapable difficulty is that the very disclosure of plans or forecasts (or the assumptions on which they are based) may have an 'announcement' effect, i.e. they may induce behavioural changes which falsify them.[29] A second problem posed by disclosure of plans or forecasts has been pointed out by the Accountants International Study Group in the context of profit forecasts: 'if forecasts were to be published regularly with explanations of variations between forecast and actual performance, the prime management objective of many companies might become the achievement of the profit forecast, this would inevitably detract from management's normal role and proper aim of improving the profitability and efficiency of their company on a medium-term or long-term basis' [1, para. 19]. In other words management may become committed to justifying the original forecast rather than abandon a particular line of action.

A third objection relating specifically to *budgetary* disclosure may be framed as follows: a budget is 'a plan detailing a period's operations and actions in physical and monetary units' [28, p. 216], therefore, it performs two functions: (1) it disseminates specific instructions and resources to various management agencies for implementing and executing a programme; (2) it may act as a motivational stimulus and serve as a measuring rod for assessing performance.

The first function is the more traditional role of budgeting [4] and it may well be that this is what is uppermost in the mind of government and trade unions when they request budget information. Stedry has pointed out, however, that 'it seems reasonable to suppose that it is the proper task of budgetary control to be concerned with strategies for constant improvement in performance' [50, p. 147]. In this particular context, therefore, budgets may be prepared in such a way as to manipulate aspiration levels and improve behaviour rather than determine detailed, specific courses of action, i.e. the primary function is to motivate rather than inform [5].

If government and/or trade unions are to be made privy to budgetary details then the motivational dimension may have to disappear altogether because non-attainment of a budget would appear to indicate failure whereas higher management may have consciously set a non-attainable standard. Consistent 'failure' of this sort would lead to union (and perhaps government) representatives questioning the efficiency of that particular level of management in circumstances where they may be performing quite well.

This particular set of objections to disclosure of company planning and budgetary information on the grounds of competitive position *vis-à-vis* foreign rivals, effects on joint ventures and the possible repercussions on the planning and budgeting process itself seem to us to be cogent arguments. Business anxiety on these points is certainly quite legitimate but nevertheless one or two points should be considered. If the argument on competitively sensitive information implies that union negotiators will *deliberately* divulge such information to the company's rivals we are doubtful. In the case of shop stewards as negotiators it is difficult to see what they would gain for themselves or their members in taking a course of action which damages the competitive ability of their own firm. In the case of official union negotiators where they bargain with different companies there may be a temptation to make cross-company references in situations where parity arguments are being deployed. In the last analysis, however, when one looks at actual practice two facts stand out: in the U.S.A. where, as indicated earlier, a limited form of disclosure has existed for many years, breaches of confidentiality have not proved a significant problem; also in the U.K., during the period of productivity bargaining when 'competitively sensitive' data was discussed with both stewards and officials, no case was reported of any trading of company secrets.

A further argument against the more liberal provision of financial information revolves around the problem of confidentiality where the rights of third persons or shareholders are concerned. The privacy of third persons can be protected by adopting specific exclusion clauses as was the case with the Industrial Relations Act 1971 and has been reaffirmed in both the Employment Protection Act and the Industry Act 1975 where information and forecasts are not to be given to trade unions if the relevant Minister considers that the information was originally given in confidence.[30] The rights of shareholders also need to be considered, however, as there is an ethical problem in disclosing certain types of information to shop stewards or trade unions while the legal owners of the firm are not consulted. The Stock Exchange has been very concerned about partial disclosure of financial information but it has largely looked at the issue in terms of mistakes or malpractices which allow some shareholders to gain at the expense of others: 'Directors should not divulge price sensitive information in such a way as to place in a privileged position any person or class or category of persons outside the company and its advisors' [51, p. 14].

There are no legal obstacles to prevent companies disclosing financial information to union negotiators: it has been common practice to allow government officials, banks and other potential creditors access to confidential information. One may, therefore, take the pragmatic view and argue that as long as shareholders are not substantially disadvantaged by disclosure to union negotiators the practice should be allowed. On balance we think that members of the company will not suffer as a result of greater disclosure, on the contrary they may well gain. Whether it is 'fair' that the owners of the enterprise should be left in the dark about certain aspects of the firm's performance is ultimately a judgement of value which each individual must make for himself, but in the light of the knowledge that other groups are already 'privileged' in this way.

A sixth argument put forward against disclosure is that it encroaches upon and diminishes 'management's right to manage'. This really boils down to a question of what constitutes managerial authority and how it is exercised. Obviously management prerogatives have been restricted increasingly over the past 30 years by challenges from inside and outside the firm [38]. The solution here is to re-establish the legitimacy of managerial authority and, as legitimacy implies acceptance, then authority may only be regained in terms of 'management by agreement'. The existence of restrictive practices and non-cooperation clearly reduces managerial discretion, so if disclosure can help to secure greater agreement it may actually extend the area of management control.

The final objection to disclosure is a development of the second argument: put simply it is that selective use of financial information, particularly about ability to pay, will result in highly inflationary wage settlements which cannot be absorbed by allowing profit margins to shrink further, thus: 'Some employers were sceptical of the whole idea that greater disclosure of information would contribute to better industrial relations and feared it might lead to *greater militancy and more inflationary trade union wage demands'* [21, para. 15, p. 14].

Given the desire to reduce inflation, it seems that disclosure may fly in the face of government policy. It is vital, therefore, to clarify the role of ability-to-pay indicators in an empirical sense by looking at their influence, if any, on the rate of increase of wages. This is the objective of our next chapter.

NOTES

1 The Liberal Party's position is too well known to require specific reference. The Conservative Party's attitude is reflected in Sections 56 and 57 of the Industrial Relations Act 1971 [32] and the White Paper on Company Law Reform [22].
2 Some game theorists have noted similar effects in studying artificial bargaining situations [29].
3 There are, of course, those who are not so sanguine about the effects of participation [52].
4 For some interesting comments on managerial ideology and attitudes to the firm see Nichols [39].
5 Parke v. the *Daily News* and others 1962 2 All 929–948 – in this case the judge ruled that making *ex gratia* redundancy payments to employees of two other newspapers was outside the legal competence of the directors that 'this was not in the interests of the company'.
6 See p. 28.
7 The implications of different behavioural views of the firm for management accounting are examined by E. H. Caplan in [17].
8 A simple introduction to these ideas is provided by Bohm [10]; similarly Pen [40] offers a simple and stimulating review of the development of this idea.
9 For the distinction between unitary and pluralistic frames of reference see Fox [26].
10 See [12] – this and other arguments against disclosure will be dealt with below.
11 See McCarthy [37 pp. 32–4]. For a less pessimistic view see Clarke, Fatchett and Roberts [19, p. 72].
12 See, however, Clarke, Fatchett and Roberts [19].
13 For a variety of conflicting views see Clegg [20], Blumberg [9] and Broadway [13].
14 Thus for example, Pigou's *The Economics of Welfare* discussed these issues in some detail in the 1920s.
15 Or may be an obstacle to trade union recruitment.
16 The benefits of the information are only apparent when it has been collected by which time costs have already been incurred: *ex ante*, one would need to assess the potential benefits according to some probabilistic calculus which will, of course, vary for different participants. The construction of such a calculus is extremely problematical.
17 See, for example [44, para. 112, p. 26] 'A guarantee against redundancy is, therefore, often regarded as in practice an indispensable prerequisite for any serious negotiations'.
18 Yet another party could be included here, i.e. customers – they too may be said to have some interest in the company's performance particularly in non-competitive industries.
19 See comments above, p. 36.
20 See also [38], [53].
21 The so-called single channel of representation school of thought is clearly seen in [34].
22 These are dealt with in considerable detail in Chapters 5 and 6.

23 See Chapter 4.
24 Lyall [36] does in fact point to the need for improvements in this area.
25 For further discussion see Chapter 4.
26 It is not simply union negotiators or employees who may be regarded as 'security risks': extensive disclosure to civil servants via the Industry Act 1975 is equally distasteful to many businesses. See also Chapter 1.
27 Thus disclosure of company information under the Companies Acts of 1948 and 1967 already goes further than is the case in other countries.
28 For a more extensive discussion of the Act see Chapter 1.
29 Thus they may cause trade unions or employees to behave in a different manner. If the information gets into the hands of suppliers or competitors similar effects may occur.
30 See Chapter 1.

REFERENCES

1 Accountants International Study Group, *Published Profit Forecasts* (A.I.S.G., 1974).
2 J. Backman, *Wage Determination: An Analysis of Wage Criteria* (Princeton, N.J.: Van Nostrand, 1959).
3 W. J. Baumol, *Business Behaviour, Value and Growth* (New York: Macmillan, 1959).
4 S. Becker and D. Green jr., 'Budgeting and Employee Behaviour', *The Journal of Business*, 35 (Oct 1962).
5 G. J. Benston, 'The Role of the Firm's Accounting System for Motivation', *The Accounting Review*, 38 (April 1963).
6 A. A. Berle, *Power Without Property: A New Development in American Political Economy* (New York: Harcourt Brace, 1959].
7 A. A. Berle, *The Twentieth Century Capitalist Revolution* (London: Macmillan, 1955).
8 A. A. Berle and G. C. Means, *The Modern Corporation and Private Property* (New York: Harcourt, Brace and World, 1968).
9 P. Blumberg, *Industrial Democracy: the Sociology of Participation* (London: Constable, 1968).
10 P. Bohm, *Social Efficiency: A Concise Introduction to Welfare Economics* (London: Macmillan, 1974).
11 British Institute of Management, Conference Series no. 10, *Financial Information and Joint Consultation* (July 1949).
12 British Institute of Management, Personnel Management Series no. 8, *Presenting Financial Information to Employees* (1957).
13 F. Broadway, *Power on the Shop Floor*, Aims of Industry Study no. 31 (1970).
14 W. A. Brown, *Piecework Bargaining* (London: Heinemann, 1973).
15 J. Burnham, *The Managerial Revolution* (Harmondsworth: Penguin Books, 1945).
16 Campbell Balfour, 'Workers' Participation in Western Europe', in *Participation in Industry*, ed. Campbell Balfour (London: Croom Helm, 1973).
17 E. H. Caplan, 'Behavioural Assumptions of Management Accounting', *The Accounting Review*, 61 (July 1966).
18 E. H. Caplan, *Management Accounting and Behavioural Science* (Reading, Mass.: Addison Wesley, 1971).
19 R. O. Clarke, D. J. Fatchett and B. C. Roberts, *Workers' Participation in Management in Britain* (London: Heinemann, 1972).
20 H. Clegg, *A New Approach to Industrial Democracy* (Oxford: Basil Blackwell, 1960).
21 Commission on Industrial Relations, Report no. 31, *Disclosure of Information* (London: HMSO, 1972).
22 *Company Law Reform*, Cmnd. 5391 (London: HMSO, 1973).

23 Confederation of British Industries, *The Provision of Information to Employees* (London, 1975).

24 Consultative Committee of Accountancy Bodies, *Accountants Comment on the Industry Bill* (London: Institute of Chartered Accountants, 1975).

25 M. P. Fogarty, 'Company and Corporate Reform and Worker Participation: The State of the Debate', *British Journal of Industrial Relations*, 10, no. 1 (March 1972).

26 A. Fox, *Industrial Sociology and Industrial Relations*, Royal Commission on Trade Unions and Employers Associations, Research Paper no. 3 (London: HMSO, 1967).

27 T. Gambling, *Societal Accounting* (London: Allen and Unwin . 4).

28 Y. Goldschmidt, *Information for Management Decisions* (Ithaca and London: Cornell University Press, 1970).

29 M. Guyer and A. Rapoport, 'Information Effects in Two Mixed Motive Games', *Behavioural Science*, vol. 14 (1969).

30 F. Herzberg, 'One More Time: How Do You Motivate Employees?', *Harvard Business Review*, 66 (Jan/Feb 1968).

31 L. C. Hunter and R. B. McKersie, *Pay Productivity and Collective Bargaining* (London: Macmillan, 1973).

32 Industrial Relations Act, 1971 (London: HMSO) ch. 71.

33 Investor's Chronicle—Editor's evidence to Company Law Committee (Chairman Rt. Hon. Lord Jenkins), Minutes of Evidence, Cmnd. 1749 (London: HMSO, 1962).

34 Labour Party, *Industrial Democracy: Working Party Report* (London, 1967).

35 R. M. Liebert, W. P. Smith, J. H. Hill and M. Keiffer, 'The Effects of Information and Magnitude of Initial Offer on Interpersonal Negotiations', *Journal of Experimental Social Psychology*, 4 (1968).

36 D. Lyall, 'Opening the Books to the Workers', *Accountancy* (Feb 1975).

37 W. E. J. McCarthy, *The Role of Shop Stewards in British Industrial Relations*, Royal Commission on Trade Unions and Employers Associations, Research Paper no. 1 (London: HMSO, 1967).

38 W. E. J. McCarthy and N. D. Ellis, *Management by Agreement* (London: Hutchinson, 1973).

39 T. Nichols, *Ownership, Control and Ideology* (London: George Allen and Unwin, 1969).

40 J. Pen, *Harmony and Conflict in Modern Society* (London: McGraw-Hill, 1962).

41 A. Rapoport, *Information for Decision Making: Quantitative and Behavioural Dimensions* (Englewood Cliffs, N.J.: Prentice-Hall, 1970).

42 L. G. Reynolds, *Labor Economics and Labor Relations*, 2nd ed. (New York: Prentice-Hall, 1954).

43 H. Rose, *Disclosure in Company Accounts*, Eaton Paper 1 (London: Institute of Economic Affairs, 1965).

44 Royal Commission on Trade Unions and Employers Associations, Research Paper no. 4, *Productivity Bargaining* (London: HMSO, 1967).

45 H. Scanlon, *Workers' Control and the Transnational Company*, Institute for Workers' Control, Pamphlet Series no. 22 (1970).

46 T. C. Schelling, *The Strategy of Conflict* (Oxford University Press, 1963).

47 B. Shenfield, *Company Boards: Their Responsibilities to Shareholders, Employees, and the Community* (London: Allen and Unwin, 1971).

48 S. Siegel and L. E. Fouraker, *Bargaining and Group Decision Making* (New York: McGraw-Hill Book Company, 1960).

49 H. A. Simon, *Models of Man* (New York: John Wiley, 1957).

50 A. Stedry, *Budget Control and Cost Behaviour* (Englewood Cliffs, N.J.: Prentice-Hall, 1960).

51 Stock Exchange, *Admission of Securities to Listing* (London, 1973).

52 G. Strauss, 'Participative Management: a Critique', *International Labour Research*, 12, no. 2 (Nov 1966).

53 B. Towers, T. G. Whittingham and A. W. Gottschalk, eds., *Bargaining for Change* (London: George Allen and Unwin, 1972).
54 A. Topham and K. Coates, *The New Unionism* (London: Peter Owen, 1972).
55 Trades Union Congress, *Annual Report, 1970* (London).
56 K. F. Walker and L. Greyfié de Bellecombe, 'Workers' Participation in Management', *International Institute for Labour Studies,* Bulletin no. 2 (Feb 1967).
57 O. E. Williamson, *The Economics of Discretionary Behaviour: Managerial Objectives in a Theory of the Firm* (Englewood Cliffs, N.J.: Prentice-Hall, 1964).

3 Disclosure, Collective Bargaining and Inflation: Some Empirical Evidence

Among the various arguments put forward against greater disclosure of company information to union negotiators perhaps the most important is that the shift in bargaining power which such a policy is expected to produce will result in an increase in the rate of wage inflation. Two questions would appear to spring directly from this argument:

(1) To what extent can trade unions, by the exercise of their monopoly power, exert continuous upward pressure on the wage level independently of general economic conditions?

(2) Will greater knowledge of company information of a financial and economic nature produce a rise in trade union pressure or 'pushfulness' and an increase in negotiated wage rates?

In Chapter 4 we shall be looking at the ways in which analytical models of bargaining have dealt with information disclosure. The purpose of this chapter is essentially empirical, i.e. to investigate the above questions in the light of the considerable volume of econometric evidence on the major determinants of money wages. The weight of this evidence may help the reader to decide whether disclosure of economic and financial information by companies is likely to add to wage inflation. This issue has, of course, been given more point by the recent inflation experienced in the U.K. and other Western economies.

We shall begin with a review of early investigations of aggregate wage behaviour and then proceed to discuss some of the more recent disaggregated studies. There were several preliminary 'skirmishes' [8], [23] prior to the now famous article published in 1958 by Professor A. W. Phillips [39] but this latter work is now regarded as *the* progenitor of the empirical investigations which followed. This seminal contribution is, therefore, highly important and deserves special attention.

A. W. PHILLIPS

On the basis of data covering the period 1861 to 1957, Phillips tested the hypothesis that the percentage rate of change of money wage rates is largely explained by the volume of unemployment, measured as a percentage of the labour force, and by the rate of change of this unemployment. Phillips had, in fact, assumed that the rise in money wage rates was really determined by the degree of excess demand for labour but as this was, and is, not directly observable, he was forced to use unemployment as a proxy. He further assumed that the relationship between wage changes (ΔW) and unemployment (U) was non-linear, arguing as follows:

> When the demand for labour is high and there are very few unemployed we should expect employers to bid up wages quite rapidly, each firm and each industry being continually tempted to offer a little above the prevailing rates to attract the most suitable labour from other firms and industries. On the other hand, it appears that workers are reluctant to offer their services at less than prevailing rates when the demand for labour is low and unemployment is high, so that wage rates fall only very slowly. The relation between unemployment and the rate of change of wage rates is therefore likely to be highly non-linear.

To estimate the relation, and in particular to capture the assumed non-linearity, Phillips used a logarithmic transform of the following equation:

$$\dot{W} = a + bU^c$$

where $\dot{W}$ is the percentage rate of change of money wage rates, U is the percentage rate of unemployment and a, b and c are constants.[1]

Two conclusions were immediately claimed on the basis of Phillips' work: first the original hypothesis seemed to be supported;[2] second, and perhaps more importantly, the structural relationship between unemployment and the rate of change of money wage rates seemed to be highly stable for the whole period. This stability was somewhat surprising given the institutional changes which had occurred over the years in question and it suggested that money wages were fundamentally determined by economic factors rather than the development of trade union activity and the extension of collective bargaining.

A stylised graphical representation of Phillips' basic equation is described in Figure 3.1 below and for obvious reasons this relation has come to be called the Phillips curve.

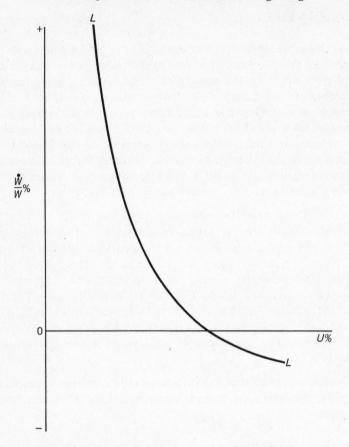

F<small>IG</small>. 3.1

While the overall regression curve *LL* relates wage changes and unemployment, Phillips explored the effects of *changes* in the level of unemployment by plotting the time path of successive observations of his primary variables. More formal methods of estimating the effect of changes in unemployment (ΔU) are used in later studies, but this fairly simple technique of plotting the time path graphically allowed Phillips to conclude that in most of the sub-periods covered there were marked loops around the basic regression line. Thus, at any *given* level of unemployment, if the rate of unemployment was falling the regression equation underestimated the associated change in wage rates; on the other hand, if unemployment was rising the equation overestimated the change in wages. These 'distortions' around the average relationship between unemployment and wage changes seemed to follow the pattern of the trade cycle: in the upswing of the cycle when unemployment was falling (i.e. ΔU was negative) the change in wages was larger than expected from the regression line, and in the downswing of the cycle (i.e. when ΔU was positive) the wage change was smaller than expected. Several hypotheses have been put forward to explain this looping behaviour but they need not concern us at this juncture.[3]

There are two further points of interest in the original Phillips analysis:

(1) assuming productivity growth of 2 % per annum it was claimed that a policy of price stability would be successful if aggregate demand were maintained so as to keep unemployment at a little less than $2\frac{1}{2}\%$;

(2) prices play a rather insignificant role in the process of wage determination and wages are assumed to respond only when very large increases in the cost of living occur, induced, for example, by import prices.

These two conclusions have clearly not stood the test of time but the study was nevertheless extremely useful as it provoked a virtual torrent of econometric work on the determinants of money wages over the following decade and a half in the U.K. and abroad, especially in the U.S.A.

In a follow-up study published in 1960 Lipsey [27] improved Phillips' approach in a number of ways: first, he demonstrated more rigorously the rationale for using unemployment as a proxy for aggregate demand; second, he developed an alternative hypothesis to explain the looped time paths and third, he included the rate of change of prices $\left(\dfrac{\dot{P}}{P}\right)$ and the rate of change of unemployment $\left(\dfrac{\dot{U}}{U}\right)$ to test for their effect as potential explanatory variables.

In general Lipsey's results supported and consolidated the Phillips' relation: unemployment was certainly the most important factor explaining wage behaviour in both pre- and post-World War I periods. Prices appeared to have a relatively more important role in the later period but the significance of the rate of change of unemployment appeared rather dubious in view of the fact that its coefficient changed from a positive to a negative sign over the two sub-periods. Despite these minor problems, however, Lipsey's study, taken with Phillips' observations, certainly seemed to show that trade unions and collective bargaining activity played no substantial part in the determination of wages.

Among several critical reactions which greeted Phillips' 1958 article [24], [43], one which is particularly interesting from our point of view came from Mr Nicholas (now Lord) Kaldor [22]. The essence of Kaldor's position was that, while he accepted the statistical association between unemployment and changes in money wage rates as well and truly established, he did not accept the inference which Phillips (and others) drew from it. Indeed, Kaldor offered a rival interpretation of the figures which he felt would prove superior. The alternative hypothesis proposed by Kaldor was that: 'the rise in money wages depends upon the *bargaining strength* of labour; and bargaining strength, in turn, is closely related to the prosperity of industry, which determines both the eagerness of labour unions to demand higher wages and the willingness, and ability of employers to grant them' [22, p. 293].

The inverse relationship between wage changes and unemployment is, therefore, attributed to:

(1) a positive causal relationship between wages and industrial prosperity; and

(2) a negative relationship between industrial prosperity and unemployment.

As it stands, however, the theory is fairly vague, as the expression 'the prosperity of industry' can be measured in a variety of ways. Kaldor did go on to make a quite specific prediction based on his rival theory: 'If instead of relating wage increases to unemployment and the rate of change of unemployment, Professor Phillips had related them to the increase in production, or to the increase in profits of the previous year, I am confident that he would have found an even better correlation – for all his periods, inter-war and post-war as well as pre-war . . .' [22, p. 294].

In general terms, some variant of this bargaining power approach is implicitly maintained by those who fear adverse consequences from greater disclosure: they believe that the ability of unions to extract concessions from employers is not constant, it varies with overall economic conditions including the state of the labour market *and* the state of the product market. The power theory is not of course inconsistent with the Phillips curve as one might well argue, for example, that high employment and tight labour market conditions weaken the employer's position *vis-à-vis* the union because:

(1) in the event of industrial action non-union labour is not readily available as a replacement; and

(2) union members are less reluctant to strike.

Bargaining power theorists would go on to argue, however, that holding conditions in the labour market constant, a significant independent influence on wages can be ascertained from the level of profits or some other indicator of ability to pay.

The Kaldor variant of the bargaining hypothesis was, in fact, exhaustively investigated on the basis of U.K. data by Lipsey and Steuer [28]. Their study was, and remains, particularly interesting for several reasons: in the first place, they specified and tested three versions of the way in which profits might affect changes in wages; secondly, the relation was investigated at both industry and aggregate levels over three sub-periods, 1949–58, 1926–38 and 1870–1913; finally, almost as an added bonus, they made some preliminary observations on other possible specifications of the bargaining power theory.

The three major versions of the wage-profits relation considered were as follows:[4]

1. The Phillips correlations between $\dot{W}$ and U can be explained away by a causal relation between $\dot{W}$ and D plus a cross-correlation between D and U. High profits *cause* wages to rise; but since high profits and low unemployment figures *happen to go together*, a statistically significant correlation will be observed between $\dot{W}$ and U.[5]

2. Although both profits and unemployment may influence $\dot{W}$, profits are the more important of the two, so that profits will be statistically a better explanatory variable than unemployment.

3. Whatever the relative importance of profits and unemployment, profits do exert a significant influence on the wage bargain and they will be statistically an important variable [28, p. 141].

For the most part the results obtained were more favourable to the Phillips 'unemployment' explanation of wage changes rather than the 'profits' theory. This was particularly true of the post-war period when, despite showing up rather weakly in the aggregate equation, the profits variable collapsed completely as an explanatory variable at industry level.

Only in the case of the inter-war period did the evidence support Kaldor's theory but even then in the attenuated form of hypothesis 2. As a parting shot, however, Lipsey and Steuer suggested three further, slightly more complex formulations of the wage-profit relation. They took as their dependent variable the difference between the rate of change of wages in each industry and the average rate of change of wages in general.[6] This was then regressed separately against:

(i) the difference between the rate of change of industry profits and the rate of change of aggregate profits;

(ii) the ratio of industry profits to aggregate profits;

(iii) the ratio of each industry's profit performance in the year in question to its average profit performance in preceding years.

In none of these cases did the variables yield a statistically satisfactory explanation for the behaviour of the regressand.

On the basis of U.K. data, therefore, the Lipsey-Steuer article dealt a severe blow to the bargaining power approach to wage determination, at least as far as the 'profits' version is representative of this theory. Their study did not conclusively dispose of the bargaining theory because, as the two authors themselves freely acknowledge, it is perfectly possible to argue that profit, i.e. last year's *realised* profit, is not the only, nor the best indicator of business prosperity or ability to pay, and that other variables would perform better. In other words the rate of change of wages may still be the product of unions' aggressive behaviour but that behaviour is conditioned by and related to a mix of financial and economic variables, some of which are examined further below. Second, further evidence has shown that profits may in fact have an independent role in wage determination. This evidence, which appeared after the Lipsey-Steuer article came from two disparate sources: an O.E.C.D. report on wages and labour mobility published in 1965 [31] and a series of investigations of wage behaviour in the American economy.

The O.E.C.D. report obtained data on profits by industry for five countries: the United States, Canada, Sweden, France and the U.K. We will shortly discuss the U.S. case separately as it certainly is the best documented. For the other four countries relative changes in earnings were correlated with the percentage change in profits in the same period and in the previous period. The result was that while the lagged relationship proved weak and unsystematic, the same period correlations yielded a majority of positive relationships. The report further pointed out that while the relation for the U.K. was considerably weaker, it was primarily because 'wage developments throughout the period [1949–58] were strongly influenced by the inter-bargain spread of arrangements made by wage round leaders. However, when a rather different question is taken up, namely whether the differentiation that did occur was in line with relative profit experience, the data appear to support the hypothesis' [31, p. 107].

Before turning to the American studies we ought to point out that foreign experience of wage behaviour may not always be relevant to the U.K. In this particular case, however, it may indeed be helpful for the following reason: demand theories of wage determination should presumably stand up, i.e. display validity, in different environmental conditions as it is precisely the nature of such theories that institutional structures make little difference to the underlying economic relationships. There is a genuine difficulty, of course, in specifying the correct proxy for aggregate demand so as to make results comparable,[7] but, given that this measurement problem can be overcome, one would normally expect a fair degree of correspondence of results. Most of the early American investigations did in fact demonstrate the negative trade-off between the level of unemployment and the rate of change of wages in the U.S., but the relationship was considerably weaker than in the United Kingdom. Thus, only tentative support for the basic Phillips relation came from Samuelson and Solow in 1960 [44], while an extensive study by Bowen [6] showed that other factors beside unemployment may play a powerful role. Further, in two consecutive articles Bhatia looked at factors affecting wages in the U.S. In the first [4], using data over the period 1900–1958, he attempted to replicate the Phillips analysis; in the second [5], he tested for the effects of profits and the change in profits as explanatory variables. In the earlier paper he found no clear-cut evidence for the unemployment/aggregate demand explanation of wage changes: in the early years of the century, 1900–1932, a rather weak association between variables was apparent, but even this fairly loose connection deteriorated in the post-war period, i.e. 1948–58. Nor did Bhatia find any relationship between wages and the rate of change of unemployment over the same period.

The second article, following up these negative conclusions, examined the influence of profits and the change in profits on wage changes. The profit variable was defined as 'the percentage rate of return on equity before tax', although Bhatia also argued that other definitions would yield similar results. Monthly data were employed and he found that, with a two-month time lag, the level and rate of change of profit explained 80 % of the variance in wage changes with each independent variable appearing as significant. With this kind of evidence he went on to argue that profit gave a much better explanation of wage behaviour in the post-war period than did unemployment. These results were prima facie a complete rebuttal of the Phillips hypothesis, at least insofar as it applies to the American environment. Insofar as each article isolated one variable at a time it may be subject to the criticism that wages are determined by the simultaneous interaction of several variables.

In the spirit of this criticism two further important studies appeared [12], [36] which demonstrated a more complex set of relationships. The investigation by Eckstein and Wilson published in the *Quarterly Journal of Economics* tested a series of hypotheses about wage determination –

some institutional and some economic. The major institutional hypothesis was that wage settlements follow a wage leadership pattern with a key group setting the example for a complete wage round. The economic hypothesis was that *both* factor market (i.e. supply and demand for labour as measured by unemployment) and product market (i.e. the profit rate) would influence the rate of change of wages. The results of this detailed investigation show that a wage round mechanism was indeed in operation in the U.S. and that both unemployment and profits affect the rate of change of wages, particularly in the key group where quite extraordinary results were obtained, even after allowing for the relatively small number of observations. Both variables proved significant at the 0.99 level and the coefficient of determination (R^2) was .9975. It must be added that nothing like the same degree of fit on profits and unemployment was found for wage determination *outside* the key group – only in three of the eleven industries did the variables come out as significant at the .95 level. Among their conclusions Eckstein and Wilson make the following comment on the weakness of the Phillips relation in the U.S.:

> Observers have puzzled over the wide scatter of points around a Phillips curve for the United States, the curve relating wage changes to unemployment. Our findings help to explain this looseness of fit. Since profits and unemployment are both important variables and *are not highly intercorrelated*, one cannot expect a curve plotting wage changes against only one of the explanatory variables to fit the data well. Further, the wage round mechanism is missing as well [12, p. 406] [Italics added].

The second important contribution to the explanation of wage behaviour in the context of a more complex model was that of Perry. The essence of his empirical study was published in an article in the *Review of Economic Studies*, 1964 [36] and was considerably extended and refined in a carefully argued book which appeared in 1966 [37]. The basic wage change function $\dot{W} = f(U)$ is made considerably more elaborate by:

(i) the addition of a price change variable to capture cost of living effects ($\dot{P}$);

(ii) a variable to test for the effect of profit (R) – defined as net profits after tax as a percentage of shareholders' equity; and

(iii) in an attempt to gauge the impact of expectations he also allows for *changes* in both the rate of profit (ΔR) and the direction of unemployment (D_u).

The general form of the model tested, therefore, becomes:

$$\dot{W} = f(U, D_u, \dot{P}, R, \Delta R)$$

The direction in which unemployment changes proved to be insignificant and added very little to the explanation of wage changes so it was eventually dropped from the final estimating equation. The empirical relation chosen by Perry as most representative of American experience was:

$$W_t = -4.313 + 0.367P_{t-1} + 14.711\frac{1}{U_t} + 0.424R_{t-1} + .796\Delta R_t$$

All the variables were highly significant and the coefficient of multiple determination, i.e. the percentage of variation explained, was 87%.

This particular analysis merits our attention for several reasons. In the first place, Perry's justification for including a profit variable is highly interesting, as he argues that:

the aspect of the bargaining situation most clearly identified with profits is the ability of employers to pay a given wage increase. It may not be entirely clear that profits are an appropriate measure of this ability. For instance, if wage changes in a firm lead to price changes for the output of a firm, all or part of a wage change may ultimately be paid for, in some sense, through increased prices. As the ability of a firm to pass on wage increases changes, say through a change in its degree of monopoly power or in the prices of competing products, so too would its resistance to a wage increase. But the first of these is a long-run effect of little importance here, and the second would surely show up in the profits of the firm in question, although imperfectly. More to the point, however, the use of profits is not meant to capture all the dimensions of a firm's ability to pay a wage increase. Rather, the fact that this ability is partially reflected in profits is one of the reasons for expecting profits to help explain wage changes [37, p. 28].

In other words, the inclusion of profits may be taken to be a direct test of the bargaining power hypothesis where profits or the profit rate act, in this instance, as a proxy for ability to pay. The fact that each of the profit variables used is statistically significant during the period studied may be interpreted as lending support to the power-bargaining explanation of wage changes, although not in the strong form originally suggested by Kaldor. Something like the Phillips curve is discernible for the U.S. but it cannot be drawn up except on the basis of very strict *ceteris paribus* assumptions, keeping, for example, the price level and the profit rate constant. In fact as Perry shows, there would be several Phillips curves depending upon one's assumptions about prevailing profit rates. Figure 3.2 below illustrates this idea.

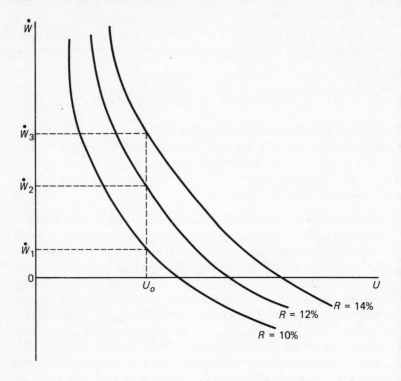

Fɪɢ. 3.2

The suggestion is that at any given level of unemployment (i.e. aggregate demand) there will be a number of possible rates of wage increase depending upon the prevailing rate of profit – thus with the profit rate at 10 % the rate of wage change associated with U_0 is $\dot{W}_1$; when the profit rate is 12 % wages increase at a rate of $\dot{W}_2$ and when R is 14 %, the rate of wage change becomes $\dot{W}_3$.

A further point of interest in Perry's model concerns the role of prices or the cost of living term. It has been suggested that the inclusion of prices (i.e. some form of general price index) in the wage determination equation will in fact capture any influence deriving from the profit variable – thus:

If profits are increased by expanding output and holding prices steady, capital's share ought to increase at the same rate as labour's share (unless the process started in a recession when labor was being hoarded, in which case labour's share was above equilibrium). However, if profits are increased through profits inflation or through diminishing returns (demand-pull) inflation, then wage earners will bargain for a share of the increased profits. In other words, wage earners will bargain for a share of the increased profits *when these profits have risen through an increase in prices*; otherwise they will not. This relationship is completely captured by the price term in the wage equation. Profits when added, make no net contribution and in fact have a slightly negative sign in the regressions we computed [13, p. 270].

The implication of this argument seems to be that there is some generally accepted 'equilibrium' distribution of income between wages and profit, and only when this equilibrium is disturbed do wage-earners react by pressing for compensatory adjustments. Such a view is difficult to accept for several reasons: it seems to regard trade unions and union negotiators as essentially defensive, whereas one of the major objectives of labour organisations has been to shift the distribution of national income in favour of labour in general and their own members in particular [50]; secondly, the gradual reduction in the profit share experienced in many Western economies since World War II [38] indicates that if such an equilibrium exists it has yet to be reached; and finally, at an empirical level, as shown by Perry's model, it is possible for both prices and profits to enter the wage equation separately and, therefore, for each to exert an independent influence.

The upshot of these studies of the American economy was to cast doubt on the simple Phillips curve as a general economic phenomenon and this in turn set off a reassessment of the relation for the U.K. Sceptics could argue that the relationship between unemployment and the rate of wage change only really held good in the period prior to World War I, that it deteriorated badly in the inter-war period and that it was less than stable in the years after World War II. This kind of destructive criticism is empty, however, unless one has a hypothesis of equal (preferably greater) explanatory power. As the profits theory had been analysed and rejected for the U.K., economists who favoured an institutional/bargaining version of wage determination sought other possible explanatory variables. Most obviously they could appeal to trade union militancy or aggressiveness. But the basic problem here was to translate this rather nebulous concept into a quantitative measure so that the hypothesis could be tested in the conventional manner. One of the first reinterpretations of wage behaviour along these lines was that suggested by Hines in 1964 [15]. He argued that pressure on the level of money wages and, therefore, the rate of change of wage rates, were related to union militancy and that *the rate of change of unionisation* could be taken as an appropriate proxy for this militancy. The 'Hines' hypothesis, therefore, is that:

$$\dot{W} = f(\dot{T}, T)$$

where $\dot{T}$ is the rate of change of unionisation and T is the level of unionisation.

When tested for the period 1893–1961 these variables accounted for more than 80% of the variance in money wage rates. For the sub-period 1921–61 his estimated equation explained nearly 90% of the variation in wage changes. This quite extraordinary set of results could quite easily have been explained in terms of the more conventional Phillips analysis if the rate of unionisation was itself determined by the level of activity in the economy. Thus if increasing union membership occurs when aggregate demand is high (producing low unemployment and tight labour market conditions) and if membership is stagnant or contracts in periods of high unemployment, then his main variable $\dot{T}$ would itself appear to depend upon the strength of demand for labour. In fact, Hines went on to show that the rate of change of unionisation could not be explained by such factors as the level of unemployment, the rate of change of unemployment or previous changes in wage rates or earnings. He found instead a strong connection with the rate of change of prices and a smaller, but still significant connection with the level of profits. Moreover, he also demonstrated that the demand theory of wage behaviour was relatively less successful than his own 'aggressiveness' index in accounting for the rate of wage change after World War I – whether demand is measured simply by the level of unemployment or unemployment minus vacancies. Indeed, in his multiple regression including U and $\dot{T}$ together the former was found to be insignificant so that Hines was led to argue that unemployment was not a determining factor in the rate of wage change – particularly since the end of World War II. Similar conclusions were derived about profits per employee, which again did not emerge as an important factor in wage determination.

Hines' theory and results which have been reiterated and further developed in successive publications [16], [17] clearly support the view that unions are an *independent* causal influence on the rate of wage inflation. Despite the apparently powerful nature of Hines' findings, however, his hypothesis has attracted a great deal of sustained criticism

[10], [14], [41], [42], [49]. As there is no underlying theory of union behaviour from which the hypothesis is derived many economists simply feel uncomfortable with what seems a rather *ad hoc* procedure: it just does not seem very plausible to argue that union recruitment campaigns are pursued in such a manner as to build up industrial muscle immediately prior to a wage demand. Other economists have quarrelled more directly with the model's detailed structure: statistical and theoretical objections have resulted in respecifying the dynamic structure [49], redefining variables [42], rerunning the time periods [41] etc. but the best that happens as far as the critics are concerned is that the significance of $\dot{T}$ is reduced *but it still remains statistically significant.*

The rate of change of unionisation is not of course the only proxy one could use to test a theory of wage behaviour based on union aggressiveness. Several studies have been undertaken in both the U.K. and abroad using a different proxy for 'pushfulness', i.e. strike activity [2], [3], [14], [48], [52]. The results obtained on this variable have been nothing like as clear-cut and unambiguous as the Hines' case for a number of reasons:

(1) first of all, strike activity is a difficult variable to define as it can mean frequency, days lost or number of workers involved;[8]
(2) second, many 'strikes' go unrecorded and other types of industrial action, e.g. overtime bans, a work-to-rule or go-slow may exert quite as much leverage as an all-out strike;
(3) finally, as the regressand is normally the union/non-union differential there is *a priori* ambiguity about the direction of causality *and* the expected sign of the relation.

Thus it is possible to argue that union militancy causes wage inflation or that wage inflation causes an upsurge in union militancy. It is also possible to argue that an increase in strike activity will widen the union/non-union differential so that a positive association between variables is to be expected; alternatively one might postulate an increase in strike activity when the differential is *compressed* – perhaps as a result of other factors – in which case a negative association is to be expected.

Nevertheless, it must be remarked that, apart from the rather negative conclusions reached by Ward and Zis in their study of 6 European economies [52], most of the studies using some definition of strike activity in their wage equations have picked up a significant positive relationship.

A number of other investigations have been undertaken to assess the possible impact of trade unions on wage inflation, these have dealt with such factors as:
(1) industry profitability;

(2) industry concentration ratios in order to reflect monopolistic product-market conditions; and

(3) the proportion of the labour force found in trade unions.

These variables are not themselves measures of aggressiveness, but 'permissive' factors insofar as they allow any given level of militancy to be more easily translated into wage increases. We have discussed in some detail the role of profitability in determining wage changes at an aggregate level. Studies by Segal [45] and Bowen [6] of the American economy illustrate that profitability may play a small but significant role in the wage equation at industry level and when combined with strong union power and a high concentration ratio a large proportion of the total variance in industry wage changes is explained. Levinson [25] has shown in a later article, however, that by redefining 'monopoly power' in terms of entry conditions rather than the conventional concentration ratio the profit variable loses its explanatory power.

Studies of the effect of the *level* of unionisation on wages have a fairly long history in economics [26] and the general view appears to have been that, while it might have an 'impact' effect, displacing the relative earnings of the newly-organized, it would not thereafter impart a continuous upward bias on the wage level. More recent research has attempted to assess the effect of unionisation by dividing the labour force into a unionised and a non-unionised sector and then estimating a Phillips relation for each. An early investigation along these lines by McCaffree [29] showed that the Phillips curve for the unionised sector ($L_u L_u$ in Figure 3.3) was less steep than that for the non-unionised sector ($L_n L_n$). The implication seemed to be that the presence of unions could be a two-edged sword: at certain levels of unemployment, e.g. greater than U_o, unions gave the wage relation an upward bias, but at levels of unemployment less than U_o they exerted a dampening effect on the normal market adjustment process. This study had been performed on cross-section data but similar effects had been picked up in Lipsey's time series analysis of the U.K. which is compatible with a hypothesis of stronger trade unionism in each of his sub-periods [27].

Two later investigations by Vanderkamp in 1966 [51] and Pierson in 1968 [40], of the Canadian and American economies respectively, indicated that the effect of unionisation may be to shift the relation between wage changes and unemployment in an upward direction throughout its length (i.e. $L_u' L_u'$ in Figure 3.3) so that at any given level of unemployment a higher rate of wage change is noted. It is also worth pointing out that many studies of wage behaviour involving trade unions indicate that the cost of living or price term becomes more significant:

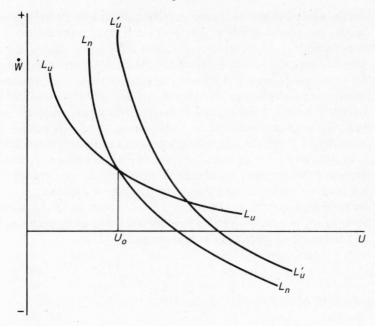

FIG. 3.3

whatever else unions do they appear capable of making wages more responsive to increases in prices.

Nearly all the research we have so far reviewed has accepted that some kind of short-run trade-off between wage inflation and unemployment exists, but it has also shown that the precise form of that trade-off can change in different environmental conditions. Thus although institutional factors such as unionisation, product market conditions, militancy, etc. may change the position and/or slope of the relation, it remains discernible in most of the analyses,[9] albeit in a modified form. In the mid-1960s, however, (i.e. towards the end of 1966 and the beginning of 1967) most of the Western economies, including the U.K., experienced the onset of a simultaneous combination of *accelerating* inflation and rising unemployment.[10] This combination of increasing rates of wage change with growing slack in labour markets was clearly not compatible with the normal inverse correlation and seemed to indicate the final demise of the whole Phillips curve approach. Some economists took it to be a final vindication of the institutional wage-push interpretation of inflation. Thus, to quote one eminent authority on the reaction to these events:

. . . the whole Phillips curve approach has suffered a severe set-back in recent years as a result of the prevalence of a combination of abnormally high unemployment and abnormally rapid inflation in the United States and the United Kingdom. These phenomena are in my view easily explicable in terms of the more sophisticated quantity theory that has emerged in recent years, and which makes use of complex models of expectation-formation and lagged responses of price and wage determination to changes in macro-economic policies; nevertheless, they have been widely interpreted by those whom I shall refer to as 'political economists' as evidence that the Phillips curve has broken down (or even never existed), that inflation is a matter of sociology or 'trade union militancy', or the abuse of monopoly power by giant corporations and that the appropriate remedy for it is some form of social control over the determination of money wages and prices, described generically as incomes policy [21].

THE COLLAPSE OF THE PHILLIPS CURVE

The apparent failure of the Phillips relation to explain the behaviour of inflation in the later 1960s produced three types of reaction:
(1) those who held a wage-push theory of inflation saw it as a justification of their argument;
(2) some economists attempted to explain the breakdown of the relationship by investigating more closely the adequacy of unemployment as an indicator of excess demand;
(3) the third approach was to introduce a price term into the wage equation to reflect price expectations and thereby construct an expectations-augmented excess demand theory of inflation.

We have already discussed much of the empirical evidence dealing with institutional influences on the wage relationship at an aggregate level, so we shall briefly deal with reactions (2) and (3) before turning to some of the less highly aggregated studies of wage behaviour which have been done recently.

The notion that unemployment ceased to be a useful indicator of the pressure of aggregate demand towards the end of 1966 has been investigated by Taylor [48] and Bowers, Cheshire and Webb [7]. Taylor finds that if adjustments are made to the unemployment variable to allow for changes in the pattern of labour hoarding and if some allowance is made for union militancy (via the number of stoppages) then the Phillips curve 'reappears' particularly when these variables are regressed against weekly earnings. Similarly Bowers, Cheshire and Webb are led, after extensive investigation, to conclude that an increase in 'structural' unemployment (i.e. a situation where job vacancies and unemployed workers can coexist because the latter do not have the correct skill, for example) had occurred. They go on to argue that if the increased 'structural' component is allowed for an excess demand explanation adequately covers the experience of the late 1960s.

The problem with both of these approaches is that while they may very well help to explain why the Phillips curve or excess demand hypothesis remains tenable until 1970/71, it becomes progressively more difficult to explain subsequent experience through to 1975. With unemployment in the United Kingdom in excess of 5% the least one would expect is a levelling off in the rate of wage inflation – instead of which it continued to climb beyond 25% per annum. Clearly in these circumstances the structural hypotheses simply will not do.

The introduction of price expectations into models of inflation appears to offer a substantial advance in our understanding of inflationary processes as they gather momentum, and, it is argued, can also help to explain the wage-price explosion which occurred from the late 1960s onward. Thus, Parkin has argued that:

> The combination of a large budget deficit and an increase in the rate of monetary expansion creates an overheated economy. The overheating normally takes the form of overtime working, longer delivery lags and inventory reductions. However, the secondary response is for wages and prices to be marked up at a faster rate. Since in a complex industrial economy the output of one stage is the input of subsequent stages of production, these initially rising prices and wages are transmitted through the economy as increased costs to others. This leads to further rounds of price and wage rises. If such a process persists for long enough, a third stage of the transmission mechanism comes into force: namely, an upward revision of inflation expectations. Such expectations, if firmly enough held, will lead firms and unions to raise wages and prices by the amount which they anticipate others will be raising theirs, quite independently of the current state of demand [32].

The basic hypothesis, therefore, is that:

$$\dot{W} = f(U) + \lambda \dot{P}^e$$ where $0 < \lambda \leqq 1$ and $\dot{P}^e$ represents price expectations.

The effect of introducing price expectations in this way makes the *position* of the Phillips curve vary in the wage-unemployment space. Thus in Figure 3.4 below, the original Phillips curve can be drawn up as C_1 and with inflation expectations of zero the normal trade-off between money wage rates and unemployment holds. As price expectations adjust to on-going inflation within the economy the money illusion disappears and in bargaining for, or being offered higher *real* wages, money wages must be notched up to cover the expected increase in prices – thus the curve shifts outwards in a north-easterly direction to C_2, C_3, etc.

The coincidence of rising wages and rising unemployment can therefore be explained for the late 1960s and the 1970s in terms of a continuous upward shift in price/wage expectations. Just such a model has been tested by Parkin, Sumner and Ward who conclude that the

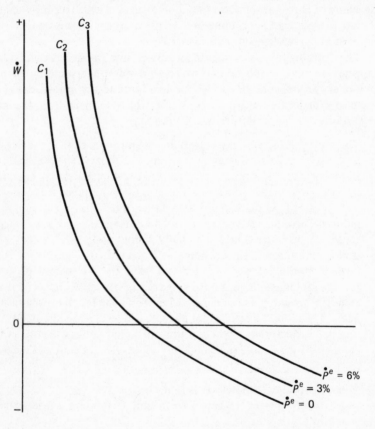

Fig. 3.4

expectations variable contributes very highly to the explanatory power of their equations [35]. The key question in this kind of research is, how are expectations conditioned and formed? Two approaches to this issue are possible and have been tried: the first is to assume at the outset that current expectations about the behaviour of future prices are simply an extrapolation of previous experience. The so-called *adaptive* expectations model therefore assumes that the present state of expectations is simply a weighted average of all past rates of inflation. As one would expect, the weights are chosen in such a way as to give greatest emphasis to recent experience [46]. The problem with this kind of approach is that one can never be sure that the weighting system is correct and it does assume that unions, firms and individuals learn in a very automaton-like fashion. There is no room here for the intrusion of one-off political/economic events like the oil price increases of 1973/74. The second approach to the formation of expectations, therefore, is to sample expectations directly via surveys like that of the C.B.I. or the *Financial Times* on the state of business confidence. This questionnaire-type study was used by Parkin and Carlson [33] to derive a series for the expected rate of change of prices in the U.K. and they found that the adaptive expectations model conformed reasonably well to the behaviour of this empirically derived series.

There is no doubt that considerable insight into wage behaviour has been gained by allowing for expectational adjustment. Studies of inflationary expectations have gone a long way towards re-establishing the demand/monetary interpretation of inflation which was badly shaken by the post-1970 wage-unemployment explosion. They have also shown that while the old-style Phillips curve may still operate in the short run, over the longer period it may become considerably steeper or, in the limit, disappear completely as inflation becomes fully anticipated.

With these models we seem to have come full circle as trade unions and institutional factors play a negligible role compared to, say, the rate of expansion of the money supply. We must, therefore, at this stage offer some tentative conclusions regarding our first problem: namely, the ability of unions to exert pressure on the wage level. While much of the evidence, especially concerning the relationship between wages and profits is open to rival interpretations of a 'demand' or 'push' type, certain other studies are much less ambiguous. Thus, investigations which proxy union militancy or which measure the 'power' variables, such as concentration ratios and degree of unionisation, demonstrate that trade union activity *does* result in greater pressure on wage levels in labour markets. To this we may add that spillover effects, wage transfer mechanisms and key bargains constitute a further dimension through which labour organisations may induce inflationary bias in the economy. There are certain high levels of aggregate demand (and presumably certain low levels) at which the trade union influence may be swamped, but within these 'extremes' there is a discernible union effect.

The second problem, with which we started this chapter, concerned the degree to which knowledge of company information might itself produce an increase in union 'pushfulness' and negotiated wages. This hypothesis is virtually impossible to test directly as we really need to compare situations which are alike in *every* respect except for availability of information to union negotiators; any difference between wage rates (or the change in wage rates) could then be ascribed to the impact of the more freely available data. The same problem bedevils all types of economic investigation but is particularly acute in this case as there is no official, systematic publication of data on wage settlements concluded at company level.

At this stage, therefore, we must content ourselves with a rather more limited question: is there any evidence to demonstrate that wage increases are related to financial and economic variables at the level of the firm? Are some of these variables more important than others? In an early study Brown [9] demonstrated that the inter-industry wage structure is influenced by ability to pay where the latter was measured by a set of different indicators, some financial, others economic. These indicators included:

(1) value added per man-hour;
(2) concentration of the industry;
(3) profitability measured by ratio of profit to sales;
(4) ratio of payroll cost to value-added;
(5) employment mix in terms of male/female composition;
(6) change in employment.

Significant, simple correlation coefficients between average annual wages and each of these variables except for (4) were obtained. In particular the productivity, market structure and profitability variables had coefficients of .471, .406 and .411 respectively. Moreover the multiple correlation coefficient between wages and expected ability to pay as measured by the 6 indexes was $R = .861$, i.e. inter-industry differences in the ability to pay variables explained almost 75 % of the inter-industry variance in wage levels. Similarly, in a study of negotiated wage increases, Sparks and Wilton [47] used a sample of 133 individual contracts collected over the period 1951–65 for a cross-section of Canadian manufacturing. The dependent variable in this case was the percentage change in hourly wage rates and this was regressed against the rate of unemployment, the rate of change of unemployment, profit as a percentage of total assets, relative productivity, the growth of employment and relative wages. In some runs the equation was extended to include a strike dummy and certain variables used to capture possible interaction effects, e.g. productivity × relative wages, unemployment × rate of change of prices. Unemployment, profitability, the price term and the unemployment/price interaction variable performed consistently well; results on the use of other variables were mixed, e.g. employment gowth and relative wages were insignificant in some equations but with the inclusion of relative productivity, relative wages become significant.

These studies, however indicative of the financial and economic factors which may determine wages, either in terms of overall structure (Brown) or in terms of individual contracts (Sparks and Wilton) are still conducted at too high a level of aggregation to answer even our modified question about the effect and importance of *company* information on *company* wage settlements. This particular issue has been taken up by Horwitz and Shabahang [18] who have looked at the relationship between published accounting information and company wage increases in the United States.[11] These authors point out that in many arbitration cases in the U.S. the concept of financial ability to pay is frequently mentioned. It is also referred to in submissions to the National Labor Relations Board and other official wage review bodies. The concept is, however, fairly nebulous and can be measured in several different ways – see for example Chapter 6 below. Horwitz and Shabahang select 7 variables which could be taken to represent various aspects of ability to pay. These variables are derived from company accounts and are as follows:

(1) net operating profit as a percentage of sales;
(2) total sales divided by net worth;
(3) rate of investment in plant and equipment;
(4) current assets divided by current liabilities, i.e. the current ratio;
(5) dividends per share;
(6) accounting net income divided by total assets;
(7) earnings per share.

The rationale for choosing this particular set of ratios is that indicators 1, 2 and 3 are to represent *productivity* at the level of the firm; 4 and 5 obviously show the short-run *liquidity* of the company as they indicate working capital and a potential call on working capital; finally 6 and 7 clearly represent the firm's *overall profitability*. These constitute the independent variables in the analysis. Horwitz and Shabahang then relate these variables taken from reported data in period $t-1$ to wage increases in period t. A one-year lag is used on the simple assumption that expectations about future financial variables help to determine current wage increases and these expectations are themselves a function of previous values of the variables.

The data on which the calculations are based comprise 205 observations taken from 15 companies over the period 1945–65. The results of their analysis demonstrate that two variables only are associated with wage increases to a significant degree, i.e. at the 95% level. These are:
(1) profit divided by sales – the mark-up variable;
(2) dividends per share.
The first enters with a positive, the second with a negative sign.

In an attempt to investigate further the results obtained by Horwitz and Shabahang the present writers conducted an essentially similar study for the U.K. Unfortunately, data limitation at this level of disaggregation is even more severe in the United Kingdom. The fact that no systematic collection of company level wage settlements is undertaken by any official body implies that rather *ad hoc* procedures had to be followed. Also, given the periodic imposition of incomes policies in the U.K. over the past 30 years, the use of time-series data becomes problematical as government intervention may distort any underlying relationships. Thus, we were confined to a cross-section analysis on a sample taken in a year when no incomes policy was in operation. In all, some 117 observations of company wage settlements were obtained for the year 1971–72.[12] The relevant financial data for the same companies were collected for the financial year preceding the settlement [taken from 30]. Percentage wage increases were then regressed against a similar set of variables to that used by Horwitz and Shabahang: a minor modification was introduced insofar as we employed the figure for gross profit in preference to the net concept in variables 1 and 6. As a test of the hypothesis:

$$W = a_0 + a_1 x_1 + a_2 x_2 + a_3 x_3 + a_4 x_4 + a_5 x_5 + a_6 x_6 + a_7 x_7 + u$$

Where:

W = percentage wage increase
x_1 = total profit/sales
x_2 = sales/net worth
x_3 = increase in plant and equipment
x_4 = current assets/current liabilities
x_5 = dividends per share
x_6 = total profit/net worth

x_7 = earnings per share

The following results were obtained:

$$W = 14.57366 + 7.75381\,x_1 + 0.28259\,x_2 - 0.00002\,x_3$$
$$(6.90)\qquad (0.51)\qquad\quad (1.76)\qquad\qquad (1.11)$$

$$ - 1.99477\,x_4 - 0.08431\,x_5 - 3.91811\,x_6 + 0.06261\,x_7$$
$$(1.78)\qquad\quad (1.17)\qquad\quad (0.48)\qquad\qquad (1.68)$$

$t_c = 1.67$ for 95% confidence level, one tail test

$R^2 = 10.4\%$

One or two comments appear to be in order, though in many ways the poverty of these results speaks for itself. First of all these results fail to support the hypothesis. Three variables come out as apparently significant:

x_2 — sales divided by net worth;
x_4 — current assets divided by current liabilities;
x_7 — earnings per share.

Considerable collinearity was expected on *a priori* grounds and was borne out from the correlation matrix, particularly between x_1 and x_6, x_5 and x_7, thus interpretation of the '*t*' statistic is in these cases fairly meaningless. In fact, only the variable indicating the short-run liquidity position was both significant *and* not strongly correlated with any other variable. The R^2 is also extremely low at 10%, even allowing for the fact that cross-section results tend typically to be on the low side.

On the basis of these results, therefore, the underlying hypothesis, that published company data on ability to pay can affect wage increases, must be regarded as very doubtful. We cannot reject the hypothesis entirely, primarily because the data on which it was tested are clearly not very satisfactory. Nevertheless, until better data are available we must make do with what very limited resources can manage to uncover. Secondly, of course, it may be that different combinations of data are used in bargaining, although from our knowledge of the use of company information in bargaining (see Chapter 5) this particular objection seems very unlikely.

If we may summarise this chapter very briefly: it is felt by some that further disclosure of company information will produce greater inflationary pressure from trade unions in the form of higher wage demands. We have seen that the first assumption implicit in this argument, i.e. that unions *can* influence the rate of wage inflation is, on balance, supported by a great deal of macro-economic evidence, although considerable disagreement remains. The second assumption, that greater disclosure *will* increase union pushfulness cannot be directly tested. When we examined the modified version of this assumption there was some conflict of evidence: Brown's study for the U.S. shows that industry wage *levels* may be determined by ability to pay, but of course here ability to pay is measured by a different set of variables than those used by Horwitz and Shabahang who tested for the effects of *published accounting data* on wage *increases*. The evidence for this particular relationship does seem to be rather weak but several caveats are in order:

(1) the absence of any correlation between wage increases and the variables used may not preclude other possible financial factors being determinants;

(2) the lag system chosen was the simplest possible and may not catch the underlying relationship;

(3) finally, other factors of a more general economic nature influence wages and these may reduce the effect of company information.

NOTES

1 The actual relation obtained by Phillips was $\dot{W} + .900 = 9.638U^{-1.394}$.

2 It was clearly not refuted.

3 The behaviour of the loops themselves was not very stable – in the 19th century they behaved according to a clockwise time-path; in the 1950s they were anti-clockwise. The interested reader may wish to consult [11], [27].

4 $\dot{W}$ is the percentage rate of change of wages.

D_t is an index of real profits, i.e. money profits deflated by a price index.

U is unemployment as a percentage of the labour force.

$\dot{U}$ is the percentage rate of change of unemployment.

$\dot{D}_t$ is the percentage rate of change of profits.

5 As Lipsey and Steuer point out, this is essentially the Kaldor hypothesis – the other two versions tested are weaker versions.

6 Hourly earnings were in fact used.

7 Unemployment figures for the U.K., for example, are not strictly comparable to those in the U.S. The American figures are arrived at by sampling techniques; the British figures are a count of those registering to claim unemployment benefit. To make some form of direct comparison, the U.K. figure should be revised upward by as much as 50%.

8 Or some composite of all three. See [52].

9 The major and important exception being that of Hines.

10 The process has been even more marked in the 1970s.

11 A further, more recent study by Tomczyk [50] has come to our attention. This extends the work of Horwitz and Shabahang by employing more variables in a multi-variate framework but is essentially similar in terms of its theoretical approach and conclusions.

12 For sources, see [19], [20].

REFERENCES

1 G. C. Archibald, 'The Phillips Curve and the Distribution of Unemployment', *American Economic Review Papers and Proceedings* (May 1969).
2 O. C. Ashenfelter and G. E. Johnson, 'Bargaining Theory, Trade Unions and Industrial Strike Activity', *American Economic Review*, 59 (1969).
3 O. C. Ashenfelter, G. E. Johnson and J. H. Pencavel, 'Trade Unions and the Rate of Change of Money Wages in United States Manufacturing Industry', *Review of Economic Studies* (Jan 1972).
4 R. J. Bhatia, 'Unemployment and the Rate of Change in Money Earnings in the United States 1900–1958', *Economica*, 28 (1961).
5 R. J. Bhatia, 'Profits and the Rate of Change in Money Earnings in the United States 1935–59', *Economica*, 29 (1962).
6 W. G. Bowen, *The Wage-Price Issue: A Theoretical Analysis* (Princeton, N.J.: Princeton University Press, 1960).
7 J. K. Bowers, P. C. Cheshire and A. E. Webb, 'The Change in the Relationship between Unemployment and Earnings Increases', *National Institute Economic Review* (1970).
8 A. J. Brown, *The Great Inflation 1939–51* (London: Oxford University Press, 1955).
9 D. G. Brown, 'Expected Ability to Pay and Inter-industry Wage Structure in Manufacturing', *Industrial and Labor Relations Review* (16 Oct 1962).
10 P. Burrows and T. Hitiris, 'Estimating the Impact of Incomes Policy', in [34].
11 J. Burton, *Wage Inflation* (London: Macmillan, 1972).
12 O. Eckstein and T. A. Wilson, 'The Determination of Money Wages in American Industry', *Quarterly Journal of Economics*, 76 (1962).
13 M. K. Evans, *Macroeconomic Activity*, (London: Harper and Row, 1969).
14 L. G. Godfrey, 'The Phillips Curve: Incomes Policy and Trade Union Effects', in *The Current Inflation*, eds. H. G. Johnson and A. R. Nobay (London: Macmillan, 1971).
15 A. G. Hines, 'Trade Unions and Wage Inflation in the United Kingdom 1893–1961', *Review of Economic Studies*, 31 (1964).
16 A. G. Hines, 'Wage Inflation in the United Kingdom 1948–62, A Disaggregated Study', *Economic Journal*, 79 (1969).
17 A. G. Hines, 'The Determinants of the Rate of Change of Money Wage Rates and the Effectiveness of Incomes Policy', in H. G. Johnson and A. R. Nobay, *The Current Inflation*, (1971).
18 B. Horwitz and R. Shabahang, 'Published Corporate Accounting Data and General Wage Increases of the Firm', *The Accounting Review*, 46 (Apr 1971).
19 *Incomes Data Reports*, nos. 106–51, 1971–2 (London: Incomes Data Services Ltd.).
20 *Industrial Relations Review and Report*, nos. 1–46, 1971–2 (London: Industrial Relations Enterprises Ltd.).
21 H. G. Johnson, 'Notes on Incomes Policy and the Balance of Payments', in [34].
22 N. Kaldor, 'Economic Growth and the Problem of Inflation', *Economica*, 26 (1959).
23 L. R. Klein and A. S. Goldberger, *An Econometric Model of the United States 1929–52* (Amsterdam: North-Holland, 1955).
24 K. G. J. C. Knowles and C. B. Winsten, 'Can the Level of Unemployment Explain Wage Changes?', *Bulletin of the Oxford Institute of Statistics* (May 1959).
25 H. M. Levinson, *Determining Forces in Collective Wage Bargaining* (New York: John Wiley, 1966).
26 H. G. Lewis, *Unionism and Relative Wages in the United States* (Chicago: Chicago University Press, 1963).
27 R. G. Lipsey, 'The Relation Between Unemployment and the Rate of Change of Money Wage Rates in the United Kingdom 1862–1957: A Further Analysis', *Economica*, 27 (1960).

28 R. G. Lipsey and M. D. Steuer, 'The Relation between Profits and Wage Rates', *Economica*, 28 (1961).

29 K. M. McCaffree, 'A Further Consideration of Wages, Unemployment and Prices in the United States 1948–58', *Industrial and Labor Relations Review*, 16 (1963).

30 *Moodies Investment Handbook*, Pt. 1. Published quarterly by Moodies Investment Services Ltd., London 1970–1.

31 O.E.C.D., *Wages and Labour Mobility* (Paris, July 1965).

32 J. M. Parkin, 'Where is Britain's Inflation Going?', *Lloyd's Bank Review*, no. 117 (July 1975).

33 J. M. Parkin and J. A. Carlson, *Inflation Expectations*, University of Manchester Inflation Workshop Discussion Paper 7305 (1973).

34 J. M. Parkin and M. T. Sumner, eds., *Incomes Policy and Inflation* (Manchester University Press, 1972).

35 J. M. Parkin, M. T. Sumner and R. Ward, *The Effects of Excess Demand, Generalised Expectations and Wage-Price Controls on Wage Inflation in the U.K.*, University of Manchester Inflation Workshop Discussion Paper 7402 (1974).

36 G. L. Perry, 'The Determinants of Wage Rate Changes and the Inflation-Unemployment Trade-off for the United States', *The Review of Economic Studies*, 31 (1964).

37 G. L. Perry, *Unemployment, Money Wage Rates and Inflation* (Cambridge, Mass.: M.I.T. Press, 1966).

38 J. Pen, *Income Distribution* (Harmondsworth: Pelican Books, 1974).

39 A. W. Phillips, 'The Relationship between Unemployment and the Rate of Change of Money Wage Rates in the United Kingdom 1861–1957', *Economica*, 25 (1958).

40 G. Pierson, 'The Effect of Union Strength on the U.S. Phillips Curve', *American Economic Review*, 58 (1968).

41 D. L. Purdy and G. Zis, 'Trade Unions and Wage Inflation in the U.K. A Reappraisal', in J. M. Parkin and A. R. Nobay, eds., *Essays in Modern Economics* (London: Longman, 1973).

42 D. L. Purdy and G. Zis, 'On the Concept and Measurement of Union Militancy', in D. E. W. Laidler and D. L. Purdy, eds., *Inflation and Labour Markets* (Manchester: Manchester University Press, 1974).

43 G. Routh, 'The Relation between Unemployment and the Rate of Change of Money Wage Rates: A Comment', *Economica*, 26 (1959).

44 P. A. Samuelson and R. M. Solow, 'Analytical Aspects of Anti-Inflation Policy', *Papers and Proceedings of the American Economic Association*, 50 (May 1960).

45 M. Segal, 'Union Wage Impact and Market Structure', *Quarterly Journal of Economics*, 78 (1964).

46 R. M. Solow, *Price Expectations and the Behaviour of the Price Level* (Manchester University Press, 1969).

47 G. R. Sparks and D. A. Wilton, 'Determinants of Negotiated Wage Increases: An Empirical Analysis', *Econometrica*, 39, no. 5 (Sep 1971).

48 J. Taylor, 'Incomes Policy, the Structure of Unemployment and the Phillips Curve: the United Kingdom Experience 1953–70', in [34].

49 R. L. Thomas and P. J. M. Stoney, 'A Note on the Dynamic Properties of the Hines Inflation Model', *Review of Economic Studies*, 37 (1970).

50 S. H. Tomczyk, *Financial Ratios and the Ability to Pay Wage Increases*, D.B.A. Thesis, University of Kentucky, 1975.

51 Trades Union Congress, *Evidence to the Royal Commission on Trade Unions* (London, 1966). See especially para. 104, p. 36.

52 J. Vanderkamp, 'Wage and Price Level Determination: An Empirical Model for Canada', *Economica*, 33 (1966).

53 R. Ward and G. Zis, 'Trade Union Militancy as an Explanation of Inflation: An International Comparison', *The Manchester School*, Mar 1974.

4 Collective Bargaining Models and the Theoretical Role of Information

Although there are a number of useful surveys of the literature on collective bargaining models already available [2], [3 ch. 2], [4, ch. 2], [13, sec. L] none of these is specifically concerned with the question of the role of information disclosure. This chapter therefore looks at the same field as earlier authors but with rather a different purpose in mind and consequently may give a slightly unusual emphasis to certain features of the models. In addition, we have found it necessary to refer to published results of empirical research from sources which may not be readily accessible to the person we imagine to be the 'average' reader. To these extents the contents of this chapter may have a certain novelty of appearance.

However, the bulk of it is certainly not novel but is nevertheless included here with the intention of providing an introductory guide (primarily aimed at the management/accounting reader) to a field of enquiry which can, on first acquaintance, be fairly overwhelming in the variety of methods of analysis employed and conflicting conclusions reached. Amongst other things we can be criticised for perhaps paying too much attention to models which are untested and often inherently untestable. Regrettably, these are often precisely those which offer the clearest insights into the possible effects of information disclosure. Our first concern has therefore been to examine a representative set of collective bargaining models from the point of view of their possible theoretical implications for the role of information. Once this 'academic incest' has been consummated we turn to the question of which of the various theoretical implications for information disclosure may rest on satisfactory empirical evidence. To have proceeded the other way around would, as we shall see, have meant dismissing the bulk of the theoretical literature without consideration and, perhaps, thrown out the baby with the bathwater from a prescriptive point of view.

COLLECTIVE BARGAINING MODELS AND INFORMATION PROVISION

There are probably as many ways in which the numerous bargaining models so far developed can be classified as there are individual models. One possible classification is that models may be characterised as basically deductive or inductive in origin. For example, some writers in the field, particularly the earlier ones, have built up almost purely deductive models of bargaining using a minimal set of behavioural axioms and institutional assumptions. A whole class of *game theoretic* models fall into this category and are characterised by their concentration on predicting the *outcome* rather than the *process* of negotiations. Indeed, the earliest models of this type virtually ignored the fact that negotiations occupy a time span. But, in practice, the fact that negotiations take time means that factors such as learning, search and expectational adjustment (each of which may be crucially related to the question of information provision) have a chance to come into play. For our purposes, then, we deduce that an explicit modelling of the negotiating *process* is necessary if we are to evaluate the effects of information on bargaining outcomes. To that extent much of the game theoretic literature proves to be of very little relevance to our primary purpose but is nevertheless fairly extensively covered because of its relationship to much of the empirical research to be discussed later. A number of 'deductive' type models do, however, exist in which the time occupied by negotiations is treated as an important variable. Not surprisingly these offer far more interesting conclusions about the role of information than the straightforward game theoretic type and we therefore spend some time examining the implications of perhaps the most influential of these *quasi-temporal* models.

The final class of models discussed, the *behavioural* models, are basically inductive in nature, usually involving a set of behavioural assumptions culled from observations of negotiations in practice.

We shall see that, typically, these assumptions are simultaneously richer in descriptive content and less quantifiable than those used by deductive modellers.[1] Thus, these models can be criticised as being of more potential use in interpreting behaviour than predicting it. A good model of the behavioural type can, however, throw light on the possible role of complex variables (such as information provision) with which the more abstract deductive models may be ill equipped to deal.

In fact, none of the models examined below can be classified as either completely deductive or inductive. Rather, a sort of spectrum seems to exist between the more deductive and inductive type models which also tends to involve a 'trade off' between quantifiability of predictions on the one hand and realism of assumptions on the other. This spectrum roughly corresponds to our order of treatment below of:

(a) game theoretic;
(b) quasi-temporal; and
(c) behavioural models of bargaining.

Non-behavioural models of bargaining are normally related to the distributive bargaining situation, i.e. one in which the possible aggregate pay-offs are already determined and the parties are simply concerned to negotiate their distribution. So, for simplicity, we can illustrate the essential features of the earlier models below by reference to management and labour (represented as 2 collective 'actors' or 'players') negotiating over the size of a single variable – 'the' wage rate to be paid. This is obviously only one, possibly over-simplified, example of a negotiating situation but is sufficient to illustrate certain fundamental points about the role of information in most bargaining models.

THE GAME THEORETIC APPROACH

Probably the most familiar form of game theoretic situation is the 2-person, constant sum game [8, ch. 4]. The essence of such 'games' is that each of the two opposing 'players' is confronted by a choice between a set of possible actions, the outcome of each of which is variable, depending on the choice made by the other player. It is assumed that the outcome of all possible pairs of action choices are known to both players in advance.[2,3]

Consider, for example, a situation in which the total 'utility'[4] available for distribution is 10 units.[5] Suppose labour is faced with a choice between putting forward a low (L) or high (H) wage claim which, if management agreed to it, would involve a split of either (5,5) (labour, management) or (9,1) of the total. Suppose also that management can take either a soft (S) or tough (T) line in negotiating. The soft line involves settling on the terms of labour's claim (whether high or low), whilst the tough line involves further bargaining which will eventually result in either a (2,8) or (4,6) split of the total of 10 depending on whether labour made a low or high claim in the first instance. This information can be shown compactly in the form of a 'pay-off table' (Figure 4.1). We have added a further column and row showing the minimum pay-offs for each action choice by labour and management respectively. As can be seen, the *best* of these *worst* alternatives for each party (4,6) corresponds to one box (*H, T*). In this case, each party should take a relatively hard line to ensure the best possible pay-off when faced with an opponent as 'rational' as himself.[6] The decision rule which involves choosing the 'best of the worst' alternatives is called the *maximin* criterion but is in fact only one alternative in a whole series of possible decision criteria which have been suggested in the game theoretic literature.[7] In fact, for the simple example given above it does not matter which of the usual decision criteria is used since the action pair *H, T* is plainly a dominant one (*H* is consistently better than *L* in terms of the pay-off for labour while *T* is always better than *S* for management whatever the other player does). This is not necessarily always the case.[8] In fact, the possibility that different decision rules may give rise to different (or even indeterminate) action choice selections is one drawback to using this form of game theoretic approach to predict the outcome of negotiations. The same difficulty applies *a fortiori* to the solution of the so called 'variable sum games' which may be met more frequently in practice than constant sum games.[9]

Whether the pay-off table indicates that we are dealing with constant or variable sum games, however, the assumptions about information built into general game theoretic analyses are similar.

As pointed out in note 11 it is assumed that both parties have perfect

		Management's choice		Minimum pay-off for labour
		S	T	
Labour's choice	L	5,5	2,8	2
	H	9,1	4,6	4
Minimum pay-off for management		1	6	

Fig. 4.1

information about the utility values involved in the pay-off matrix (both their own and the other player's). What they do not know directly, however, is what choice the other player will make from amongst his alternatives. Assumptions may be made about the *probability* of the opponent choosing a particular course of action but this is a different matter from having information on what the choice will actually be. Nevertheless, on the assumption that the opponent is a rational decision maker, a prediction of what the opponent will do may *sometimes* be derived from knowledge of the pay-off table (as in the above example).

It has already been noted that the pay-off values may themselves be the predicted outcomes of a series of sequential choices on the part of the player, i.e. they are valuations of alternative *strategies*. Thus, perfect knowledge of the pay-off table implies perfect predictions of all factors affecting the outcome of alternative strategies taken to infinity for both parties. From our point of view this means that all information relevant to both parties in negotiations is assumed to have been taken into account in arriving at the pay-off table values (presumably in some 'pre-play' phase of the negotiations). In effect then, any elements of the negotiating process which involve information provision as a variable, e.g. bluffing, persuading and rationalising tactics, are taken to be completed before the game theoretic analysis begins.[10] Thus, three assumptions of general game theoretic modellers – rationality, perfect knowledge and play independence of pay-offs – preclude the possibility that disclosure of information can have any significant role to play *within* such models. Even with the benefit of these simplifying assumptions, however, many games 'solved' by such methods simply yield a set of potential solutions rather than pointing to a unique outcome.

There are, however, a series of game theoretic bargaining models which do generally predict a unique solution and which, since they have also had an important seminal effect on later model builders, are worth looking at individually. We refer to the models of Nash [9], Zeuthen [18] and Pen [10].

J. P. Nash [9]

Although we have just used an illustration in which each player has only two possible alternative strategies to choose from, in practice the 'pay-off matrix' will probably be characterised by a very large number of possible cells. In such cases the pairs of pay-off utilities available to the parties may be more conveniently shown in graphical form. Thus, in Figure 4.2, U_m represents the utility of management and U_l the utility of labour. If we assume that utility can be represented in the Von Neumann-

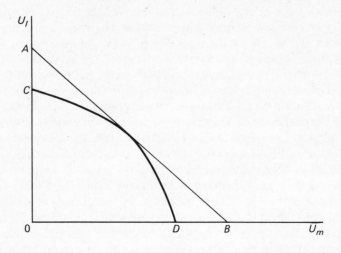

F<small>IG.</small> 4.2

Morgenstern [15] sense, i.e. with arbitrary origin and arbitrary measuring units (like the Fahrenheit scale on a thermometer),[11] we can conveniently assign the value of zero utility to the 'no-agreement' outcome for both players.[12] Points on the line *AB* then represent the possible incremental utilities to be gained by the players when they adopt the various alternative strategies which lead to agreement. A line such as *AB* will therefore represent the utility frontier for a pair of bargainers. (Where the locus of possible utility pairs is a straight line such as *AB*, we clearly have a constant sum game situation, as in the earlier example.) It will be determined by the joint objective pay-off possibilities and each player's utility function for goods and/or money. In the more general case, therefore, non-linearity of either utility functions or the objective pay-off substitution rate may lead to the frontier taking a non-linear form such as *CD*.

Of the possible outcomes represented by lines such as *AB* or *CD*, the Nash analysis is able to predict a particular solution which is usually unique. This is done by prespecifying certain conditions which a *solution* should fulfil. These conditions are:

(a) Pareto optimality – the outcome will lie on the northeast frontier of the set of possible outcomes, i.e. on *AB* or *CD* in the diagram, which means that no better outcome for one player can be obtained without simultaneously reducing the other player's utility.[13]

(b) Symmetry – if the sets of attainable pairs of values of U_l and U_m is symmetrical with respect to the line $U_l = U_m$ the solution point should lie on that line.

(c) Independence of irrelevant alternatives – the solution should not be affected by the removal of possible outcomes from the game which are neither the solution nor the non-agreement point.

(d) Transformation invariance – order-preserving, linear transformations of the utilities do not change the solution, i.e. the same 'real' outcome must result whatever the scale on which we choose to measure the players' utilities.[14]

Using these axioms, Nash showed that the outcome of the game would be that one which maximised the *product* of the players' utilities.[15] In general, this would predict a unique agreement point. Because of the restrictiveness of the assumptions however, it has been suggested that, rather than predicting what *will* happen in a bargaining situation, Nash's model shows what *should* happen. As such it may be of some interest as a comparative yardstick, e.g. for the use of arbitrators concerned with finding a 'fair' solution. Whether or not Nash's model has normative or descriptive value the fact remains that for our purposes it encapsulates the drawbacks with respect to the general role of information in game theoretic models mentioned earlier. That is, the incremental use of information is essentially buried in the concept of a strategy and thus already summarised in the pairs of utility values from which the Nash analysis *starts*.

F. Zeuthen [18]

Zeuthen's bargaining model is earlier in origin than that of Nash but has more recently been shown [6] to predict a point of agreement corresponding to that of Nash, although the Nash solution is reached from rather a different angle. Zeuthen's model is of interest to us in that it seems to extend the Nash analysis so as to include a description of the bargaining *process*. We begin, in Figure 4.3, with a management-labour utility frontier, *CD*, as before. It is then assumed that each party begins with a demand for an outcome on the frontier which is relatively favourable to themselves. Thus, U_{ij} represents the utility of the ith party as proposed by the jth ($i = l, m; j = l, m$) (i.e. U_{ml} is the utility for management proposed by labour etc.).

Using expected utility as a decision criterion Zeuthen asks what will be the maximum probability of non-agreement a bargainer will accept in the risky option of either holding out for his own demand or accepting the other's offer. In the case of labour immediate agreement to management's offer would give a pay-off of U_{lm} with certainty, whilst

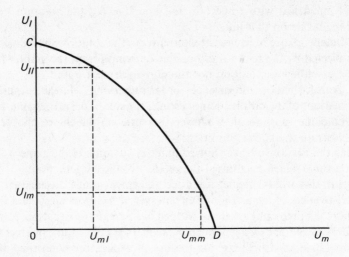

Fig. 4.3

holding out for labour's own demand will have an expected value of $(1 - P_l)U_{ll}$, where P_l is the probability of non-agreement as perceived by labour (with the utilities of non-agreement being set at zero, as before). Thus, a critical value of P_l will be given by:

$$U_{lm} = (1 - P_l)U_{ll}$$

i.e.
$$P_l = \frac{U_{ll} - U_{lm}}{U_{ll}}$$

and similarly, for management:

$$P_m = \frac{U_{mm} - U_{ml}}{U_{mm}}$$

Zeuthen then assumes that each bargainer compares his critical value of the probability of non-agreement (his 'risk willingness') with his perception of the probability of non-agreement. The player will concede if the perceived probability of conflict exceeds his risk willingness. To articulate the model, Zeuthen makes the rather questionable additional assumption that the perceived probability of conflict is equal to the risk willingness of the other party (which he can compute, having full knowledge of the other's utilities). As a result, the player with the lower risk willingness will make the first concession, i.e. labour will concede first if $P_l < P_m$ and vice versa. The concession is assumed to take the form of a lowering of the relevant player's demand to the 'next feasible outcome',[16] from which stage the process can be repeated. By a succession of such concessions it can be shown that, in general, the final outcome will be the same as that predicted by Nash, i.e. that at which the product of the players' utilities is maximised.[17]

Zeuthen's model is intuitively appealing in that it appears to fit most observations of the course of negotiations in practice – offer and counter-offer with concessions converging on an intermediate settlement point. However, there are two important reservations about the model's practical usefulness:

(a) specifically: the essentially arbitrary equation of the perceived probability of conflict with the actuarially computed risk willingness of the other party;

(b) more generally: the underlying (perfect knowledge) assumption that each bargainer is, in any event, able to estimate correctly the probability of the other party rejecting a particular settlement. It is the lack of this kind of knowledge which, in practice, permits differing opinions on the part of bargainers as to what the outcome will be. Without these differing opinions, the collective bargaining process would be reduced to a set of mechanical rules for arriving at a solution which could, from the start, be predicted solely from knowledge of the combined utility frontier.[18]

Thus, under Zeuthen's (and the other game theoreticians we have already covered) assumptions of perfect knowledge we can gain no insight into the possible effects of varying elements in the bargaining *process* because the process is essentially irrelevant to the outcome. It is precisely because bargaining is characterised by different degrees of ignorance and perceptive ability in practice that the process may be relevant to the outcome and hence that the provision of information or misinformation may be important.

J. Pen [10]

Pen's model is essentially an extension of Zeuthen's but (crucially) distinguishes between the actuarial probability of conflict and a negotiator's subjective estimate of the other's risk willingness. From the point of view of labour it is assumed that its preference structure is contained in a utility function for wages $U_l(W)$ which has a maximum at $U_l(\overline{W}_l)$. At a particular stage in bargaining labour must therefore decide whether to accept a wage offer of W, with associated utility $U_l(W)$, or to press for the best rate $\overline{W}_l$. The possible gain involved is $U_l(\overline{W}_l) - U_l(W)$ but there is the consideration that continued bargaining involves a probability of breakdown (P_l) with which a particular conflict utility (U_{lc}) is associated.[19] The rational labour bargainer will therefore continue to bargain as long as the expected value of the gain from an increased claim is greater than or equal to the expected loss due to possible non-agreement, i.e. as long as

$$(1 - P_l)\left[U_l(\overline{W}_l) - U_l(W)\right] \geqq P_l U_l(W) - U_{lc}$$

$$\text{or } U_l(W) \leqq (1 - P_l). \, U_l(\overline{W}_l) + P_l. \, U_{lc}$$

The question thus arises as to how labour arrives at an estimate of the probability of conflict P_l. Pen argues that this is derived from the management's 'net conflict utility' ('ophelimity').

For management, with utility $U_m(W)$ for wage rate W, with a maximum value at $\overline{W}_m$ and U_{mc} utility in the event of conflict, the net contract utility is $U_m(W) - U_{mc}$. Clearly, if this is negative, a conflict is preferable to the W settlement as far as management is concerned, i.e. P must be either 0 or 1 *in fact* for a particular W. However, each party is assumed to be uncertain as regards the utility function of the opponent, thus rather than knowing that $P = 0$ or 1, labour's estimate of P will vary between 0 and 1 depending on labour's *estimate* of $U_m(W) - U_{mc}$. Labour is thus assumed to have a *correspection function* which relates the net contract utility of management to labour's estimate of P, i.e.

$$P_l' = F_l\left[U_m(W) - U_{mc}\right]$$

Correspondingly, for management we have the equilibrium condition

$$U_m(W) \leqq (1 - P_m) \, U_m(\overline{W}_m) + P_m U_{mc}$$

and a correspection function which relates management's perception of P to labour's net contract utility at wage rate W,

i.e. $\qquad P_m' = F_m\left[U_l(W) - U_{lc}.\right].$

$U(\overline{W}_l)$ and $U(\overline{W}_m)$ can be thought of as corresponding to U_{ll} and U_{mm} in the Zeuthen model so that the parties may begin with two opposing 'bids'. However, in Pen's model it is assumed that the (compromise?) wage rate W somehow comes 'under consideration'. Then, providing it adopts an 'actuarial mentality', labour will be prepared to accept any probability of disagreement up to

$$P_l = \frac{U_l(\overline{W}_l) - U_l(W)}{U_l(\overline{W}_l) - U_{lc}}$$

(this corresponds to the 'risk willingness' of the Zeuthen model). The essentially new element in the Pen model is thus the subjectively assessed risk of disagreement[20]

$$P_l' = F_l[U_m(W) - U_{mc}]$$

Labour will concede, from $\overline{W}_l$ to W, when $P_l' > P_l$ and hence will be on the point of agreeing to an outcome W when

$$F_l[U_m(W) - U_{mc}] = \frac{U_l(\overline{W}_l) - U_l(W)}{U_l(\overline{W}_l) - U_{lc}}$$

which gives an equilibrium wage rate for labour (W_l). A similar equilibrium equation can be determined for management (with equilibrium wage rate W_m). In general these equalities will not simultaneously hold for the same W for management and labour $(W_l \neq W_m)$ and so Pen suggests that the bargaining process essentially consists of producing shifts in the functions and parameters until the two equations do apply for the same W. Although Pen has been criticised for not explicitly dealing with the way in which this equilibrium is reached it can be recognised that Pen's model does at least provide for a real role for the bargaining *process*. The eventual outcome is not independent of the manner by which it is reached since the equilibrium W is determined by whatever shifts in the parameters take place during the negotiating process. To see more clearly how this may come about consider the Pen model in diagrammatic form. In Figures 4.4a and 4.4b, which apply to labour and management respectively, we show Pen's two implicit functional relationships between P and W. (The position and shape of the lines actually shown are based on plausible but highly simplified assumptions about the exact form of the relationships.) For full equilibrium W_l must be made to equal W_m. This can be brought about by inducing appropriate shifts in *any* of the 4 lines shown on the graphs.[21] It seems to us that one way of bringing this about would be for one or both of the parties to introduce new information which will cause the opponent to change either his perception of his own value function directly (by, e.g. making his desired alternative appear less attractive to him) or indirectly to influence his estimate of the other's utility function.

However, Pen himself is rather sceptical in his views on the possible use of communication of information in this tactical way. In relation to the possibility of being able to influence the utility function of one's opponent by communication of information he writes: 'It is rather futile to try to do it when faced with a more sophisticated bargainer . . . One tries to persuade him that he does not see his own interests clearly and that he should, therefore, listen to the well meant advice of his opponent' [10, pp. 139–40]. However, this quotation seems to put rather a heavy strain on the meaning of the word 'sophisticated'. Clearly, if sophisticated is intended to mean 'fully informed' then Pen's point is probably valid, but in that case why introduce the device of correspection functions? If, however, 'sophisticated' merely means worldly wise or skilled in argument then clearly even the best negotiator, in this sense, may be operating under a misconception or a lack of information and there is no reason why his correspection function, based on error, should not be shifted by the emergence of new and unforeseen information.

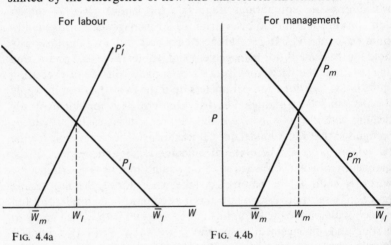

FIG. 4.4a   FIG. 4.4b

Thus, from our point of view, for the first time in this chapter we are dealing with a model in which information disclosure *could* have a role to play within the model. It is important to recognise that the reason for this innovation is that the previous strait-jacket of a perfect knowledge assumption is dropped and the bargainers are allowed to entertain different and mistaken views of one another's preferences. Unfortunately however, the failure of Pen to fully articulate his model means that a precise outcome is not predicted. Thus, we also come across the first instance of a sacrifice of predictive precision for increased realism in describing the bargaining process. Nevertheless, for our particular purposes, it is necessary to have an even more 'realistic' model, i.e. one which probes deeper into the determinants of the 'correspection functions' (or their equivalent) if we are to explore the role of information in any specifically useful way. As we shall see, however, models which do 'dig deeper' in this way tend to suffer to an even greater extent than Pen's from a lack of predictive power.

QUASI-TEMPORAL MODELS

Perhaps the most obvious omission from the models already dealt with is an explicit consideration of the effects of the passage of time on the bargaining process and hence on the outcome of negotiations. This is perhaps hardly surprising in the game theoretic models discussed earlier, since it is of the essence of them either that the bargaining process is essentially irrelevant to the outcome, or at the least that it cannot affect the pay-off possibilities, or perceptions of them, during play. Such models are, therefore, essentially static. On the other hand, the bargaining process in practice is recognisably dynamic with, as noted in note 10, constant changes being made to the perceived pay-offs on which the final action choices, and hence outcome, will depend. To explain the possible impact of information on outcomes we must therefore recognise bargaining for what it is in practice: a dynamic, adaptive, process in which information provision at different times may have differential effects.

An influential model which explicitly considers negotiations from a dynamic point of view is that of Cross. It also has particular interest in that its predictions can be claimed to fit the empirical findings of Siegel and Fouraker [12] (see later discussion).

J. G. Cross [4]

In this model the effects of time are included in three ways:
(a) through the discounting of future agreement values;
(b) through changes in the absolute value of agreements over time (e.g. for technological reasons); and
(c) through the effects of bargaining costs which are incurred per unit of time (these costs are set at zero in our exposition below, for simplicity).

Cross begins by making an assumption that negotiations are concerned with the question of how to distribute a variable which is fixed in aggregate terms. (Let the total utility available for division $= Q$.) Crucial to his model is the supposition that each party expects the other to concede at a constant rate but does not expect to have to shift his own demand.

Thus, let Q_l be labour's current demand (in utility terms)

Q_m be management's current demand (in utility terms)

C_l be labour's current concession rate, as expected by management

C_m be management's current concession rate, as expected by labour.

From labour's point of view, on the assumptions made, agreement will be expected at time $T = (Q_l + Q_m - Q)/C_m$. Assuming r_l to be labour's discount rate, and continuous compounding, the present value of the agreement which gives labour Q_l will therefore by $Q_l e^{-rlT}$.

Assuming labour wishes to maximise its utility from such an agreement we may therefore predict the optimal value of the current demand by labour.[22]

$$Q_l^* = \frac{C_m}{r_l}$$

A similar expression can be obtained for management. However, clearly if both management and labour stick to these optimal demands then their respective estimates for C_l and C_m will prove to be wrong.

Cross thus introduces a learning effect whereby errors in estimates of the opponent's concession rate cause expectations to be revised over time as the actual concession rate becomes evident. Using the simple adaptive assumption that the change in estimated concession rate is proportional to the absolute error in the last estimate, we get, for labour for example:

$$\frac{dC_m}{dT} = -A\left[\frac{dQ_m}{dT} + C_m\right]$$

where A is a constant. (A similar equation is assumed to hold for management, with coefficient B.) As a result of this change in expectations quite clearly labour's own optimal demand will change and bring about a change in management's demand leading to a further change in labour's expectations and so on. Thus Cross's assumptions essentially result in a dynamic system of interdependent adjustments of demands by labour and management which can be represented as a closed loop adaptive system, as shown in Figure 4.5.[23] Normally the adjustment process will result in the two parties' initial demands being moderated over time until an agreement is reached, such that $Q_l + Q_m = Q$ (i.e. the process is convergent).[24] The actual solution values of Q_l and Q_m may be

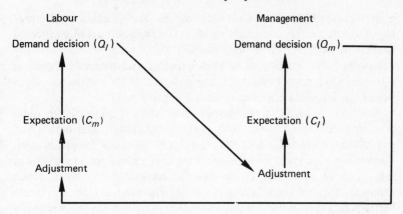

FIG. 4.5

obtained by solving the two simultaneous differential equations (one for each party) produced by combining the optimising demand equations with the learning equations given above. When this is done the final outcomes for each party may be shown to depend on: discount rates, learning coefficients and *initial* expectations about concession rates [4, ch. 4]. For example, in the symmetrical case, where $r_l = r_m$ and $A = B$, Cross's final equation (with some adjustments)[25] gives the solution outcome for labour as:

$$\overline{Q}_l = \frac{Q}{2} + \frac{C_m{}^0 - C_l{}^0}{2\,r_l} \cdot \left[\frac{Q\,r_l}{C_l{}^0 + C_m{}^0} \right]^{\frac{r_l + A}{r_l - A}}$$

where $C_m{}^0$ and $C_l{}^0$ refer to the *initial* values of these variables.

It is interesting to note that the second term on the right-hand side represents the deviation from the 'ideal' (Nash) solution (in which the total quantity available would be divided equally). Thus labour can apparently gain more than their 'fair share' by ensuring that $C_m{}^0 > C_l{}^0$, i.e. that management's concession expectations are relatively 'subdued' compared with labour's.

In addition to this effect of initial expectations, where learning rates differ between the negotiators there will apparently be a tendency for the final pay-off to the *more sensitive* (better?) learner to be reduced.[26]

These two effects, of differing initial expectations and differing learning abilities mean that there is implicit in the Cross model a possibly crucial role for information. Notice, however, that in the Cross model as in the earlier game theoretic models information has an effect in the pre-negotiation state, i.e. on the setting of *initial* expectations. Once expected concession rates are established initially the process will be inevitably determined by comparison between expected and realised concession rates and adjustments made at a rate governed b' the parameter values (which are assumed unchanged during negotiations).

However, whereas in the earlier game theoretic models an independent relationship has to be hypothesised between information and pay-offs if we are to predict the incremental effects of information on bargaining outcomes, at least in the Cross model we are given an indication of *how* information may be related to outcomes, albeit indirectly, through the influence of intervening variables (concession rate expectations and learning rates) which may in themselves be more easily identified with the provision of specific kinds of information.

To summarise, the implications of the Cross model which seem to be interesting from our point of view are that a party should seek to provide information to its opponent which would tend to:

(a) decrease the other's expectation of the party's own initial concession rate; and/or

(b) increase the other's learning rate.

However even these fairly vague conclusions can be tentative only, since the Cross model has not proved tractable to empirical verification and its predictive use would depend on the specification, *inter alia*, of parameters such as the parties' learning rates, C_l^0, C_m^0, r_l and r_m which are essentially subjective, probably transient and almost certainly specific to particular bargaining situations.

In addition Cross's model contains an important logical inconsistency, which, if not completely fatal to its possible predictive usefulness casts doubt in that direction. That is, Cross assumes that a player expects the opponent to concede, but not to do so himself. However, the player *will* then generally concede himself after comparing the other's actual concession rate with his prior expectations of it. In addition, although a player expects the opponent to concede at a constant rate *in fact* the opponent will concede at varying rates in the adjustment process. Thus, Cross essentially denies the ability of a player to learn by experience to the effect (a) that he himself will concede and (b) that the other will concede at varying rates.

Thus, although the players are assumed to be rational in their decision making (they optimise their demands), they are simultaneously assumed to be essentially irrational in the formation of *expectations* – an implausible inconsistency.[27]

BEHAVIOURAL MODELS OF BARGAINING

So far, the reader may have observed a progression in the models discussed, from denial of the relevance of the bargaining process (game theoretic, Nash, Zeuthen), through process relevant but unspecified (Pen), to process relevant and specified (Cross) models. Even in the last case, however, the parameters which determine the process and hence the outcome have no clear predictable causal relationship with the provision of information, even if we restrict our requirements to directional predictions alone. Hence, it is necessary to proceed to models which deal with the mechanism of the bargaining process in much more detail than has been done so far. As we shall see, however, although this will take us closer to the complexities of the real world, it will also take us further away from the ability to make precise (quantified) predictions about the outcome of negotiations. There is, as always, a great deal to be said for using the simplest model which gives reliable and relevant predictions. Unfortunately, in relation to our particular needs – predicting the effects of information disclosure – *no* bargaining model, simple or complex, has yet been shown to give predictions which are both precise and relevant. What the behavioural models which we shall deal with next do, however, is to enable us to trace much more clearly the possible causal relationships involving information provision, which in turn may enable us to make certain predictions, of at least a qualitative nature, about the possible effects of disclosure on bargaining outcomes. Nevertheless, it is always difficult to know how far one can defend behavioural approaches to collective bargaining as 'theories' at all since they are often very largely *descriptive* in character, i.e. they tend to 'explain' (after the event) rather than predict.

Two major approaches which are based on theories of behaviour independently established in the literature of psychology (and to that extent do not 'hang by their own bootstraps') are those of C. M. Stevens [14] and Walton and McKersie [16]. Both of these models have potentially interesting implications for the impact of information on collective bargaining.

C. M. Stevens [14]

The models described earlier all rely on a theory of human decision making which is the one most commonly identified with 'rational' behaviour in economic theory, i.e. utility maximisation. As opposed to this Stevens classifies the bargaining situation, from the point of view of the negotiators, as a 'conflict choice situation'. What this implies is that a negotiator, faced with a choice between two competing alternatives may attempt to find an intermediate equilibrium situation rather than opt immediately for the alternative which maximises utility.

Stevens' characterisation of the bargaining situation is of a negotiator faced with two, normally differing 'goals' – holding out for one's own claim or settling on the opponent's terms. For reasons discussed later both of these goals may be considered as having a negative expected value, such that the negotiator will seek to avoid choosing either of them directly. The negotiator is, in fact, assumed to have a set of attitudes towards each goal which can be expressed in the form of a subjective 'avoidance gradient' which shows an inverse relationship between the strength of tendency to avoid a goal and the distance from it.

Thus, in Figure 4.6, which applies to the labour negotiator, AA is the avoidance gradient with respect to goal A, etc. Since we are still dealing with a single bargaining variable, the wage rate, we can show 'distance' from a goal in terms of the wage rate. For simplicity alone, we also show the avoidance gradients as straight lines. With the avoidance gradients shown (solid lines), the negotiator would have an equilibrium wage rate at D, since for any other wage rate the strength of tendency to avoid one goal would exceed that with respect to the other goal. In general, the consequence will be that a negotiator will have an equilibrium wage rate which is intermediate between goals A and B.[28]

It is important to realise that a diagram such as Figure 4.6 applies to one negotiator only (in this case, the labour side). A quite separate diagram, with different subjective avoidance gradients, will apply to the other party. A necessary, but not sufficient[29] condition for a settlement is, therefore, that the equilibrium wage rates for the 2 parties are equal. In this respect the model is similar to that of Pen discussed earlier, since two individual equilibria must be reconciled. In the case of the Stevens model, however, the means by which this occurs has been much more explicitly dealt with, at least at a descriptive level.

To see what this involves we must return to the question of the assumed negativity of the 'goals'. Each goal is assumed to be viewed by the negotiator concerned in terms of its expected value to him, i.e. a combination of pay-off values and associated probabilities. From the point of view of the labour negotiator it is relatively straightforward to see how this may result in a negative expected value being attached to Goal A (settle on management's terms). On the other hand, in terms of Goal B (maintain one's own position) the possible outcomes, apart from the possibility of gaining a higher wage, will include the possibilities of breakdown of negotiations, a strike or a lock out. Such events, contrary to popular opinion, are not usually viewed with favour by labour organisers (and hence negotiators) since they may involve paying strike pay to members, loss of subscriptions, executive time being tied up etc. If these latter (negative pay-off) events are estimated to have a relatively high probability of occurrence as a consequence of holding out for labour's claim, the weighting process may result in an overall negative expected value being attached to Goal *B* as well as Goal *A*. (An analogous argument may be used in relation to management's attitudes towards the two goals.)

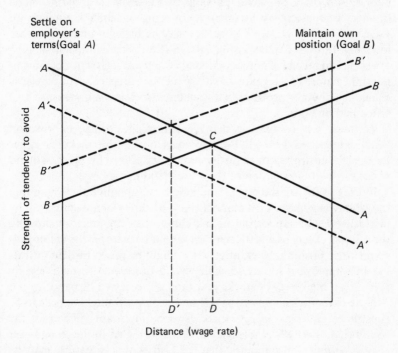

FIG. 4.6 (for labour)

The fact that 'values' of goals can be seen to be the compound result of risk perceptions on the one hand and subjective utilities on the other is the key to the advance in explanatory power, for our purposes, represented by the Stevens model as compared with that of Pen. As in the Pen model differing individual equilibria may be reconciled by shifts in the parameters (avoidance gradients). However, in the Stevens model it is clear that this comes about by influencing the risk and/or the valuation (preference function) perceptions of negotiators. Put in this way we can trace more distinctly the possible influence of disclosure of information on outcomes.

Fairly clearly the tactics of each side in the negotiations will be to try to move the outcome in their own favour. In terms of Stevens model this may be achieved by shifting one or both of the 'opponent's' avoidance gradients and hence shifting his equilibrium position. (It is, of course, through such shifts that the necessary conditions for a settlement are eventually achieved.) However, let us consider the positive use of information disclosure as a possible management negotiating tactic (termed 'persuasion' by Stevens). A lowering of labour's equilibrium wage rate to, say, D' (see Figure 4.6) may be brought about by either lowering AA to $A'A'$ or by raising BB to $B'B'$ (or some combination of the lowering and raising of both functions). To achieve such shifts, bearing in mind the nature of the goals, management may direct its tactics towards changing labour's probability estimates, its estimated valuations of outcomes, or both.

To lower AA, for instance, management might produce information which emphasised the relative generosity of its offer, thus making it easier for the labour negotiator to justify acceptance of it to his principals and hence raising his valuation of the corresponding outcome.

Raising of BB, on the other hand, might be brought about by raising the labour negotiator's estimate of the probability of a dispute, e.g. by disclosing results supporting an 'inability to pay' argument or showing the adverse effects of a settlement on labour's terms on the employer's competitive position. Alternatively, BB might be raised by demonstrating the employer's ability to withstand a protracted dispute, e.g. by revealing a high level of stocks at a time of depressed demand.

Note that although lowering AA and raising BB might appear to be substitutes in this respect, there is one important difference: the equilibrium 'strength of tendency to avoid' is higher in the second case *ceteris paribus*. This implies that the bargaining situation may be invested with a higher degree of tension on the part of the negotiators which may in turn have adverse strategic effects on future negotiations. In terms of the model the position and shape of the avoidance schedules is likely to be heavily influenced by the history of industrial relations between the parties, and the question of information disclosure as a management policy must therefore be considered in a longer term context for this reason alone. (We return to the possible influence of the 'atmosphere' of negotiations later in dealing with the Walton and McKersie model.)

Although Stevens' model, and its graphical presentation in particular, gives the impression of being deterministic it suffers in this respect in much the same way as that of Cross. That is, it is unlikely that in practice the (essentially subjective) functional forms of the avoidance gradients could be estimated and even if they were they would, in any case, probably prove to be both transient and unstable. In addition, to use the Stevens model for prediction of outcomes we should need to know precisely how the avoidance gradients were affected by factors such as information provision. Nevertheless, even in a relatively unspecified form the Stevens model does, as we have seen, provide a framework for examining the possible causal connections between information provision and outcomes which may be used to draw, at the very least, some conclusions about *directional* relationships.

In the Stevens model, as in previous ones, we have used the simplifying assumptions of a single bargaining variable (the wage rate) and, implicitly, a distributive bargaining situation. Many of the arguments raised in practice against the disclosure of information by management in collective bargaining also implicitly assume distributive bargaining. But, as we have seen above, it is by no means clear that disclosure of information will *always* result in a shift in outcomes unfavourable to management, at least according to the models discussed here, even in a distributive bargaining situation.

On the other hand, many of the arguments in favour of information disclosure cannot be properly put by reference to distributive bargaining alone. It is, therefore, one of the virtues of the Walton and McKersie model (which follows) that negotiating situations other than purely distributive bargaining can be dealt with and thus the possible effects of information in more complex (closer to the real world) situations analysed.

Walton and McKersie [16]

It is difficult to do justice to the analytical complexity of Walton and McKersie's 'Behavioural Theory' in the space available here. But, as they themselves point out, its constituent parts are not novel, and to that extent they rest on the deductive and inductive foundations of earlier model builders, some of which have already been covered in this chapter. What is particularly useful about their model, from our point of view, however, is the way in which these constituent parts are articulated. For a description of what the theory encompasses we can do little better than quote them directly:

Labour negotiations . . . [are] comprised of four systems of activity, each with its own function for the interacting parties, its own internal logics, and its own identifiable set of instrumental acts or tactics. We shall refer to each of the distinguishable systems of activities as a *subprocess*. The first subprocess is *distributive bargaining*; its function is to resolve pure conflicts of interest. The second, *integrative bargaining*, functions to find common or complementary interests and solve problems confronting both parties. The third subprocess is *attitudinal structuring* and its functions are to influence the attitudes of the participants toward each other and to affect the basic bonds which relate the two parties they represent. A fourth subprocess, *intra-organisational bargaining*,[30] has the function of achieving consensus within each of the interacting groups [16, p. 4].

We have already dealt in some detail with the distributive bargaining process which essentially consists of establishing a point on the pre-specified joint utility frontier of the two parties such that the total pay-offs available are divided between them in agreed proportions. We have also indicated, in writing about the Zeuthen model, that in practice each of the parties usually begins with a demand/offer which, if agreed to, would afford them a relatively favourable pay-off. This gives rise to an *explicit* bargaining range which, typically, is successively narrowed by a series of concessions until a mutually agreeable solution is reached.

In terms of Walton and McKersie's model we can think of this bargaining range as being based on the *implicit* aspiration zones of each of the parties. These aspiration zones are in turn delimited by *target* and *resistance points* which are based on subjective expected utility estimates similar to those met earlier in the valuation of the 'goals' in Stevens' model.

Both target and resistance points represent aspiration levels, the first being essentially optimistic, the second pessimistic (see Figure 4.7).[31] Resistance points may be set, for example, by beliefs about the minimum level of achievement the principals (employees and employers) require of their respective negotiators (which might, for instance, in the employer's case, be based on some concept of 'ability to pay'). On the other hand, the target level probably represents a best estimate of the other party's resistance point. Although other relationships may apply the relative positions of demands (D), target (T), and resistance points (RP) will usually result in some positive possible *settlement range* being indicated, as in Figure 4.8 (Note that the settlement range is, strictly, solely determined by the position of the resistance points). In fact, where the

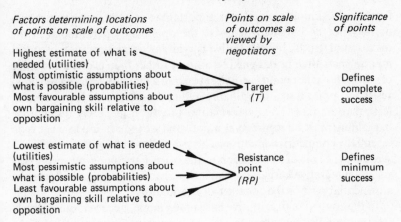

Factors determining locations of points on scale of outcomes	Points on scale of outcomes as viewed by negotiators	Significance of points
Highest estimate of what is needed (utilities) Most optimistic assumptions about what is possible (probabilities) Most favourable assumptions about own bargaining skill relative to opposition	Target (T)	Defines complete success
Lowest estimate of what is needed (utilities) Most pessimistic assumptions about what is possible (probabilities) Least favourable assumptions about own bargaining skill relative to opposition	Resistance point (RP)	Defines minimum success

Fig. 4.7

two parties have relatively accurate pictures of each other's utilities (i.e. they are reasonably well informed – perhaps by having access to the same information sources), targets (based on opponent's anticipated resistance points) are likely to be set fairly close to the opponent's actual resistance points and the result is therefore more likely to be a positive settlement range.[32]

The method of arriving at a solution is then similar to that suggested in the Stevens model, i.e. the players seek to influence each other's preferences and perceptions in a way which will successively narrow the range until a settlement point is reached. One typical way in which Walton and McKersie suggest this may be done is through *commitment* tactics. 'Commitment' means the act of pledging oneself to a course of action (e.g. making preparations for a strike or lock out) in order to influence the opponent's perception of one's own probability function

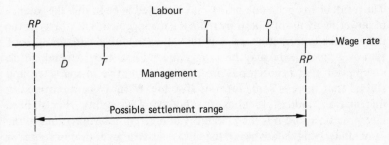

Fig. 4.8

for taking actions [11, ch. 2]. It is important to note that such tactics may or may not be intended to revise the opponent's perceptions in the direction of 'truth'. In distributive bargaining communication of 'information' may often be designed to obscure rather than clarify knowledge of where resistance points *actually* are, since if one side revealed its actual resistance point it would probably induce the other side to press for at least that amount. Thus, information provision in purely distributive bargaining must be regarded as a potential weapon of use in what is an essentially competitive situation. This poses a crucial conflict, as we shall see, with the role of information in the other bargaining sub-processes, such as integrative bargaining and attitudinal structuring, which may be an essential part of the *same* set of negotiations.

In the context of distributive bargaining alone, however, quite clearly information disclosure may be used to operate on the constituents of the opponent's aspiration levels so as to move the settlement range, and hence the eventual outcome in one's own favour, as in the Stevens model. This can be done by lowering the opponent's valuation of his own preferred pay-offs and/or altering his subjective estimates of the probabilities of attaining them or, as in commitment tactics, altering the opponent's perceptions of one's own pay-off utilities and/or probability function. Note in particular that 'It is not necessary for the objective conditions to change; it is only necessary for the perceptions of these conditions to change in order for a negotiator to alter his position. In contract negotiations objective knowledge virtually never becomes complete in the sense that the true nature of all factors is accurately understood by all sides. Thus, it is only necessary to change the other's *perceptions* in order to alter his bargaining position' [16, p. 60] [Italics added].

Such a statement goes some way to explaining why managements may be reluctant to allow uncontrolled access by labour negotiators to a company's internal information sources such as the accounting records. The result of an open book policy may be feared to be to shift the balance of power in favour of labour by reducing management's flexibility in the use of such information as a potential distributive bargaining tool. However, such fears may be exaggerated. First, they depend on an assumption that negotiations are purely distributive in character, and second that there is some form of absolute 'truth' to be discovered in information sources such as the books of accounts. 'Facts' need interpretation and it is the possibility of different interpretations of the same underlying data which must always leave a great deal of room for differing perceptions in negotiators with different objectives.[33] In any event when a set of negotiations is at least partly *integrative* in nature a policy of complete disclosure of information to labour negotiators, as we shall see, may be a necessary condition for *increasing* the pay-off to management.

A purely integrative bargaining situation would, in fact, be one in which negotiations created increases in pay-offs for both management and labour, i.e. the possible pairs of pay-offs resulting would lie on a positive sloping line, as in Figure 4.9, rather than forming a negatively sloping utility frontier, as for distributive bargaining (e.g. Figure 4.3). This arises from the fact that integrative bargaining is essentially a joint problem-solving approach to questions of mutual concern to management and labour (the search for bona fide 'productivity' bargains may be an example of a potentially integrative situation). A line such as that in Figure 4.9 must therefore represent the locus of points on successively higher utility frontiers. (Of course, this interpretation implies that there is a simultaneous question of distribution, but we shall deal with that problem later.)

As usual, problem solving should involve at least these 3 steps:
1. identify the problem;
2. search for alternative solutions and their related consequences;
3. evaluate the alternatives in terms of preferences and select one.

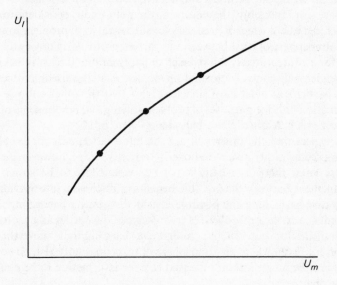

Fig. 4.9

Information is clearly crucial to this process, i.e. 'when information is low, the result will be a less adequate definition of the problem; fewer alternatives will be generated; and the potential consequences of these alternatives will be less explored. Finally, when the information is relatively low, the parties will produce relatively low grade solutions' [16, p. 140].

In order to gain maximum benefit from an integrative, problem-solving situation then, it is essential that management employs a liberal disclosure policy to labour representatives. On the other hand, there may be fairly substantial information collection and processing costs associated with such an information policy, and thus it may be considered important to ensure that a problem has reasonable integrative potential before the mechanics of full disclosure are invoked. In this connection, Walton and McKersie observe that 'agenda items involving strictly economic values are much less likely to contain integrative possibilities than are items referring to rights and obligations of the parties' [16, p. 129]. In fact, it is doubtful whether this is fully valid – certainly there may be more opportunity for 'economic' issues to involve distributive as well as integrative relationships with labour, but the history of productivity bargaining (not all of which has been a mechanism for disguising straight wage increases) shows the potential for joint management/labour problem solving even on economic issues.[34]

Apart from, possibly, the nature of the item under consideration, a further ingredient which is necessary for successful joint problem solving is an atmosphere of trust between the parties, particularly in view of the need for a comparatively full passage of information: 'If trust is lacking, the sender will control information or deliberately miscommunicate. Each participant must have sufficient trust that the other will use the information only for purposes of problem solving and not for some other purpose (such as distributive bargaining)' [16, p. 142].

To expect that the other will use the information *only* for problem solving seems rather a vain and overly restrictive hope, however. As we discuss later, there is usually a balance which has to be struck by management between the possible benefits of disclosing information in integrative bargaining and possible costs in distributive bargaining. The dependence on an atmosphere of trust between the parties as a probable prerequisite for constructive integrative bargaining is nevertheless important. Even where an atmosphere of trust does not exist, however, there may be an important potential role for information in helping to create one.

In other words, a liberal disclosure policy may well provide maximum benefits to management in the short term when an atmosphere of trust already exists such that joint problem solving can be undertaken immediately, but it may also provide benefits in the longer term in other situations by helping to foster trust which in turn may lead to integrative bargaining possibilities.

The aspect of bargaining which relates to influencing the overall relationship pattern between management and labour is called by Walton and McKersie *attitudinal structuring*. They characterise overall relationships between a set of management and labour negotiators as falling along a spectrum, ranging from conflict, through containment, to accommodation, co-operation and collusion. Amongst factors which create and perpetuate these different patterns are: '(1) the technological, market and power contexts of the parties; (2) the basic personality dispositions of key individuals in the relationship; (3) the social belief systems of the individuals . . . ; and (4) the actual bargaining experiences that they have shared' [16, p. 190]. These factors are listed in ascending order of their probable susceptibility to change. Thus from a practical point of view we must look for the possible effects of information disclosure on the bargaining relationship primarily in terms of their influences on attitudes arising from shared experiences.

Walton and McKersie make use of psychological 'Balance Theory'[35] in putting forward suggestions for bringing about attitudinal changes. Briefly, this theory involves emphasising shared attitudes (either positive or negative) towards some third object (event, idea or third person) which in turn should lead to a more positive relationship between the two parties. Thus, Walton and McKersie suggest that a 'way for [management] to be identified with an event which benefits [the labour negotiator] is to structure a situation which confers legitimacy, respect or status on [the labour negotiator]' [16, p. 236]. Our suggestion in turn is that the gesture of providing information to labour negotiators over and above any statutory requirements might most obviously qualify as an attitudinal structuring tactic in this sense.

On the other hand, the direct communication of information to employees 'over the heads' of their negotiating representatives may often be an example of a tactic which has negative attitudinal effects in that it would tend to reflect adversely on the self-perceived status of the negotiator.

However, such a tactic may clearly have value for management in a distributive bargaining situation. Thus, we cannot continue to ignore the series of dilemmas created by the possibly conflicting roles of information in distributive bargaining, integrative bargaining and attitudinal structuring. One such dilemma relates to the fact that the tactics required for integrative and distributive bargaining may be contradictory:

> In the integrative process Party makes maximum use of voluntary open, accurate discussion of any area which affects both groups, and he attempts to avoid consequences that would present new difficulties for Opponent. Just the opposite is involved in the distributive process. Party attempts to gain maximum information from Opponent but makes minimum disclosure himself – in fact he often tries to manipulate and persuade Opponent. And he explores the implications of action for possible unfavourable consequences for himself but does not concern himself with the consequences for Opponent.
>
> In brief, integrative bargaining is tentative and exploratory and involves open communication processes, whereas distributive bargaining involves adamant, directed and controlled information processes [16, p. 166].

Worse is to come in that a basically integrative situation almost always involves a distributive phase and that the general case is, in any case, one of 'mixed' bargaining – where the issues of negotiations have, potentially, both integrative and distributive aspects.

In addition, as we have seen above, the optimal tactics of distributive bargaining and attitudinal structuring may be in conflict with respect to information disclosure: 'A tactic designed to promote a better relationship frequently entails a sacrifice of the substance of distributive bargaining, and conversely a tactic designed to achieve a distributive gain often adversely affects the relationship' [16, p. 270].

If we accept Walton and McKersie's analysis then, these dilemmas appear to make it essential for management to formulate a policy on information disclosure which takes account of its possible effects (present and future) on integrative situations and attitudinal structuring *as well as* the more visible effects on distributive bargaining.

THE EFFECTS OF INFORMATION DISCLOSURE – SOME THEORETICAL CONCLUSIONS

In Table 4.1 we have tried to summarise, in a very broad way, some of the conclusions already reached about the possible effects of information disclosure on bargaining outcomes according to the predictions of the various models we have discussed here. Obviously, the table is not a substitute for reading the discussion since a number of the 'conclusions' are very tentative, as well as (necessarily) vague. What is fairly obvious,

TABLE 4.1 Summary of implications for information disclosure derived from bargaining models

Model		Process relevant	Information affects outcomes through:		Likely effect of 'full' disclosure by management on own pay-offs
General game theoretic					
Nash	Distributive bargaining	No	Pay-off utilities		Not applicable (perfect information)
Zeuthen		No	,,		,,
Pen		Yes	Corresepaction functions		,,
Cross		Yes	Learning rates Initial concession expectations	}	Unpredictable Favourable? Variable: depends on content
Stevens		Yes	Avoidance } Probability estimates Gradients } Valuation functions		,, ,, ,, ,,
Walton & McKersie:					
(a) Distributive bargaining		Yes	Aspiration } Probability estimates Levels } Valuation functions		,, ,, ,, ,,
(b) Integrative bargaining			Problem-solving process		Favourable
(c) Attitudinal structuring			Bargaining relationships		,,

however, is that, even given this vagueness, certain contradictions appear to be present. To a certain extent, therefore, what you believe about the role of information may depend on the model (if any) in which you put your trust.

Because of its potential relevance to the selection of the most appropriate model for this purpose, we have summarised below a representative selection of what empirical evidence there is on the effects of information on bargaining.

THE EFFECTS OF INFORMATION ON BARGAINING – SOME EMPIRICAL EVIDENCE

A number of experiments have been carried out by social science researchers which have a possible bearing on the role of information in bargaining. A desire to control, as far as possible, variables other than those under direct consideration has meant that these investigations have generally taken the form of laboratory experiments rather than field tests. Thus, most of the results indicated below have been obtained from observations of a series of 2-party bilateral monopoly (buyer-seller) experiments involving students as subjects. The effects of information on bargaining have then usually been deduced by experimenters from comparisons of the results of giving these subjects 'complete', as opposed to 'incomplete' information. In this context complete information means being given a schedule of the pay-offs ('profits') of the other player as well as one's own for all possible sets of action choices. That is, in terms of the pay-off table of game theory (e.g. Figure 4.1.) the 'completely' informed subject has full knowledge of all the values in the table. On the other hand, the 'incompletely' informed subject knows only his own pay-offs. These details are emphasised in order to make it clear just how 'artificial' are the conditions under which the experimental findings below have generally been established, and, therefore, to enter a caveat from the start about the utility of the respective conclusions in relation to possible practical predictions.

Perhaps the most influential experimenters/authors in this area are Siegel and Fouraker [12]. They studied the effects on bargaining outcomes of (a) complete versus incomplete information; (b) variations in the structure of pay-offs and (c) variations in the 'level of aspiration' (the target level of Walton and McKersie). From their results the following tentative conclusions about the effect of information have been drawn:

(a) increasing the amount of relevant information available to the

bargainers strengthens the tendency towards Pareto optimal solutions [12, p. 41];
(b) increasing the amount of information available to bargainers tends to lead to a more equal division of the joint pay-off [12, p. 70];
(c) if both bargainers have 'complete' information they tend to be more modest in their initial demands than they are in the cases of incomplete information [12, p. 59];
(d) there is *some* (but not statistically significant) evidence that increasing the information to one player alone tends to decrease his pay-off at agreement[36] [12, pp. 57–8].

Findings (a) and (b) may be of potential interest to legislators in formulating disclosure regulations to apply to collective bargaining since Pareto optimality and 'fair shares' could be considered to be socially desirable features of bargaining outcomes. Finding (c) if it led, in turn, to a reduction in overall bargaining time – by presumably reducing the opportunities for bluffing – might also be considered socially desirable. Finding (d) suggests that information disclosure in distributive bargaining may act to the positive benefit of the discloser and, as such, is perhaps the most controversial conclusion.

On the other hand, the research of Liebert, Smith, Hill and Keiffer [7] suggests that there is an additional interaction between the information available to a player and the degree of favourableness of the opponent's first demand. Their evidence supported the hypothesis that incompletely informed bargainers tend to use their opponent's first bid to set a target level so that the final outcome is less favourable to them when the opponent's first bid is unfavourable, and vice versa. On the other hand, completely informed bargainers use the opponent's first bid to assess the reasonableness of the opponent's target and use their counter-bids to influence the opponent towards a solution they consider to be reasonable on the basis of the information they have. Extrapolating from these findings of Liebert *et al.* the likely result of creating 2 'fully informed' players (by disclosure) is to render the outcome less dependent on the level of initial demands. For the discloser this implies a worse (better) outcome as compared to the strategy of his making a high (low) first demand when faced by an incompletely informed opponent. Thus, the Liebert *et al.* findings suggest that the phenomenon listed as finding (d) above for Siegel and Fouraker is likely to be reversed, unless the discloser engages in a rather altruistic bidding policy (i.e. he intends in any case to make an opening bid favourable to his opponent).

A more recent study, by Harnett and Hamner [5], points out that, in addition to the effects of differential information and opening bids, the share of total pay-offs a bargainer eventually receives is likely to depend on individual differences, such as attitudes toward conciliation, risk-taking propensity, experience in the negotiation process and financial needs. Their own empirical work was, however, limited to the interaction of 'expectancy' (the amount of money the bargainer expects to earn) and information on bargaining outcomes. Significant differences in pay-off were found both between low and high expectancy cases and for complete versus incomplete information. Directional effects were such that while high expectancy tended to increase the pay-off, complete information worked in the opposite direction. They also found a significant interaction between the two factors. The overall result was, however, such that the average player with complete information was consistently worse off than with incomplete information, whatever the state of his expectancies. This tends to confirm the controversial Siegel and Fouraker finding (d) and Schelling's hypothesis (see note 36). However, 'the model may only apply to inexperienced bargainers, since one would expect professional negotiators to handle information much more effectively than the college students who participated in this research. Certainly no implication is intended that a completely informed bargainer with high expectancy must *always* be at a bargaining disadvantage' [5, p. 88] [Italics added].

CONCLUSIONS

Since none of the empirical research described above has been directly concerned with testing the predictions of the bargaining models discussed earlier it cannot be used to justify adoption of any one of them for predictive purposes to the exclusion of the others. Nevertheless, one interesting conclusion does seem to emerge from the sparse evidence which is available – that the effects of information appear to be correlated with a number of other variables in the bargaining situation such that disclosure does not always necessarily weaken the position of the discloser. This falls far short of confirming the Schelling conclusion 'that if two bargainers have different amounts of information, the bargainer with less information often will receive a greater share of the joint pay-off than his bargaining position would indicate' [5, p. 81]. But, when it is realised that the studies have been concerned with purely distributive bargaining situations the conclusion that information disclosure might not *always* be to the disadvantage of management even in that context may be important when added to considerations of the effect on whatever other processes may be involved in bargaining relationships in practice. Evidence that there may, in fact, be sub-processes involved in most negotiations apart from the immediately obvious distributive one is largely of a descriptive, anecdotal, nature rather than deriving from strictly controlled experiments.[37]

Nonetheless, Walton and McKersie's characterisation of the negotiating process as one which involves distributive, integrative and intra-organisational bargaining and attitudinal structuring is intuitively appealing. Whether or not bargaining relationships can be best categorised in the precise way they suggest, there seems little doubt from the weight of observational evidence available that management/labour negotiations in practice are crucially influenced by factors such as mutual attitudes, intra-organisational politics (e.g. the ability of the union to control its members) and joint problem-solving activities. To that extent the distributive bargaining situation cannot adequately be considered in isolation from the inter-related processes Walton and McKersie call attitudinal structuring, intra-organisational bargaining and integrative bargaining.

It is necessary to remember, in this context, in discussing the issue of disclosure of *accounting* information in collective bargaining, that such information originates, in general, from only one party to the negotiations – management. Arguments in favour of disclosure made above have therefore been primarily couched in terms of identifying the possible benefits and costs to management.

However, direct communication of information between management and labour can, in fact, take place in two sets of circumstances:
(a) discretionary disclosure on the part of management, either as a unilateral move or in response to a request from labour; or
(b) socially regulated disclosure as a result of specific regulations, case law or guidelines laid down in a code of practice arising out of legislation.

From the point of view of being able to measure information value and so justify disclosure on a strict benefit/cost basis in either of the above situations we have seen that no collective bargaining model yet available gives sufficient predictive precision to quantify the incremental effect of information on bargaining outcomes confidently.

Thus, we have had to fall back on making general *directional* predictions about the probable effect of information on bargaining outcomes and it is in this context that a clearer identification of all the possible constituents of the negotiating process may have been important. It is perhaps too easy for management, and particularly those involved most closely in day to day negotiations, to equate the effect of information on collective bargaining as a whole with its possible effect on distributive bargaining alone.

Thus, an acknowledged possibility (but *only* a possibility) that information disclosure may have adverse distributional effects from management's point of view may be sufficient for a risk-averse management negotiator to fail to draw attention to the possible simultaneous benefits linked to integrative bargaining possibilities and attitudinal structuring for the purposes of reaching a decision on disclosure. This is particularly understandable in a situation where, in the short term, with a poor relationship already existing between labour and management, an experiment in integrative bargaining can lead to the realisation of a manager's worst fears about the possible effects of information disclosure, since: 'The shift [back] from integrative to distributive decision processes is difficult because precisely what one has revealed in discussing the item in order to establish the greatest joint gain can weaken his position in bargaining over the shares of that gain' [16, p. 166]. To accept such (real) dangers as a continuing justification for a negative policy on information disclosure to labour negotiators is, however, to get trapped in a vicious circle.

In the long run the potential benefits to management from integrative bargaining may be considerable but may not be obtainable without some restructuring of attitudes. Both attitudinal structuring and integrative bargaining may require a liberal disclosure policy, one element of the costs of which may be the possibly adverse effects on management's distributive bargaining position in the short term. It is not denied that these adverse effects may be occasionally so important as to endanger the organisation's ability to survive to reap any longer-term benefits. Rather, what is argued is that while the possible distributional bargaining costs and risks of disclosure cannot be ignored by management they must be properly weighed against all the associated possible benefits before a decision is reached.

It seems to us, in this respect, that the self-preservational instincts of managers engaged directly in distributive negotiations may already be a more than sufficient lobby for risk aversion in relation to disclosure decisions. We think it imperative, therefore, that top management become involved in formulating an organisational policy in this field since it is they who may, from a longer term and broader perspective, be better able to balance the possible requirements of attitudinal structuring and integrative bargaining against those of distributive bargaining.

From the point of view of legislators, on the other hand, the disclosure argument cannot be conducted solely in terms of possible costs and benefits to management. On this point we have seen above, in discussing the Siegel and Fouraker research, that 'full' disclosure of information *could* bring about certain socially useful results such as a tendency towards Pareto optimal agreements, 'fair' shares and a shortening of bargaining time. Whether or not these particular results do hold, and a lot more research is necessary before we can be adequately assured that they do, these are the kinds of issues it is suggested that governments, and their advisers, should be looking at in the process of drawing up disclosure regulations. Certainly there should be no question that governments, in formulating regulations, should be restricted to the criterion of possible benefits to management as a justification for requiring disclosure.

On the other hand, if there is any outstanding lesson to be learnt by management from a survey of collective bargaining models such as that carried out here it is that the list of possible benefits of disclosure may be more extensive than appears at first sight. To the extent that this results in more of the relevant benefits being recognised and weighed against the more obvious costs of a disclosure policy in the future, one intriguing possibility is that many more managements may find themselves taking decisions to move ahead of statutory disclosure regulations in this field, purely as a matter of organisational self interest.

NOTES

1 This is not to say that the more deductive models have, in fact, proved any more successful in prediction than the inductive ones. Some possible reasons for this are indicated later in the chapter.

2 This is the so-called perfect or complete information assumption. It implies that each player knows, and is known to know, with certainty, the pay-offs for both players associated with every possible pair of action choices.

3 Strictly, each choice for a player represents a possible strategy rather than a single action. Thus, the perfect information assumption implies that the results of all possible future actions on the part of both the player and opponent are known to infinity. Uncertainty exists only insofar as the precise actions the opponent will take to complete his alternative strategies are unknown.

4 Game theoretic and most other models are based on a behavioural assumption that the player is a utility, as opposed to money value, maximiser.

5 Which may be measured in 'utils'. As to the measurability to utility, see note 11 and [15].

6 Herein lies another implicit set of assumptions – that the player knows, and is known to know, that his opponent adopts certain decision criteria consistent with 'rationality'. For an explicit consideration of what this involves, see [13, chs. 3 and 7].

7 Other suggested decision criteria include minimum regret, Hurwicz and Laplace. For a discussion of these, see [8, ch. 13].

8 Consider, for example, the game: which has no unique solution using the maximin criterion (but note that (L, T) involves relatively 'perverse' pay-offs in this case).

	S	T
L	5,5	7,3
H	9,1	4,6

9 Any pay-off matrix involving 'cells' in which the totals are not c ˙ is a variable sum game. Obviously, in relation to the whole range of combinations of pay-offs which are possible, constant sum games are only a small proportion. For example, a game which has a zero cell (see diagram) is a variable sum game, and also, if we interpret (H, T) as the non-agreement (strike, lockout) result, is an example of a 'fixed threat' game (see note 12).

	S	T
L	5,5	2,8
H	9,1	0,0

10 However: 'The fact is that evaluations of the outcomes are not constant during the course of negotiations. Indeed, apart from the final single moves of the two negotiators by which they make a choice and conclude negotiations, the negotiators' bargaining activity serves primarily to estimate these utilities and to alter them' [16, p. 48].

11 The measurability of utility is the subject of considerable theoretical disagreement but, with the proviso that the necessary Von Neumann-Morgenstern assumptions are fulfilled, most model builders in the bargaining field seem to be agreed that utility functions such as AB in Figure 4.2 can be constructed which are determined up to a positive linear transformation and have preferred to express their models in such utility terms rather than monetary values. We may, therefore, rephrase our earlier comment on the assumptions of perfect information to say that each player knows, and is known to know, all relevant data, including each participant's Von Neumann-Morgenstern utility function. For a critical review of the Von Neumann-Morgenstern axioms see [1, ch. 22].

12 We are here implicitly assuming a 'fixed threat' bargaining situation in which the origin of both players' utility functions can be associated with a single, non-agreement point, which is the worst that either player can threaten. For an introduction to the added difficulties involved in 'variable threat' games see [2].

13 This means in effect that the outcome will always be an 'efficient' one from a welfare economics viewpoint.

14 This assumption coincides with the Von Neumann-Morgenstern cardinal utility axioms.

15 Consider a utility frontier of the form $U_l + U_m = K(AB$ on graph): By the symmetry axiom, outcome should be at mid point $(K/2, K/2)$. Let product of utilities $U_l . U_m = P$

For maximum P, $\dfrac{dP}{dU_l} = U_m + U_l \dfrac{dU_m}{dU_l} = 0$

i.e. $-\dfrac{dU_l}{dU_m} = \dfrac{U_l}{U_m}$ But, at mid point $-\dfrac{dU_l}{dU_m} = \dfrac{U_l}{U_m}$ (by congruent triangles)

So outcome (mid point) also represents the maximum utility product. By the transformation invariance axiom this applies also for any other straight-line utility frontier since the mid point always represents the same 'real' outcome. Thus, outcome is always at the mid point of *any* straight-line utility frontier. By invoking the independence of irrelevant alternatives axiom, we can say that, for any continuous concave-to-the-origin frontier, such as CD, since we can always find a straight line which is tangent to it at the mid point of the straight line (this can be seen to be true by rotating a tangent line around the boundary), that point must be the outcome and must

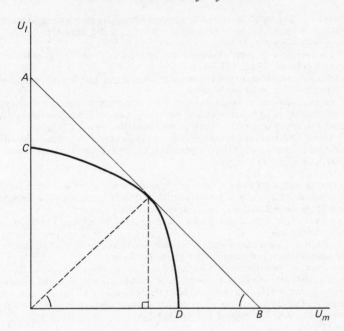

also maximise the utility product. It can only be said to divide the total pay-off equally, however, if we associate the pay-off possibilities with *AB*.

16 $P_l < P_m$ means $\dfrac{U_{ll} - U_{lm}}{U_{ll}} < \dfrac{U_{mm} - U_{ml}}{U_{mm}}$

i.e. $U_{ll} \cdot U_{ml} < U_{lm} \cdot U_{mm}$

– the utility product proposed by labour is less than that proposed by management. Thus, the 'next feasible outcome' must be a point for which the inequalities change in sign.

17 For a concave-to-the-origin outcome set each concession to a 'next feasible outcome' will raise one of the utility products, the other remaining constant. This will continue until the two utility products are equal, and at their maxima.

18 Even the size of the initial demands is irrelevant to the solution in the Zeuthen model (as interpreted by Harsanyi), so there is no question of even being able to use information disclosure to influence initial demands in the hope of influencing the outcome.

19 To compare directly with previous models we have to set U_{lc}, and later U_{mc}, equal to zero.

20 Actually, Pen brings a further element of uncertainty into the model by applying a 'risk valuation function' to the actuarial computation, but this does not introduce anything new for our purposes.

21 The eventual outcome will thus depend on the precise shifts which take place and hence is not determinate within the confines of Pen's model.

22 Obtained by setting the differential du/dQ_l equal to zero, in the usual way.

23 Adapted from [3, p. 14, Figure 1.4].

24 The system could, however, be an unstable one, see [4, pp. 74–7].

25 From [4, p. 83], with adaptations to meet the simplifying assumptions adopted here and also to correct for the error pointed out in [13, p. 245, note 90].

26 For a fuller discussion of these conclusions, see [4, ch. 4].

27 This is a result of the 'level' of decision rule adopted by Cross. The point is very well covered in [3, ch. 4] and [13, sec. L. 5].

28 Although if one avoidance gradient lies everywhere above the other the negotiator will choose one of the goals immediately.

29 A sufficient condition would be that the coincidence of the two equilibria is communicated to both parties without disturbing those equilibria. The mechanism by which this might be achieved is not covered here (see, instead, [14]).

30 This is not discussed here, but see [16, chs. 8 and 9] and note that intra-organisational bargaining can influence the labour negotiator's utility function for the purposes of the other bargaining sub-processes.

31 Taken from [16, p. 42].

32 Where the settlement range is not positive, no settlement is possible which would be minimally acceptable to both parties, with the probable result that a strike will occur, to be followed by enforced revision of aspiration levels.

33 This is not of course to say that perceptions cannot also be influenced by the impact of 'new' information.

34 For instance: 'Union examination of company books has not always been destructive. Occasionally, such analysis has shown clearly that the lack of profit sufficient to provide an increase has been the result of factors other than wages. For example, in the [U.S.] clothing industry, unions have co-operatively aided management in the reduction of operating costs and thus in effect created an ability to pay. In this type of "backhanded" creation of ability to pay the union sometimes steps up productivity to enable the employer to meet the increase' [17, pp. 320–21].

35 See [16, pp. 212–21].

36 As well as, possibly, fitting the predictions of the Cross model [4, p. 60], this fits the hypothesis of T. C. Schelling, [11], that the lack of knowledge by the less informed bargainer of what is fair or reasonable will generally induce him to concede more slowly than his opponent.

37 For an introduction to such evidence, see [16, *passim*].

REFERENCES

1 W. J. Baumol, *Economic Theory and Operations Analysis*, 2nd ed. (Englewood Cliffs, N.J. : Prentice-Hall, 1965).

2 R. L. Bishop, 'Game-Theoretic Analyses of Bargaining', *Quarterly Journal of Economics*, 77 (1963) pp. 559–602.

3 A. Coddington, *Theories of the Bargaining Process* (London: George Allen and Unwin, 1968).

4 J. G. Cross, *The Economics of Bargaining* (New York: Basic Books, 1969).

5 D. L. Harnett and W. C. Hamner, 'The Value of Information in Bargaining', *Western Economic Journal*, 11 (1973) pp. 81–8.

6 J. C. Harsanyi, 'Approaches to the Bargaining Problem Before and After the Theory of Games', *Econometrica*, 24 (1956) pp. 144–57.

7 R. M. Liebert, W. P. Smith, J. H. Hill and M. Keiffer, 'The Effects of Information and Magnitude of Initial Offers on Interpersonal Negotiation', *Journal of Experimental Social Psychology*, 4 (1968) pp. 431–41.

8 R. D. Luce and H. Raiffa, *Games and Decision* (New York: J. Wiley, 1957).

9 J. F. Nash, 'The Bargaining Problem', *Econometrica*, 18 (1950) pp. 152–62.

10 J. Pen, trans. by T. S. Preston, *The Wage Rate under Collective Bargaining* (Cambridge, Mass: Harvard University Press, 1959).

11 T. C. Schelling, *The Strategy of Conflict* (Cambridge, Mass: Harvard University Press, 1960).

12 S. Siegel and L. E. Fouraker, *Bargaining and Group Decision Making* (New York: McGraw Hill, 1960).

13 I. Stahl, *Bargaining Theory* (Stockholm: Economic Research Unit, Stockholm School of Economics, 1972).

14 C. M. Stevens, *Strategy and Collective Bargaining Negotiations* (New York: McGraw Hill, 1963).

15 J. Von Neumann and O. Morgenstern, *Theory of Games and Economic Behaviour*, 2nd ed. (Princeton, N.J.: Princeton University Press, 1947).

16 R. E. Walton and R. B. McKersie, *A Behavioral Theory of Labor Negotiations* (New York: McGraw Hill, 1965).

17 M. S. Wortman and C. W. Randle, *Collective Bargaining: Principles and Practices* (Boston, Mass: Houghton Mifflin, 1966).

18 F. Zeuthen, *Problems of Monopoly and Economic Warfare* (London: Routledge and Kegan Paul, 1930).

5 Trade Union and Management Uses of Company Accounting Information

The reader will no doubt have observed that, so far in the book, we have been mainly concerned with the issue of what information *should be* disclosed in bargaining. In addition, because of the lack of sufficiently specific predictive models, we have been treating 'information' as if it were some homogeneous commodity, i.e. we have been concerned about the possible effects of a change in the general *level* of information disclosure rather than its constituents.

In this chapter, in contrast, we shall look mainly at aspects of the current and past use of *particular* types of company level information in collective bargaining. We shall also examine some arguments for the (future) disclosure of specific items by companies. The reason for dealing with such proposals at this stage, rather than earlier, is that demands for the disclosure of particular items seem mainly to arise out of practical experience of information deficiencies and/or knowledge of practice elsewhere. To that extent we feel that analysis of specific disclosure proposals cannot logically precede a discussion of past and current disclosure practice (whereas arguments relating to disclosure *in general* may be a necessary prerequisite for understanding much current disclosure practice). The subject matter of this chapter is, therefore, a discussion of sources and uses of company (mainly accounting) information in collective bargaining, together with some specific proposals for extending company disclosure practice. For this purpose, the chapter is divided into two sections, one relating to the trade union (labour) side of negotiations and one to management, although the two are necessarily interdependent.

It should also be mentioned that, for the U.K. in particular, there appears to be far more documentary evidence available for the trade union side than management. This is perhaps a reflection of the relatively one-sided nature of pressures for increased disclosure in collective bargaining. As a result, for evidence on the management side we rely mainly on U.S. sources. We feel that U.S. material is relevant to the U.K. also, however, on the grounds of general economic and societal comparability and, specifically, the fact that the U.K. appears to be moving towards a legislative position on disclosure which parallels that established some time ago in the U.S.A.[1]

TRADE UNIONS

We deal with trade unions in relation to information disclosure, rather than labour negotiators in general, because all the evidence which is available relates to unionised employees and, in any case, the organisational resources of the unions mean that practice in relation to labour negotiators' information usage is likely to be at its most developed in union/management negotiations. The trade unions have, in fact, devoted considerable resources to research in connection with preparation for negotiations.[2] Most of the larger unions have their own full-time research departments staffed by specialists.[3] The services of these departments are available to negotiators for the preparation of 'briefs' and documentation supporting claims and, often, to shop stewards for answering queries relating to their employing organisations.

Perhaps the most spectacular and well publicised instances of use of financial information by unions in the U.K. have been in the 'prestige' analyses supporting wage claims prepared by the Trade Union Research Unit at Ruskin College, Oxford.[4] Although these are not necessarily typical of the way in which financial information may be marshalled in arguments by union negotiators, they do give an indication of the sophisticated nature of the resources to which unions potentially have access.[5]

We have already discussed, in Chapter 4, the role played by information in negotiations, whether it be in distributive bargaining, integrative bargaining or attitudinal structuring (to use the terminology of the Walton and McKersie [47] model). Another role, also mentioned previously, is that of 'rationalising' the union's demand in order to influence third parties such as the general public, government or potential arbitrators, and hence indirectly influence management's (as well as the union membership's) attitudes.
For example:

During the 1970 dispute the Ford management went over the heads of the union negotiators and offered an extra £3 a week straight to the men. They hadn't dreamt of money like that and immediately accepted the offer.

But last year we circulated the claim to the rank and file. They might not have understood all the figures but they certainly got the message that Fords could afford to pay more. So when the management again took its offer straight to the workers, it was they who walked out before the shop stewards even suggested it.[6]

This is a perhaps unusual illustration of the way in which union members' attitudes can be changed by the presentation of information by the union. A more common instance of the same type of effect is where management and the union by making use of information jointly or separately may 'rationalise' a settlement they have both agreed upon in order to make it acceptable to the union members who have to accept it formally.[7]

Despite this, a number of union sources appear to play down the significance of financial information in wage negotiations, viz.:

In relatively few negotiations does management or the union emphasise the company's or industry's financial experience in great detail. Most of the bargaining is based primarily on the factors other than profits and financial status. The issue is normally willingness to pay and not ability to pay . . . Profitability and the level of business is usually significant as a background and psychological consideration [4, p. 18].

In fact, this description fits the Walton and McKersie model, discussed in Chapter 4, in which information may have a psychological role to play which, if not direct, is nevertheless real. In apparent contradiction of this, however 'there does exist a point of view, perhaps held by the more hardened practitioners in the industrial relations world, that the actual impact of mere facts and figures in the wage-bargaining situation is minimal, compared to some unspecified "forces" allegedly at work in the negotiating process. The mountains of statistics and other factual information are only put forward, so the theme runs, to give the useful illusion of rationality to the whole affair' [2, p. 6]. This is, in fact, a description of the school of theorists and practitioners who maintain that negotiating outcomes are determined by the relative 'power' of the participants.

As has been pointed out [16, p. 17] such power 'theories' may, in fact, be mere tautologies. This is because in them 'power' is often defined synonymously with 'the ability to get a better outcome' and the result is a completely circular argument which cannot add anything to knowledge in a predictive sense. On the other hand, a definition of power which is linked to the *determinants* of the outcome, which is a suggested way out of the circularity [16, pp. 17–18], could well restore a meaningful role to information, since the possession of information may be one important constituent of 'power'.

In practice the constituents of *wage claims*, at least, seem to be clearly linked to information provision, for example:

The % Net Increase required includes three increases:
1. *The cost of living increase*
   (The minimum demand necessary to hold the line on the real standard of living.)
2. *The productivity increase*
   (The workers'share of increased output per worker at the factory or firm – necessary to hold the line on the workers' share of the Gross National Product.)
3. *The parity increase*
   (An attempt to alter the national distribution of income in favour of workers, by bringing their pay up to the level of workers doing equal work in another area) [5, p. 2].

Using this as an example of the construction of a 'typical' wage claim it can be seen that factors (2) and (3) will depend mainly on the use of organisational 'labour force' information (see below). Organisational financial information, on the other hand, rather than entering into the direct computation of the claim, seems, typically, to be referred to 'after the fact', i.e. in rationalising the organisation's 'ability to pay' the claim. This would appear to fit union views that the primary factor in constructing a wage demand should be what the workers are 'entitled to' rather than what the organisation is able to pay.

Indeed, it has been questioned whether a union should be at all concerned that an organisation may possibly be 'unable to pay' a wage increase, viz.:

There is of course a question of principle, of whether it is a responsibility of workers to subsidise a company by accepting wages which lag far behind those paid elsewhere ... The financial difficulties of some companies are due to reasons which cannot begin to be met by restricting wages ... Unions are aware that, if an employer knows they will relax efforts to raise wages, he will be more inclined to let his business slide along as in the past, hoping that some broad economic change will come along to better his position. But if the union keeps pushing firmly for wage advances, the employer is forced to find better ways to run his business to offset the costs of higher wages . . .

If acceptance of an inadequate wage increase might seriously jeopardise the union's negotiations at other companies, the union may be unwise to accept it. The union must consider not only the situation of members at one company, but the interests of its membership as a whole.

Also, in fairness to other employers who have already agreed to certain terms, and in consideration of its future bargaining relations with them, the union may not want to undercut them by agreeing to lower wages from competitors . . .

At some time, a laggard company must find a way to take higher wages in stride. If it cannot, and must go out of business, that may mean the loss of some poorly paying jobs. But even though any job loss is serious, this may be only a temporary blow, for the bulk of the workers involved very likely will then gradually improve their position as they gain better paying jobs elsewhere [4, pp. 19–20].

Clearly there are a number of institutional assumptions built into these opinions which may or may not apply in a particular negotiating context. What the quotation does suggest, nevertheless, is that there may be a number of negotiating situations in which financial information (relating to ability to pay) appears to be irrelevant, at least from the union viewpoint.

There is, however, no reason why such a view should be accepted at its face value. In terms of the computation described previously, measurements of ability to pay may influence the calculation of item (2), in particular, where this is based on some estimate of the marginal or average revenue product. In addition, although ability to pay may appear to have merely a 'ratchet' influence in that it appears to be used in wage demand rationalisations only when it is favourable to the union case, in fact 'inability to pay' may also depress the union's expectations generally, and hence implicitly affect the computation of factors (2) and (3). Thus, financial information would appear always to have, at least potentially, an implicit effect on wage claims (where it is known to the union).

Clearly, though, we must also bear in mind the distinctions between explicit wage demands, negotiators' implicit expectations and settlement outcomes. We have already (in Chapter 4) put forward reasons for believing that financial information can have a role to play, through the adjustment of expectations, in the determination of outcomes.

Whatever the relationship between documented wage claim arguments and union negotiators' 'actual' expectations, it is apparent that the information used in circulated documents *can* play an effective role in determining wage settlements simply by influencing the expectations of union members. [8] The fact that documented wage claims *could* play a 'real' role, then, gives relevance to an analysis of their informational content.

We can analyse the type of information used by unions in terms of the three factors listed in the illustration of a computation of a typical wage claim [9] above i.e.:

(a) cost of living;
(b) productivity;
(c) comparability (or parity).

(A) COST OF LIVING DATA

As rates of inflation have increased, the cost of living element in wage claims has become increasingly important, e.g. 'The cost of living will remain a principal issue which needs to be taken into account in collective bargaining' (T.U.C., *Economic Review*, 1974).

In the U.K. the statistic most frequently used by trade unions for measuring cost of living changes is the Retail Price Index. This has the advantage that it is published monthly, although its conceptual disadvantages, as regards coverage for example, appear to be well recognised by the unions. [10] The need to take account of *expected* inflation rather than experienced inflation has also been recognised in a period of accelerating price rises. A further sophistication has been the suggestion that the percentage cost of living increase should be adjusted to take into account the incidence of taxation, i.e. % Gross Cost of Living Increase Required

$$= \frac{\text{Expected Inflation Rate } \% \, (1 - \text{Average Tax Rate})}{(1 - \text{Marginal Tax Rate})}$$

where the 'tax rate' includes items such as National Insurance contributions as well as Income Tax. [11] To employ this method, it is obviously necessary to work with the statistics of a 'typical' worker, since specific assumptions need to be made about tax allowances etc. The result, if the increase were granted, is then supposed to insulate such a 'typical' worker from the effects of inflation on take-home pay.[12]

In the U.S.A. rather than using the equivalent of the Retail Price Index, unions have tended to use statistics taken from 'family budget surveys', the scope of which is deemed more appropriate to unionised workers.[13] It is interesting to note, incidentally, that a switch to using family budget data rather than the 'cost of living' index occurred in the U.S.A. in the 1930s when the cost of living index actually *fell*.[14]

One obvious extension of the use of cost of living data by unions is to demonstrate, where appropriate, that wages and/or earnings have not been maintained in 'real' terms and that, therefore, an element of 'catching up' is necessary.[15]

(B) PRODUCTIVITY DATA

Productivity has a fairly long history of separate consideration in collective bargaining.[16] It appears to find favour with participants in the bargaining process for a number of reasons:

(1) from the union or shop-floor negotiator's point of view, productivity growth, when expressed as changes in output per man, or per man-hour, is a succinct way of characterising labour's contribution to the productive process (whether this contribution is active or merely passive is not necessarily a material issue as far as the negotiating ploy is concerned);

(2) management may be more amenable to productivity arguments because wage increases commensurate with productivity change may be absorbed without increasing final prices;

(3) finally governments have also welcomed productivity based arguments in collective bargaining precisely because they are more likely to result in non-inflationary settlements. In fact during the mid 1960s in the U.K., productivity growth became one of the most important gateways by which increases above a specific norm were allowed.[17]

In the absence of any direct internal data union negotiators may be forced to approximate productivity growth by referring to such statistics as changes in sales value per employee [24, p. 18] calculated directly from the published accounts. Other, similar, indicators used have been wages and salaries as a proportion of sales [34, p. 26] and value added per employee [19, p. 17]. Clearly there is a good deal of room for argument over the relevance of different productivity indicators and their various methods of computation even given the restrictions on what is available in published accounts. One question which seems appropriate, therefore, is whether a particular indicator of productivity can be considered 'best' in some sense.

Economists have long been aware that productivity data are extremely tricky to use and can be quite misleading when employed uncritically – particularly when making short-run comparisons. The concept itself has a deceptively simple definition – it is the ratio of outputs to inputs – but problems begin to arise immediately one tries to apply it in specific cases. For instance, some types of activity, e.g. research and development or servicing jobs, may not have any immediately recognisable outputs. Output measures, even when available, may be based on gross concepts rather than net concepts; product data may be crudely lumped together into broad categories; quality variations may be quite marked between batches or at different times and finally technological change may affect the basic nature of the product such that one is no longer comparing like with like. Similar problems arise on the input side: where labour is the denominator, employees and man-hours of different skills may be treated as equivalent; the data may be based on hours clocked instead of hours actually worked; the effectiveness of work may vary; changes in the quality of other inputs may go unrecorded and the scope of the input data may not coincide with the scope of the output data. Value measures of productivity are no less susceptible to these criticisms and suffer from the further disadvantage of relative price fluctuations.[18]

Nevertheless 'productivity' has played a significant role in many pay claims. The measurement problems imply, however, that considerable confusion may arise in the use of productivity criteria. Thus, bargaining activity might arguably become more efficient if *both* parties were aware of the various data currently used by management to construct production control systems and internal productivity indexes since these should be inherently more relevant than data obtained from the published accounts.

The C.I.R. report on disclosure [14, p. 32] indicated that some U.K. companies were, in fact, willing to give information on such items as standard performance levels, output per man and production schedules as well as costs of different shift systems and costs of overtime.

Knowledge of currently used performance indicators may also serve to indicate areas of potential improvement. In the particular case of productivity bargaining which emerged in the U.K. in the early 1960s disclosure of plant efficiency indicators appears to have been a necessary component of successful agreements. As this form of collective bargaining requires comprehensive and detailed reassessment of working practices it is self-evident that union officials, shop stewards and employees, need internal data. These data are crucial at two phases in the programme:

(1) in the 'problem solving' phase of 'mixed' bargaining[19] when *possible* changes and objectives are under discussion. Here they assist the definition of the range of potential actions and relative rewards; and

(2) in the evaluation or follow-up stage. There may be the suspicion that management does considerably better out of productivity bargaining than the workers – this can only be determined by continuous access to, and monitoring of, the relevant data by stewards and/or union officials.

As productivity bargaining demands a considerable amount of management time and commitment of company resources there should normally be a periodic post audit of the agreement.[20] From the management point of view it is probably most important that the package successfully controls unit costs, checks wage drift and reduces overtime. Union representatives will similarly be interested in these things but will in turn want to know the effect of the bargain on the level, distribution and stability of earnings.

(C) COMPARABILITY

In relation to the construction of arguments over comparability and what 'parity' adjustment may be necessary, unions make use of two major classes of information:

(i) external wage data; and

(ii) internal wage data.

Many claims based upon comparability arguments require external data since the reference group may be in another industry or in another region. This is particularly true in national negotiations but such comparisons are made at all levels of bargaining. The level of wage rates and earnings in *other* plants or companies induces claims for parity of treatment especially when the work done is similar. Thus, many union officials negotiate with several companies in the same industry and are certainly aware of rate of pay and nationally negotiated skill differentials in different firms; similarly shop stewards, through combined committees or informal contacts, get to know data on rates paid in other plants. In these circumstances they will quite naturally frame their claim in terms of wage data external to their own particular bargaining unit. What union negotiators are not always fully informed about, however, is relative *earnings* or relative wage structures in other plants and firms. Even data on *wage rates* paid by comparable companies are often not easily obtainable.

The result is that, unless unions also bargain with comparable companies they may not have systematic access to relevant external wage data (and the same partial ignorance may, of course, apply to management). There are two dangers in using wage comparisons in situations where the bargainers are only partially informed: firstly, often quite unrepresentative cases may become the focus of attention; secondly, word of mouth is the main way in which information is transmitted between union negotiators and this is itself notoriously unreliable.

It is certainly arguable, therefore, that bargaining might be considerably improved if more systematic data on relative earnings on a company basis were made available. This could perhaps be done on similar lines to the U.K. Department of Employment's *New Earnings Survey*. As well as *average* hourly and weekly earnings, the *Survey* also provides information on the *dispersion* of earnings in each case. Two measures of dispersion, within any given classification, are provided, the first shows the upper and lower quartiles and deciles of the distribution, as well as the median; the second gives a cumulative frequency distribution indicating the percentage of that particular group earning less than a specific amount – for example, in the 1975 survey 18.4 % of full-time male, manual workers in engineering were estimated to earn less than £45 per week compared with only 9.2 % in U.K. shipbuilding and ship repairing [18, p. B11].

The advantages of presenting data in this way may be appreciated with two examples:

(a) in many cases the median is a more representative indicator of 'typical' wages in a firm or an industry than the arithmetic mean, which tends to be distorted by extreme values in the distribution;

(b) if the structure of earnings is highly skewed this will be signalled by the data so that it may be possible to spot and renegotiate a more equitable wage structure before it becomes a source of conflict.[21]

The main point here, however, is that statistics of this nature allow negotiators to test the validity of claims based upon comparability arguments for industry level bargaining. It would seem quite feasible, as well as advantageous, for employers' associations to collect and make available to both management and unions systematic surveys of this type for their particular industry to be used in company and plant level bargaining.

Many wage claims are, of course, based on intra-company or intra-plant comparisons. In fact, with the growth of shop-floor bargaining it can be argued that these have become the most important preoccupation of the work-force. Brown, for example, points out that: 'the main force behind the bargaining process becomes one of comparison in an unending stream of fragmented bargains between individual workers and junior managers' [12, p. 16]. Quite clearly, where the reference group is internal to the particular firm or plant, wage discussions would be facilitated if management and unions were fully appraised of earnings levels, changes in wage structure and the composition of relative wages in terms of over-time, shift premia, bonuses etc.

It has been commented, however, that 'Unions use internal wage data infrequently; and when they do use them they do so primarily to show inequities among the wages and working conditions of the employees' [6, p. 56]. This obviously refers to the explicit, tactical use of information by unions. As emphasised many times in this book, however, the implicit effects of information on expectations have also to be taken into account and the selective (explicit) *use* of information is not necessarily a sound reason for its selective *provision*.[22]

ABILITY TO PAY

As already indicated, statistics on ability to pay seem to be referred to by unions as a 'permissive' rather than 'determining' factor in wage claims. A very wide range of 'ability to pay' indicators have been used at various times. Some indication of the variety involved may be gathered from the following list of ability to pay indicators derived from (only) 16 arbitration cases in the U.S.A.:

1. Accumulated profits, accumulated surplus and past profits.
2. Profits of the industry (in industry wide bargaining).
3. Amount of dividend payments and dividends per share (on all classes of stock).
4. Working capital (amount and changes in).
5. Changes in invested capital – total and per share.
6. Effects of loss of line of credit on working capital.
7. Income before interest on income bonds.
8. Relationship of labour cost to total costs.
9. Rate of return (profit/capital funds invested).
10. Rate of profit on sales.
11. Profits before and after taxes.

12. Relationship of par value and market value of shares.
13. Profit after fixed charges (before dividends).
14. Departmental or divisional (versus entity) profits.
15. Earnings per share.
16. Profits in the future.
17. Net book value of plant and equipment.
18. Expenditure for ordinary maintenance of equipment.
19. Gross revenues (changes over a period of time in physical units of output and dollars).
20. The amount of company securities retired.[23]

In relation to the U.K. the range of ability to pay indicators used appears to be just as diverse. For example, during 1972 the authors were allowed access to records of the research departments of 2 of the larger U.K. trade unions. We examined a large number of 'briefs' prepared by staff of the research departments for the use of union negotiators. From a sample of 102 such briefs, dated between 1957 and 1972, the information in Table 5.1 was extracted.

In referring to the table, it is necessary, above all, to stress the possibly non-representative character of such 'evidence' of union uses of financial information. Only 2 unions were involved and we had no means of estimating the total population from which our 'sample' was drawn. In addition, we were working with information at least 'once removed' from negotiations, i.e. we do not know whether it was actually used, or even considered relevant by negotiators. It was also noticeable that the briefs we examined were of a fairly stereotyped nature with identifiable 'switches' in the pattern of uses of information which seemed to be associated with changes in 'fashion' (e.g. the onset of productivity bargaining) or changes in the research staff involved. Nevertheless, in the absence of other, better, evidence we can offer certain comments on what may be shown by Table 5.1.

Firstly, it will be noticed that almost all the information appears to be obtainable from published accounts. There are two possible reasons for this: one, that it is used simply because it is available and relevant (but, possibly, as a surrogate for less accessible but more relevant information); and the other, that the information provider and/or user is 'conditioned' to its use by familiarity (this is obviously a function of the availability). It is, in fact, not possible to say definitely whether all the information is derived from published sources since precise definitions of the terms used were not given. Interviews with current research staff indicated, however, that published accounts were a major source of their information in preparing such briefs.

In relation to 'ability to pay' it is noticeable that the most popular measure of profits referred to was also the 'grossest' (trading profits) although the separate provision of depreciation figures meant that the recipient of the brief (the union negotiator) could also 'add back'

TABLE 5.1   Financial Accounting indicators quoted in negotiating briefs

Indicator	Frequency
Turnover	77
Trading profit	66
Dividends	61
Profit before tax	55
Capital employed	52
Directors emoluments	49
Mark up (gross profit/sales)	49
Net profit/capital employed	49
Gross profit/capital employed	47
Aggregate remuneration	41
Gross assets	39
Net assets	38
Depreciation	37
Reserves	32
Sales/employee	32
Labour cost/total cost	31
Profit after tax	28
Trading profit/employee	24
Remuneration/employee	21
Output	15
Earnings for ordinary shareholders	9
Output/employee	8
Gross profit, before tax and interest	5
Cash flow	4
Investment grants	3
Output/man hour	3
Exports	2
Gross profit/employee	2
Labour costs	2
Scrip issue	2
Assets/income	1
Capacity utilisation	1
Cash outflow	1
Dividend yield	1
Fixed assets	1
Fixed assets/employee	1
Sales/man hour	1
Share price	1
Total income	1
Trading profit/capital employed	1
Value added/employee	1
Total no. of Briefs	102

depreciation if thought necessary. That measures of profit 'grosser' than trading profits may be used by union negotiators can be seen, for example, in the 1971 I.C.I. claim prepared by the Trade Union Research Unit, in which 'gross trading profit, before depreciation' is referred to [34, p. 33].[24]

The tendency to use as large a measure of profits as possible is, of course, explainable in terms of the 'tactical' use of information. (Although in Chapter 6 we discuss another possible reason.) Clearly other items, such as directors' emoluments and dividends, could also be made use of tactically by emphasising their possibly discretionary nature.

It is also noticeable that a number of financial ratios were used, whilst the separate provision of basic information such as turnover, aggregate remuneration, gross assets etc. enables the negotiator to derive further ratios if necessary. To a certain extent the popularity of standard ratios (mark up, net or gross profit/capital employed etc.) may be a function of the stress placed on them in accounting text books and courses i.e. of the *conditioning* of research staff to their use. It is feasible, however, that such ratios satisfy certain underlying 'real' information needs of negotiators.

One possible reason for using ratios rather than absolute financial values is that they may assist comparability by taking the 'scale factor' out of the comparison. For instance, it should be theoretically possible to compare validly a profitability ratio for different 'sized' firms, either cross-sectionally or longitudinally (*ceteris paribus*). The difficulties introduced by varying accounting practices, *inter alia*, however, make ratio comparison a tool of doubtful validity in practice, although this need not deter the negotiator from making use of it for tactical reasons.

On the other hand, as suggested in Chapter 6, ratios may also serve the purpose of assisting in the prediction of *future* ability to pay. Since negotiations are concerned with future conditions it is *future* ability to pay which is presumably directly relevant. To the extent that past measurements are actually referred to in negotiations, they are therefore classifiable as either direct predictions of future ability to pay (e.g. the 'profit measures') which implicitly assume no change, or else as tools to assist the prediction of future ability to pay (e.g. ratios). The first of these classes (which assumes the past is to be repeated in the future) seems at first sight to represent a rather perverse use of information in the face of the known fluctuating nature of year to year company financial results.

The use of such information, which seems on the face of it not to be directly relevant may, however, occur simply because the information base for making anything other than a 'no change' assumption is not available.[25] On the other hand, it is possible that information which is known to have faults may be quoted by labour negotiators in order to provoke management into providing more relevant measurements. As one possible example of this,[26] in the 1971 I.C.I. claim the unions derived a measure of the change in 'productivity' from 1965–70 by comparing constant (1963) price sales per employee. In so doing, in the absence of other information, the union made use of statistics for I.C.I.'s U.K. activities as a whole [34, pp. 26–7]. The company's response was to produce similar information referring to 'those parts of the company directly affected by the current negotiations' [31, p. 13].

It is possible in this particular case, of course, that I.C.I. simply did not know in advance what information the union side required, and this explanation is, in fact, supported by the company's offer to provide certain requested information in the future [31, p. 7]. On a more general level, however, this case may serve to illustrate one argument for a liberal disclosure policy – i.e., if the unions are not given access to information which they consider relevant, then they will estimate it themselves – and their assumptions are hardly likely to favour management's case!

In general, the major sources of financial information to trade unions are published company reports[27] and government publications (for industry wide data). The snag about such sources is that they are not necessarily best suited to providing information for collective bargaining.[28]

As is well known, the traditional focus of company reporting has been shareholders and creditors. Whilst it is possible that such users may have many specific information needs in common with negotiators, on some items (such as manpower data) it is likely also that their needs will differ. The expansion of published information to meet negotiators' needs may, however, exacerbate problems of 'information overload' for existing users as well as adding to reporting costs.[29]

'Information overload' is only one implicit cost of increased disclosure as far as the *recipient* is concerned. More obviously, the use of financial information by unions in bargaining implies processing costs for them. We have already noted that many of the larger unions have research departments which provide 'financial information services' to negotiators and that, in the U.K. for example, the Trade Union Research Unit at Oxford has also been used by unions for preparation of sophisticated 'prestige' claims, whilst other smaller unions, and individual negotiators, may make use of the services of the Labour

Research Department. As a result, where several unions may be negotiating with the same employer, there could be a considerable amount of duplication of effort in obtaining and processing relevant organisational information.

In the U.K. there is, in fact, no central research agency for unions. The T.U.C. acts as a focus for research activities in that it publishes relevant literature and organises conferences on the subject but it does not keep any kind of central record of company financial information as does, for instance, the Industrial Union Department in the U.S.A.[30] However, the T.U.C., in its representative capacity, has frequently commented on the drawbacks associated with current sources of information for collective bargaining and made suggestions for 'improving' (by increasing) the current level of disclosure.

General union criticisms of company financial information have, however, perhaps best been expressed by an American union source, i.e.:

(a) The typical financial statement summarises business experience in a past period . . . A financial statement is therefore not an adequate tool for measuring likely future effects of a wage bargaining settlement [4, p. 21].

(b) Profitability can be understated because (1) financial policies and/or the choice of accounting methods can significantly alter the amount of reported profits, (2) temporary or non-recurring expenses can affect a year's operating figures, and (3) some companies are not run merely to make a profit [4, p. 23].

(c) The typical published financial statement is a highly condensed or summarised statement which masks many of the distinctions meaningful for bargaining purposes. It fails to give breakdowns on various costs and other data often needed for sensible evaluation, for example, on productivity, unit labor costs, and the role wage increases might play in the company's operations [4, p. 21].

The *ex post* nature of accounting results means that comment (a) must necessarily be true where it is *future* ability to pay that is at issue. On the other hand, it is possible to use past results to *predict* the future. Thus, in order to make accounting reports more relevant we may *either* present direct predictions *or else* provide information which has improved predictive ability. Ways of 'improving' disclosure according to both of these alternatives are examined in Chapter 6.

Criticism (b) relates partly to the discretionary nature of accounting practices. To the extent that 'Statements of Standard Accounting

Practice' [30, Sec. M] succeed in reducing the variety of practices adopted, it may be considered that this criticism is now being met in the U.K. However, there is a danger that such standardisation will result in *less* relevant accounting reports. This could happen if an organisation was prevented from using a non-standard accounting practice which 'best' suited its own peculiar circumstances. For this reason, the U.K. Accounting Standards Steering Committee has been careful to preserve a certain amount of flexibility in the Standards.[31] But such 'flexibility' reintroduces problems for comparability.

To meet such problems it seems necessary to know how the accounts are constructed, so that, if necessary, they can be reconstructed on a preferred alternative basis.[32] For this purpose what is ultimately needed is access to the 'building blocks' of the accounts, not merely a statement of accounting policies. (As we shall see in Chapter 6 such a solution may also be necessary for predictive purposes.) But this, in turn, increases the possibility of 'information overload'. (We return to this discussion in Chapter 6.)[33]

Criticism (c), although superficially different, again suggests the same solution, i.e. that more 'basic' information should be disclosed. One obvious problem with expanding disclosure to cope with this is that the usual counter-arguments about effects on confidentiality etc. may be raised by management (see Chapter 2). To a certain extent these arguments may be met on a practical level by pointing out that in the U.S.A. both the general level of disclosure in published accounts and specific disclosure to trade unions in collective bargaining have been more extensive than that practised in the U.K. as a result of legislation and extra-statutory regulation. The comparative economic records of the two countries do not lend support to the hypothesis that such disclosure disadvantages companies *as a whole*. Of course, disclosure may sometimes disadvantage individual organisations – but that has not been felt by regulators to be an overriding objection in the development of previous disclosure legislation (e.g. in the U.K. Companies Acts).

Other 'problems' stressed in relation to the use of financial information during interviews the authors had with research officers of most of the larger U.K. unions were:
(1) the need for information related to the bargaining unit;[34]
(2) the lack of information on multi-national companies;[35]
(3) defects in the present system of filing accounts.[36]

The first two of these issues could again, in principle, be met by an increase in the general level of disclosure.

In the case of (1), a satisfactory solution would seem to require not *replacement* of what is currently disclosed by more disaggregated information, but rather its *supplementation*. This is because the degree to which inter-related units *could* 'manipulate' their accounting results is already recognised as a potential problem by unions, viz: 'The profit total also has little significance in the case of some subsidiary companies which accept contracts from their parent company on pretty nearly a cost basis and so make little profit . . . Or the reverse is sometimes true' [4, p. 22].

In fact, it was problems of this kind which led, in the U.K., to legal requirements for more aggregated accounting reports (consolidated accounts). Thus, while on the one hand unions seem to want the benefit of 'seeing the whole picture' (in consolidated accounts), they are simultaneously pressing, for understandable reasons, for financial reports on sub-group and sub-organisational bargaining units. But to give such results inevitably involves the use of yet more accounting discretion with respect to the allocation and transfer pricing policies adopted. [37] Again, one possible way out seems to be to give sufficiently detailed information to rework the calculations, if considered necessary. [38]

These problems, of course, occur also with respect to the subsidiaries of multi-national companies. An added complication here is that access to even the overall (group) accounts has not always been straightforward, at least in the U.K. Enforcement of the provisions of the 1976 Companies Act should, however, remedy this situation.

Similarly, criticism (3) above relating to defects in the current filing system may also prove to have been alleviated by the passage of the 1976 Companies Act. In particular, one of the commonest complaints in the past has related to the average length of time expiring between the completion of a company's reporting period and the date on which the accounts are made available for public access. The 1976 Act has introduced new time limits for filing accounts with the Registrar of Companies and lays down penalties for defaulters in this respect. This is potentially significant for unions in that for predictive purposes it is obviously necessary that the information available to negotiators should be as 'up to date' as possible.

Apart from the resolution of such administrative questions, the overall impression is that what the unions are asking for is an extension in the detail disclosed in company accounts. This is evidenced, for instance, by the 'shopping lists' for information which have been issued through the T.U.C., e.g.:

The disclosure of information to trade union representatives should cover the following points: Manpower: Numbers of employees by job description; rates of turnover, short time, absenteeism, sickness and accidents; details of existing provisions for security, sickness, accidents, recruitment, training, redeployment, promotion and redundancy. Finance: Sales turnover by main activities; home and export sales; non trading income including income from investments and overseas earnings; pricing policy. Costs: distribution and sales; production costs; administrative and overhead costs; costs of materials and machinery; labour costs including social security payments; costs of management and supervision. Incomes: directors' remuneration; wages and salaries; make up of pay-negotiated rates, payment by results, overtime and bonuses. Profits: before and after tax and taking into account Government allowances, grants and subsidies; distributions and retentions. Performance indicators: unit costs, output per man, return on capital employed, value added etc. Worth of company: details of growth and up to date value of fixed assets and stock; growth and realisable value of trade investments. Prospects and plans: Details of new enterprises and locations, prospective close downs; mergers and takeovers. Trading and sales plans: investment plans including research and development. Manpower plans: plans for recruitment, selection and training; promotion, regrading and redeployment; short time and redundancy provisions. General information: A description of the company's activities and structure: details of holding companies and subsidiaries; organisational and managerial structure; outside contracts. Details of ownership: Directors and shareholders in the company and in holding companies; beneficial control of nominee shareholdings [45, pp. 17–18].

This rather long quotation serves to illustrate the type of information and the degree of detail which unions seem to be seeking. In this respect it is by no means the longest such 'shopping list' for information.[39] We do not intend to comment on the specific information involved here, or on what part of it represents an extension of current U.K. disclosure regulations,[40] but rather we shall concentrate on the general nature of the proposed extensions of disclosure.

Firstly, there seems to be one primary conceptual novelty as compared with disclosure under the present U.K. Companies Acts – that extensive information should be required on prospects and plans, i.e. direct predictions.[41] We have already noted the direct relevance of *future* information to negotiations about *future* conditions. The provision of direct predictions is, however, only one possible way of meeting this need. A discussion of the advantages and disadvantages of *predictions* as compared with *predictive information* is, however, left to be dealt with as a topic in Chapter 6.

Apart from extending disclosure to cover predictions, the other noticeable feature of the shopping list given is that it seems to be divisible into 2 classes of information. Firstly, there is a request for information of the 'labour force' type, i.e. that which relates to wages, terms and conditions of work. Such information is obviously necessary for the union to assess the productivity and parity elements in constructing wage claims and to react to the employer's offers. It is also clearly a prerequisite for rational bargaining on non-wage issues. It may also be required for the post audit or 'policing' of the agreement. In addition: 'manpower information may be needed in order to allow unions to recruit members, collect subscriptions and to provide adequate services to their members particularly in the handling of individual and other grievances' [14, p. 13].

For these purposes, unions may be seen to have a potential need for almost any conceivable class of information relating to labour usage, payment and outputs. This perhaps explains the almost 'open-ended' access the Courts in the U.S.A. have granted to unions for obtaining such information from employers.[42] Similarly, under the U.K. Employment Protection Act it may be considered that most of such information *could* fall within the terms of Section 17 (1), although the constraints of Section 18 may limit disclosure of information which is otherwise relevant. The interpretation of Sections 17 and 18 are, of course, a matter for the Courts, although, on the face of it, the 'loopholes' of Section 18 seem to be wider than those allowed by the U.S. Courts.[43]

What seems important to stress, however, is that the relevance of a particular item can only be judged in the knowledge of the particular circumstances applying. More than this, relevance, in the sense of 'bear[ing] upon or be[ing] usefully associated with the action [the information] is designed to facilitate or the result it is desired to produce' [3, p. 9], depends, *inter alia*, on the quantitative dimension of the information. That is, a piece of information may be relevant at a particular time simply because it signals some extraordinary or unexpected event. For instance, 'consultancy fees paid' may not in itself appear to be a very relevant item in the normal course of events. However, if the level of consultancy fees paid to members of a holding company by its subsidiary were suddenly to increase, then the information might become relevant to negotiators with the subsidiary. Thus the disclosure of relevant information implies flexibility (or alternatively, completely open-ended access to the records).

In particular, a requirement that relevance has to be *demonstrated* is overly restrictive, since without access to the information it is not possible for the union to tell whether it may be 'material' enough to be relevant to negotiations.[44] On the other hand, a requirement that all information which is potentially relevant should be disclosed is effectively a directive to 'open the books', since, as already stated, almost any piece of information *could*, under certain circumstances, be material enough to be relevant. It is, therefore, not possible to have a conceptually satisfactory (and non-exhaustive) set of disclosure regulations or an information agreement which specifies the list of (relevant) items to be disclosed. From this point of view, then, proposals such as the T.U.C. shopping list can be regarded as unsatisfactory. They are likely to result both in the disclosure of non-relevant (immaterial) items and in the non-disclosure of relevant (material) items in a particular situation.

To be fair, the T.U.C. shopping list and its ilk must probably be looked upon as suggestions for the kinds of items which will most usually be found to be relevant in negotiations, so that they represent an idea of the *minimum* level of disclosure required based on *expected* relevance.

As with the Companies Act regulations, it will probably be found, however, that minimum disclosure becomes typical disclosure. Thus it is important that in U.K. case law the overriding necessity to provide *all* relevant information is established[45] since, unless a relatively 'liberal' disclosure policy, based on a conscious examination of user needs, is seen to be part of the law's requirements from the start, the development of disclosure regulations in collective bargaining is likely to follow the same unsatisfactory, 'fire fighting', course as statutory disclosure under the Companies Acts.[46]

It may be objected that this could place unions in a better position than shareholders and other interested groups. Insofar as 'labour force' data are concerned this is undoubtedly the case. Such a situation can, however, be justified in that much of the employment data being discussed here are of specific relevance to negotiators. In any case, the fact that shareholder disclosure regulations are unsatisfactory is not an argument in itself for formulating unsatisfactory regulations with respect to collective bargaining.

There are, of course, more valid reasons for concern where the information disclosed to negotiators is 'price sensitive'. In this respect it has been pointed out that: 'It is wrong to suggest that the requirements of the Companies Acts and the Stock Exchange Rules inhibit employers from disclosing financial information to employees. These requirements are not restrictive in what should be disclosed but are designed to safeguard the interests of shareholders by seeing that information likely to influence share values is not disclosed in a way which might create privileged interests' [14, p. 25].

The moral to this particular story, then, is that if management feel that certain price sensitive information is relevant to labour negotiators it should ideally be simultaneously disclosed to them and to investors at large.

Such a situation is, of course, more likely to arise in respect of the second category of items the T.U.C. would wish disclosed, i.e. financial information, including expectations.

Much of this can be claimed to be of simultaneous relevance to investors and negotiators. Indeed 'price sensitive' information must necessarily be relevant to investors. Once again, then, the 'ideal' solution (based on relevance) would seem to be simultaneous disclosure. In practice, however, there may be significant costs to such a solution. To the extent that legislators accept the social significance of such costs they can, of course, impose constraints on the information which labour negotiators are entitled to demand (as in Section 18 of the U.K. Employment Protection Act).

This does not, of course, then prevent an employer from voluntarily disclosing information which is so 'protected'. Where such information was price sensitive its circulation would, however, need to be restricted unless investors were simultaneously informed. To the argument that information cannot be restricted once it is passed on to labour negotiators, the response is a practical one. That is, while unions and management must have experienced shared price sensitive information under U.S. law for many years, we have been unable to find a single documented reference to consequential 'abuses' with respect to the release of 'confidential' information. There is no reason to suppose U.K. unions to be less trustworthy in this respect than their U.S. counterparts.

One implicit problem may certainly arise, however, despite the 'good faith' of bargainers. That is, unions do have shareholdings held both for investment purposes and on behalf of their pension funds. To ensure that there is no suspicion of a division of interest in this respect it might be best if unions were prohibited from holding shares, either directly or through nominees in companies with which they engage in bargaining.[47] Where this may be unduly restrictive, e.g. for a large national union with bargaining relationships throughout industry, some form of neutral trustee arrangement could possibly be made.

To summarise, trade unions have basically requested the disclosure of organisational information of two types: manpower or 'labour force' data and 'ability to pay' related data. The primary purpose of the labour force data appears to be for the construction and evaluation of arguments related to the productivity and comparability elements in negotiations. 'Historic' or 'actual' data would often seem sufficient for this purpose. On the other hand, financial data seem to be required for constructing ability-to-pay arguments, for which purpose it is *future* ability to pay which needs to be predicted. Whilst we shall have more to say about the conceptual background to such predictions in Chapter 6, it is clear that it is this aspect of information usage which gives rise to the most serious objections as far as management is concerned. This is because in order to satisfy theoretical union needs on this point *either* direct predictions (budgeted or planned information) of critical financial variables *or* sufficient details to form the basis of informed forecasts – or both – need to be provided.

MANAGEMENT

In this section we shall be concerned with what information management may need for decision making in relation to collective bargaining. Essentially there appear to be three phases into which bargaining activities fall for this purpose:

Phase 1 – those activities which relate to preparation for negotiations;

Phase 2 – activities carried out during the period of negotiations;

Phase 3 – activities associated with the interpretation and administration of the contract.[48]

PHASE 1 – PREPARATION FOR NEGOTIATIONS

Preparations for negotiations can themselves be divided into 2 sub-phases: (a) the collection, analysis and interpretation of data, and (b) the setting of bargaining policy based on the results of (a).[49] It is to the first of these that we direct our attention here.

Thorough (but somewhat dated) surveys of management practice in this area have been published in the U.S.A. [6], [11], [41]. Because we feel that U.S. practice to some extent points the way for the U.K. also, as well as because of the dearth of U.K. evidence, we have drawn almost exclusively on these sources in what follows.

One example of a practice developed in the U.S.A. which seems to be equally applicable to the U.K. is the preparation of a *bargaining book*:

> Many companies today spend a considerable amount of time marshalling factual information prior to the beginning of negotiations. Company executives try to anticipate union demands, estimate their costs and weigh the pros and cons of each possible demand carefully. When this is done they can determine the course of action they expect to follow and perhaps even develop countermands of their own as to revising the collective bargaining agreement.
>
> To back up their arguments, company negotiators assemble a great mass of information. Wage and fringe benefits surveys, and significant settlements in the area or the industry provide part of the source data. Analyses of the internal problems that have arisen during the term of the contract also provide strong bases for possible contract changes.
>
> As an aid to bargaining, many companies bring together all or part of the information they have gathered in what is known as a bargaining book. The format of these books varies from a simple listing of union demands and company counter demands in a looseleaf notebook to elaborate tomes that include the historical development of each contract provision, many types of cost data and comparative statistics and detailed outlines of the company's position [6, ch. 2].

One class of information which is presumably always necessary for determining management's bargaining policy is that related to the evaluation of the costs of alternative 'packages', i.e. feasible negotiating outcomes. For the prediction of what 'packages' are most likely to be demanded by, and acceptable to, unions, knowledge of 'comparability', i.e. external wage, data may be crucial. This will most obviously be the case where the employer is a 'pattern follower', i.e. where wages etc. are likely to be largely determined by comparison with a prior settlement elsewhere in the industry, area or economy.

The other source of information on what 'packages' are likely to be of interest to labour is, of course, an independent computation by management of the expected union claim. For this purpose management will obviously need information on the elements entering into the union's calculation of the gross increase required.

From the above it is deducible that the information normally necessary for management's bargaining book is similar to that already discussed in relation to unions i.e.:

(a) external wage data;
(b) internal wage data;
(c) productivity data;
(d) cost of living data; and
(e) ability to pay data.[50]

(a) External wage data

Relevant comparative wage data are likely to be of two sorts:

 (i) data on wage rates, earnings etc., of a comparable group of workers in other companies;
(ii) increases and other changes involved in other recent negotiations.

The purpose of collecting such data may obviously be to predict, and if possible counter, the union's parity arguments. Another reason, however, may be to determine the 'going rate' which may need to be paid to retain workers in a tight labour market.

The difficulties involved for management in obtaining such data to a certain extent parallel those of the union discussed earlier. That is, there may be no systematic source of statistics on wages and earnings in comparable organisations.

To the extent that information can be shared between employers on industry or area bases, voluntarily and informally, then the employer may be in much the same position as unions who often do likewise. Of course, there is always the possibility that information sharing can be arranged formally, through, e.g., the employers' federation. Otherwise, it may be necessary to fall back on national statistics such as the *New Earnings Survey* discussed earlier.

The use made of external wage data in bargaining, in a U.S. context, has been succinctly described by Ryder *et al.*:

Both parties use their external wage data in a selective manner. The parties frequently differ about the external wage criteria that are appropriate for comparison purposes; the most common disagreements are over the use of area versus industry criteria. If one of the bargaining parties has consistently favoured the use of a particular criterion, however, it becomes difficult for that party to shift ground in a year when the previously favoured criterion operates against its interest.

In a number of firms, the parties have agreed on the external wage criteria they will rely on during negotiations. Through such agreements, management and union have been able to remove a considerable part of the controversy that surrounds wage bargaining [41, ch. 5].

A possible reduction in bargaining time and effort associated with a diminution in the opportunities for confusion are also reasons for trying to come to such agreements about relevant external comparisons in a U.K. context. The dangers involved are, of course, a possible freezing of inappropriate differentials and 'leap-frogging' settlements. Nevertheless, since collection of data on external wage comparisons is in any case an essential element of managerial planning for collective bargaining, explicit consideration should be given to the possible advantages (and disadvantages) of sharing such information with unions.

(b) Internal wage data

One possible reason for collecting this type of information for bargaining purposes is, once again, to try to anticipate union calculations. Another important reason is to enable the costs of the various 'packages' of feasible outcomes to be estimated. If carried out on a strict 'opportunity cost' basis this estimation process gives rise to serious theoretical and practical difficulties, which we shall leave for discussion to Chapter 6. Here we shall assume that management merely wishes to arrive at approximations of the 'direct' (labour) costs of packages which may come under discussion, i.e. that: 'Internal wage statistics are most frequently used by company executives to provide wage cost estimates. They feel they need reliable estimates of the total wage costs that would be entailed by any union demands or company counter proposals. To facilitate the calculation of wage costs, many companies, before bargaining, develop tables that show the cost to the company of any possible wage demands' [6, p. 56].

Examples of types of internal data found useful for this purpose in practice are:

'1. Average hours worked.
 2. Number of employees – by job class, by step within each job class, by seniority and by sex.
 3. Number of employees on incentive and amount of incentive earnings.

4. Number of employees on each shift.
5. Straight time and gross weekly earnings by job class.
6. Costs of fringe benefits.
7. Chronologies showing when firm gave increases in wages and fringes' [6, p. 67].[51] The use of break-even charts to demonstrate the effects of alternative wage levels may also be found useful.[52]

One possible use of internal wage data, mentioned in the Bambrick and Dorbant survey, is to determine what would be an acceptable settlement. The criteria suggested for a 'fair' settlement are that it:
'(a) maintains proper differentials between various job classes;
(b) ensures that no one group gets the lion's share of the increase;
(c) will be acceptable to the union membership' [6, p. 69].

Fairly clearly internal wage statistics of the type suggested above should enable management to predict the effects of various outcomes on different employee groups, so making it easier to evaluate the 'politics' of alternative outcomes and hence their chances of being accepted by the union. Perhaps the most effective use of internal wage data is, however, *during* negotiations, i.e. Phase 2 – which we discuss below.

(c) Productivity data

Organisation-wide productivity information serves two possible purposes in bargaining. Firstly, unions may seek to use *past* 'increases in productivity' as a justification for increased payments to their members. This is obviously an attempt to *redistribute* possible gains and may be connected with such questions as the *equity* of relative rewards to labour and other 'contributors' to the organisation – relevant information for the evaluation of which we discuss in Chapter 6.

Secondly, productivity information may be used in an *ex ante* sense, i.e. to explore possibilities for productivity increases in the future (by joint problem solving), the expected benefits of which become the subject of distributive negotiations. For such purposes, the more detailed the information, the more likely it is to be useful in identifying opportunities for improvement. Where management is interested in obtaining future increases in productivity from negotiations they would therefore seem to have a vested interest in focusing attention on disaggregated, rather than organisation-wide data. This in itself implies a need to go further in disclosure than the information in published accounts.

As well as negotiating a full-blown, once-for-all productivity agreement, e.g. for buying out restrictive practices, some companies have attempted to formalise the productivity element in wage settlements by linking future wage increases to changes in an agreed productivity index. For example, an Institute of Personnel Management report, published in 1968 [27], indicated that a large engineering firm with plants in the Midlands had used an 'Index of Competitive Ability' to ascertain the latitude for wage increases. This index was simply

$$\frac{\text{Output per hour}}{\text{Hourly wage rate}}$$

If output per hour increases faster than the hourly wage rate, then unit wage cost is falling, which in turn presumably implies the competitive ability of the firm is improving. Such an improvement would then justify the payment of a bonus. Output per hour was calculated on a 'net' or added value basis, allowing for changes in final sale prices and deducting the cost of bought-in materials.

Clearly, in respect of negotiations which are expected to be solely distributive (i.e. do not involve any proposed future change in productivity), the major concern of management in preparing for negotiations as far as productivity data are concerned, may be to try to anticipate (in order to counter) union calculations of any 'productivity increases' which have taken place.

Thus, overall 'productivity' indicators may, for example, have a tactical value for management in 'demonstrating' low productivity to be the reason for not making a high offer to the union. This is, of course, management's counterpart to union arguments about high achieved overall productivity levels.

Another reason for computing overall productivity indicators may simply be in order to resolve uncertainty about labour's demands and expectations whether or not *ex post* productivity change is a factor which in itself 'justifies' a wage increase.[53] In this connection there are no fixed statistics which may be considered independently relevant to management; rather the whole range of 'productivity' indicators most likely to be available to, and used by labour negotiators – e.g. sales/employee, value added/employee etc., should find a place in the bargaining book. On the other hand, if negotiations are expected, or hoped to be of a 'mixed', partly problem solving character as well as partly distributive, then what is theoretically needed is freedom of access by negotiators, both management and union, to detailed organisational data if maximum joint benefits are to be obtained.[54]

In such a situation it appears to be counter-productive and too space consuming to suggest here a list of information which *might* be of use. Since the demise of productivity bargaining in the late 1960s, productivity arguments seem, in any case, to have resumed a subsidiary role in negotiations, at least in the U.K.[55]

(d) Cost of living data

Clearly in times of high inflation (as at present) the need to maintain employees' 'real' wages may become a major determinant of union claims and expectations. In such conditions it is obviously necessary for management negotiators to have information available on the cost of living statistics most likely to be used by the union side, i.e. in the U.K., movements in the Retail Price Index.

One possible positive approach management may make to counter union claims is to try to demonstrate that the organisation's wage rates and/or earnings have increased in line with the cost of living. For such purposes internal wage data and an appropriate index are clearly necessary.

If cost of living changes are regarded as a legitimate determinant of wage increases then ideally an index appropriate to the workers covered by negotiations should be used. The Retail Price Index may, for example, not be wholly satisfactory for this purpose in terms of coverage.

Clearly the choice of an index becomes most critical where a cost of living increase is built formally into the labour contract, e.g. in 'threshold agreements'. In such cases it may be advantageous to commission a special family budget survey to obtain an appropriate index. However, expenditure surveys of union members whose earnings may depend on the results of the survey obviously need careful designing to avoid abuses. This in itself implies such a survey may not be cheap, and that such statistics as the R.P.I. may be a good enough approximation in cost/benefit terms.

(e) 'Ability to pay' data

This section is limited to consideration of organisational financial information not already dealt with above. For instance, we have already discussed the use of internal wage data to estimate the direct costs of bargaining outcomes. In addition we have deferred until Chapter 6 consideration of the opportunity costs of outcomes, i.e. their effects on profits etc. However, other financial information of a wide variety of classes, as we have already seen, may be used by unions to 'rationalise' the organisation's 'ability to pay' a wage claim. We discuss a suggested theoretical concept of ability to pay, and the way it may be measured in practice in Chapter 6. Where management wish to counter the unions 'demonstrations' of ability to pay we believe the material of Chapter 6 should assist them in constructing relevant arguments.

One issue which remains to be discussed here is that attempts by management to show 'inability to pay' may create a potential entitlement, on the part of the unions, to a wide range of organisational information, on the grounds of relevance. This has been most clearly established in a U.S. context, where the National Labor Relations Board has stated: 'An employer's duty to bargain also included the obligation to furnish the bargaining representatives with sufficient information to enable the union to bargain intelligently *and to understand and discuss the issues raised by the employer in opposition to the union's demand.* The extent and nature of such information depends upon the bargaining which takes place in any particular case'[56] [Italics added]. As a result the 'fail safe' rule operated in the U.S.A. has been: if an organisation wants to avoid the possibility of being compelled to disclose additional financial information to unions it should not plead 'inability to pay'.

That such a situation could arise in the U.K. as a result of current legislation is pointed to in the 'guidelines' of the C.I.R. Report: 'The relevance of financial information depends both on the bargaining area and the arguments used, e.g. the argument of inability to pay on the part of the employer creates its own need for information to justify the argument' [14, p. 29]. Although the C.I.R. is now defunct, the force of this argument seems to be of an enduring nature.

Of course, 'confidential' information, of various types, should still be protected under the 'loophole' clauses of section 18 of the U.K. Employment Protection Act, the interpretation of which in turn depends on the establishment of case law. That it may not always be in the best interests of management to take full advantage of such loopholes, i.e. to pursue a minimum disclosure policy, is, however, indicated by the analysis of Chapter 4.

Detailed discussion of the types of information which are theoretically needed to support arguments about ability to pay and relative equity are postponed until Chapter 6, but it is worth pointing out at this stage that, whether or not company financial information is believed to have a direct influence on labour negotiators, it may be useful for 'rationalising' the employer's case to third parties, including the union membership, who may have an indirect influence on bargaining outcomes. For that reason, it is to be recommended that a whole range of ability to pay data (including forecasts) is prepared for the use of management negotiators, whether or not it is to be passed on to unions.

Guidance as to the useful content of negotiators' 'primers' in this respect can be found in the section on union uses of ability to pay data earlier in this chapter and the relevant material of Chapter 6.

PHASE 2 – DURING NEGOTIATIONS

Decisions on the timing of information use during negotiations and its precise effects are, of course, dependent on specific circumstances. To generalise, however, the preparation of information as previously described, and its availability in the bargaining book make possible the following types of benefit during negotiations:

(a) management can produce more effective counter-arguments to the union's demands: 'The union tends to accept statements as to costs, knowing that we refer to specific figures, whereas the union tends to discount broad statements. We gain by being factual and, to a degree, documentary' [6, ch. 2].

(b) Management negotiators' decision-making ability may be improved: 'Information gained during the process of setting up the bargaining book, and the knowledge that many useful data are at hand, negotiators say, helps to increase the assurance of the management team' [6, ch. 2].

(c) The support of third parties can be gained, e.g. management may publish its case in the form of newspaper advertisements, or simply circulate employees.[57]

(d) Decisions may be made more quickly and effectively with a possible shortening of negotiations resulting: 'We have in the bargaining book the cost figures for every demand the union can make. Instead of just saying that the union's demand for a specific item is too expensive we add up the costs and show the union's negotiators just how much it will cost. Of course, if the union's proposal is reasonable, our bargaining books cost figures show that too and we're in a position to readily accept' [6, ch. 2].

In the case of (a) and (d) it is internal wage data that are likely to be most useful to management, whilst for (c) all forms of data discussed above (i.e. internal and external wage, productivity, cost of living and ability to pay) may be useful in 'rationalising' management's position.

PHASE 3 – POST NEGOTIATIONS

Disclosure of organisational information after completion of bargaining is necessary for at least three purposes: (a) the joint interpretation and administration of the agreement, including the processing of grievances; (b) the immediate need to 'sell' the agreement to union members and/or influential third parties (e.g. the government); and (c) the continuing need to justify the 'fairness' of the outcome arrived at, again to unions, employees and, possibly, third parties.

(a) Information for interpreting and administering the agreement will obviously depend on the specific contents of the agreement, e.g. cost of living data will be crucial where a threshold agreement is employed, etc. Internal wage and 'manpower' data will presumably almost always be necessary for this purpose, however.

(b) 'Selling' the agreement will, in principle, involve rationalisation using a range of types of available data — essentially selecting what is judged will be most effective in the circumstances. In relation to government policy, of course, 'selling' the agreement may involve demonstrating conformity with specific guidelines, e.g. on productivity or allowable cost of living increases.

(c) In demonstrating the 'fairness' of an outcome, consideration must obviously be given to effects on individuals — and for this purpose grievance records and reference to internal wage data may be important. In addition, however, 'ability to pay' data may be employed to demonstrate to employees the equity of distributions of rewards, e.g. in the form of 'employee reports', statements of value added etc.[58] It may be equally important, in this respect, to demonstrate *ex post* fairness to union negotiators since collective bargaining is a continuing process and, if one side feels it has been totally out-manœuvred on one occasion, attitudes will tend to become more uncompromising in future.[59]

THE COSTS AND BENEFITS OF INFORMATION DISCLOSURE – A SUMMARY

Immediately above we have been concerned with the types of information management negotiators may find it useful to have. In some cases its disclosure to unions was also implied, e.g. when we spoke about 'rationalising' management's case. In general, however, both the fact of disclosure and its timing will be a matter for management's discretion. Clearly there may be tactical advantages in the selective disclosure of information, which will be dependent on circumstances.

What we wish to examine here, however, is the general nature of some of the advantages (benefits) and disadvantages (costs) associated with the disclosure of specific sorts of information by management to unions. 'Disclosure' presumably means the communication of information in management's possession which is not otherwise available to unions, i.e. generally, that related to productivity, internal wage data and (some) ability to pay data.

One significant cost of disclosure of such information would appear to be the extra processing costs involved in its collection and presentation in a form relevant to the unions. As far as collection and processing are concerned, in fact the *incremental* costs of these should be negligible since we have argued that information which may be relevant to unions should be available to management negotiators in any case. The presentation of information in a *form* specifically useful to unions, where this would involve 'an amount of work or expenditure out of reasonable proportion to the value of the information in the conduct of collective bargaining' is presently excluded from being the subject of compulsory disclosure.[60] There is nothing, of course, to prevent management voluntarily preparing information in a form specifically useful to unions where the benefits in bargaining relationship terms are thought to be sufficiently high.

Nevertheless, it can be seen that, in general, 'disclosure' involves information which should have little *incremental* effect on processing costs. The more significant costs and benefits therefore have to be looked for in terms of the possible effects on bargaining outcomes.

Clearly there is always the possibility that the effect of disclosure of information in bargaining may make for a worse outcome, from management's point of view, than would otherwise be the case. As we have argued in Chapter 4, however, collective bargaining is a continuing relationship and the effects of disclosure have to be evaluated for the long as well as short run. Even in a purely distributive bargaining context the argument has to be weighed that: 'demands made in complete ignorance of the true picture are much more likely to be unrealistic than demands made after a study of figures which both parties can accept'[61] – although demands can be 'unrealistic' downwards as well as upwards!

However, a successful shift from distributive towards integrative bargaining relationships seems to require an atmosphere of mutual confidence between management and unions – one useful instrument for the encouragement of which could be a 'liberal' disclosure policy. Certainly fullest disclosure is logically necessary if the maximum potential benefits from integrative bargaining are to be realised.

This is, of course, an argument we have already developed in Chapter

4, but in the present context it is necessary to point out a particular conclusion in terms of specific disclosure policy. This is that, if joint problem solving activities are to be encouraged, clearly the information most relevant to such activities must be provided. Since 'problems' involve future choice it is *future* information (i.e. budgets, forecasts and plans) which is most relevant. There is therefore an uncomfortable paradox for management in deciding on disclosure policy: that the information which management usually seek most to protect on the grounds of its disclosure costs to them (which for the inverse reason may also be that most sought after by unions) could also, in the long run, be the information whose disclosure would bring the greatest *joint* benefits to both management and union.

NOTES

1 See Chapter 1.

2 Although there are reasons to feel that more could be done in the U.K. to improve the research facilities available to smaller unions, e.g. by setting up a central research agency – see [20].

3 For a description and analysis of one such U.K. union's research facilities, see [36] and [9, pp. 115–16].

4 For an easily accessible example of the work of the Trade Union Research Unit, see [28].

5 Another reason for giving emphasis to prestige claims in this chapter is that they are so well documented. In the case of the 1971 I.C.I. claim [34] a very full reply by the employers, giving extensive attention to the informational aspects of the claim, was also circulated [31].

6 John Hughes, Trade Union Research Unit, quoted in the Sunday Times, 27th February, 1972.

7 Here, information can be said to serve an 'intraorganisational bargaining' purpose, see [47, chs. 8 and 9].

8 See the quotation above by John Hughes (referenced in note 6).

9 Unions need information for purposes other than constructing wage claims, of course. Indeed many negotiations are not concerned with wages as such – but we believe the discussion below is general enough to cover union's non-wage bargaining needs also.

10 See, e.g. [9, p. 117] and [43, pp. 33–4].

11 See [5, pp. 3–4] and [33, pp. 35–7].

12 To achieve this, the marginal tax rate has to be calculated on the total wage *after* the proposed increase and the inflation index will need to reflect the expenditure pattern of the 'typical' worker.

13 See [6, pp. 86–93].

14 [6, p. 86].

15 For an illustration of a cost of living argument which contains most of the features mentioned above, see [34, pp. 18–19].

16 See, for example [40].

17 For a useful survey of U.K. government policy with respect to incomes since W.W. II, see: 'The Uses of Prices and Incomes Policies in Britain', *Midland Bank Review*, August 1973, pp. 11–20.

18 These and related difficulties are discussed in [21] where 15 possible definitions of the concept are listed.

19 See [47] and Chapter 4.

20 A comprehensive list of the control data which *management* should collect is offered by [23]. For a discussion of the system used by one major U.K. *union* to classify and monitor agreements, see [49].

21 Another advantage of having this type of data applies to industry level bargaining: 'In a situation, for example, where only wage or salary *minima* are being negotiated, the basic need is no longer for data on average earnings, but for the frequency distribution type of statistical survey . . . It must be ascertained how many employees will be affected by new minimum rates, where they are employed, and which firms will have to sustain the maximum cost' [2, p. 7].

22 Here we are alluding, basically, to the possible effects on bargaining relationships, i.e. 'attitudinal structuring' (see Chapter 4).

23 D. Kleinerman, *Ability to Pay Wages: Concept and Measurement*, Ph.D. thesis, University of Chicago, 1961, quoted in [50, p. 66].

24 Note also the comments of one trade union researcher: 'The I.C.I., Ford and Pilkington wage claims demonstrated that the unions consider profitability to be measured by trading profits before depreciation and interest charges, as this represents the employees' contribution to profits' [43, p. 35].

25 In this connection it has been observed that: 'Unless financial data of management are made available to unions, they will of necessity rely primarily on data from published financial reports and will, therefore, be estimating the firm's ability to pay in terms of past profits. Management, on the other hand, equipped with data which probably would not be published, tends to estimate the ability of the firm to pay in terms of future profits' [26, p. 629].

26 Another possible instance is the 1973 Ford claim [24], about which it has been said: 'This kind of case is clearly inviting confirmation or correction of the data which have been estimated, so that the negotiation can proceed on a firm basis. Any data which are released may provide the union and its advisers with a basis for developing further, more detailed estimates' [48, p. 4].

27 Sometimes 'once removed', e.g. in the form of Extel data or the information services of the Labour Research Department, which itself mainly relies on information from published accounts.

28 As is well recognised by the unions, see [45, p. 6].

29 For an analysis of the 'data expansion' method of improving disclosure, and the problems of 'information overload', see [37, pp. 8–19].

30 See, e.g. [25].

31 See [30, sec. M].

32 'The trade unionist would prefer being able to recalculate the corporation's statement according to his own views. It is for this reason, that is [*sic*] would petition for detailed supplementary statements necessary for such recalculations' [7, p. 756].

33 Criticism (b) (3) – 'Companies are not run merely to make a profit' seems to allude to the discretionary *level* of certain expenses – this again could, in theory, be met by access to sufficient 'basic' information to identify and recompute the 'necessary' level of such items.

34 See also [14, p. 13].

35 See also [46, p. 7].

36 See also [10, p. 13].

37 See Chapter 6.

38 Although this appears to lead potentially to the kind of situation warned against by the AFL-CIO: '[Union representatives] should be aware that, unless they are experienced in evaluating company finances, it is easy for a company to steer them away from the main financial points and to muddy the picture with complicated explanations of

bookkeeping practices . . . It is usually not enough merely to hire an accountant to examine the books, because he may only certify that the books are "correct" or that "proper accounting procedures" were used or he may end up having the union debating accounting techniques rather than the merits of a wage increase' [4, p. 21].

39 See, for instance, [8] for a much fuller list of suggestions.

40 Instead, refer to [14, Appendix 7] for a comparison with disclosure under the U.K. Companies Acts, and [15, Appendix] for the information required by other Acts.

41 The present Companies Acts require this to only a *very* limited extent, e.g. 'where practical', contracts for capital expenditure should be disclosed (1967 Companies Act, Schedule 2, Section 11 (6)).

42 See Chapter 1 and [35].

43 See, e.g. [48, p. 6].

44 Thus, in a U.S. context it has been ruled that: 'Since the employer has an affirmative statutory duty to supply relevant wage data his refusal to do so is not justified by the union's failure initially to show the relevance of the requested information. The rule governing disclosure of data of this kind is not unlike that prevailing in discovery procedures in modern codes. Any less lenient rule in labor disputes would greatly hamper the bargaining process, for it is virtually impossible to tell in advance whether the requested data will be relevant except in those infrequent instances in which the inquiry is patently outside the bargaining issue'. (NLRB v Yawman & Erbe Manufacturing Co.). Although a different ruling has, in fact, been applied in the case of financial information (White Furniture Co.), the logic of the situation would in fact appear to be unchanged.

45 There is a particular danger if 'relevance' is too narrowly interpreted in terms of the value of information, see [22].

46 For a critical view of legislative developments on disclosure under the U.K. Companies Acts, see [39, pp. 20–23].

47 Rules against 'insider trading' would also need to be extended to cover union officials who obtain privileged access to price sensitive information. This point would appear to be covered by the proposals in [32, ch. 8].

48 This analysis is suggested in [13].

49 See [41, ch. 1].

50 Again, this list is primarily applicable in the case of wage bargaining, but covers the types of information likely to be useful in non-wage bargaining also. 'Wage' data has, however, to be read as including information on fringe benefits, where applicable.

51 Extensive examples of the way in which such information may be usefully presented are given in [6, ch. 4].

52 As is suggested by [17, p. 553].

53 Questions of equity – which are essentially what *ex post* productivity arguments are about – may be better envisaged in terms of the 'divisible fund' of the organisation (discussed in Chapter 6), although settlements can, of course, always be 'rationalised' in terms of productivity changes – where this seems advantageous.

54 Although an atmosphere of mutual trust will also probably be a requirement viz: 'One can observe in productivity bargains financial and operating data of a sort never published by companies being used responsibly by shop stewards and management to improve wages and conditions by increasing the efficiency and profitability of companies. Such information, given voluntarily in an atmosphere of trust and constructive discussion, really is potent information'[38, pp. 112–13].

55 Valedictory surveys of productivity bargaining are provided in [29] and [44].

56 16th Annual Report of the National Labor Relations Board (for Year Ended 30th June 1951) as quoted in [42, p. 382].

57 Although this can have adverse effects on the longer term bargaining relationship if it is regarded as 'going behind the backs of the union,' see Chapter 4.

58 See Chapter 6 and the suggestion for an 'Employment Report' put forward by the

Accounting Standards Steering Committee in 'The Corporate Report' [1, pp. 51–3].

59 The need for *ex post* information is only one of the reasons why information useful in bargaining should be collected on a continuing basis – the need to prepare and maintain the bargaining book is another. Hence: 'The collecting and analysing of facts and figures is a continuous responsibility and should not be an emergency operation just prior to or during negotiations' [11, Research Finding no. 13].

60 The quotation is from the U.K. Employment Protection Act, Section 18 (2) (b), but similar restrictions on the need to go to unreasonable or impossible lengths in supplying relevant information, and on supplying it in a specific form, appear to apply also in the U.S.A. (see [35, p. 42–4]).

61 L. Kirkland, American Federation of Labor Researcher, quoted in 'What Kind of Information Do Labor Unions Want in Financial Statements?', *Journal of Accountancy* (May 1949) p. 371.

REFERENCES

1 Accounting Standards Steering Committee, *The Corporate Report* (London: Institute of Chartered Accountants in England and Wales, 1975).

2 D. Alexander, 'The Information Explosion and Collective Bargaining', *Industrial Relations Review and Report*, no. 9 (June 1971) pp. 5–10.

3 American Accounting Association, *A Statement of Basic Accounting Theory* (Evanston, Ill: author, 1966).

4 American Federation of Labor, Congress of Industrial Organisations, *Collective Bargaining Report*, 3 (March 1958) pp. 17–24.

5 Amalgamated Union of Engineering Workers, Engineering Section, *Briefing*, a bulletin issued by the Research Department (Jan/Feb 1971).

6 J. J. Bambrick and M. P. Dorbant, *Preparing for Collective Bargaining*, Studies in Personnel Policy no. 172 (New York: National Industrial Conference Board, 1959).

7 S. Barkin, 'Financial Statements in Collective Bargaining', *Labor Law Journal*, 4 (1953) pp. 753–8.

8 M. Barratt-Brown, *Opening the Books* (Nottingham: Institute for Workers' Control, 1968).

9 D. Basnett, 'Disclosure of Information – A Union View', in *Conflict at Work*, eds. S. Kessler and B. Weekes, (London: BBC Publications, 1971).

10 C. Beever, 'Disclosure of Information', *Incomes Data Study*, no. 34 (Aug 1972).

11 E. Brooks, N. A. Tolles and R. Dean, *Providing Facts and Figures for Collective Bargaining* (New York: The Controllership Foundation, 1950).

12 W. Brown, *Piecework Bargaining* (London: Heinemann, 1973).

13 W. G. Caples, 'The Computer's Uses and Potential in Bargaining: A Management View', in *The Impact of Computers on Collective Bargaining*, ed. A. J. Siegel (Cambridge, Mass.: M.I.T. Press, 1969) pp. 69–120.

14 Commission on Industrial Relations, Report no. 31, *Disclosure of Information* (London: HMSO, 1972).

15 Confederation of British Industry, *The Provision of Information to Employees* (London: author, 1975).

16 J. G. Cross, *The Economics of Bargaining* (New York: Basic Books, 1969).

17 E. Dale, 'The Accountant's Part in Industrial Relations', in *Handbook of Modern Accounting Theory*, ed. M. Backer (Englewood Cliffs, N.J.: Prentice-Hall, 1955) pp. 541–60.

18 Department of Employment, *New Earnings Survey 1975*, Part B (London: HMSO, 1975).

19 M. Evans, *The Ford Wage Claim* (London: Transport and General Workers Union, 1970).

20 Fabian Society, Fabian Tract 373, *The Trade Unions: on to 1980* (London: author, 1967).

21 R. W. Fenske, 'An Analysis of the Meaning of Productivity', *Productivity Measurement Review*, no. 42, OECD (Aug 1965) pp. 16–22.

22 B. J. Foley and K. T. Maunders, 'The CIR Report on Disclosure of Information: A Critique', *Industrial Relations Journal*, 4 (Autumn 1973) pp. 4–11.

23 R. K. Fleeman and A. G. Thompson, *Productivity Bargaining: A Practical Guide* (London: Butterworths, 1970).

24 Ford National Joint Negotiating Committee Trade Union Side, *The Ford Claim 1973* (London: Transport and General Workers Union, 1972).

25 W. L. Ginsburg, 'The Computer's Uses and Potential in Bargaining: A Trade Union View', in *The Impact of Computers on Collective Bargaining*, ed. A. J. Siegel (Cambridge, Mass.: M.I.T. Press, 1969), pp. 26–8.

26 T. P. Goggans, 'The Accountant's Role in Wage Negotiations', *Accounting Review*, 39 (1964) pp. 627–30.

27 M. Harris, ed., *The Realities of Productivity Bargaining*, Industrial Relations Committee Report (London: Institute of Personnel Management, 1968).

28 J. Hughes and R. Moore, eds., *A Special Case? Social Justice and the Miners* (Harmondsworth: Penguin, 1972).

29 L. C. Hunter and R. B. McKersie, *Pay, Productivity and Collective Bargaining* (London: Macmillan, 1973).

30 Institute of Chartered Accountants in England and Wales, *Members' Handbook* (London: author, updated continuously).

31 Imperial Chemical Industries Limited, *Company Reply to the Argument Contained in the Signatory Unions Claim of 2nd April 1971* (I.C.I., 1971).

32 Labour Party, *The Community and the Company* (London: author, 1974).

33 Labour Research Department, *How to Get the Facts about Profits and Prices* (London: author, 1975).

34 J. Miller, *A Positive Employment Programme for I.C.I.* (London: Transport and General Workers Union, 1971).

35 M. J. Miller, 'Employer's Duty to Give Economic Data to Unions', *Journal of Accountancy*, 101 (Jan 1956) pp. 40–49.

36 G. Radice, 'Research and the Unions', *Management Today* (Nov 1971) pp. 27–34.

37 L. Revsine, *Replacement Cost Accounting* (Englewood Cliffs, N.J.: Prentice-Hall, 1973).

38 E. J. Robertson, 'Disclosure of Information – A Management View', in *Conflict at Work*, eds. S. Kessler and B. Weekes (London: BBC Publications, 1971).

39 H. B. Rose, *Disclosure in Company Accounts*, Eaton Paper no. 1, 2nd ed. (London: Institute of Economic Affairs, 1965).

40 A. M. Ross, 'Productivity and Wage Control', *Industrial and Labor Relations Review*, 7 (1954) pp. 177–91.

41 M. S. Ryder, C. M. Rehmus and S. Cohen, *Management Preparation for Collective Bargaining* (Homewood, Ill.: Dow-Jones, Irwin, 1966).

42 J. E. Shanklin, 'Employer's Duty to Supply Data for Collective Bargaining', *Monthly Labor Review* (1952) pp. 381–7.

43 R. Stephens, 'Playing the Numbers Game', *Personnel Management* (Sept 1972) pp. 32–5.

44 B. Towers, T. G. Whittingham and A. W. Gottschalk, eds., *Bargaining for Change* (London: Allen and Unwin, 1972).

45 Trades Union Congress, *Good Industrial Relations: A Guide for Negotiators* (London: author, 1971).

46 Trades Union Congress, *Review of Collective Bargaining Developments*, no. 2 (1972).

47 R. E. Walton and R. B. McKersie, *A Behavioral Theory of Labor Negotiatons* (New York: McGraw Hill, 1965).
48 T. Watson, *The Accountant's Role in Industrial Relations: An Outsider's View*, paper presented to 21st Summer School of the Institute of Chartered Accountants of Scotland, 15–19 June, 1973.
49 D. Whitaker, 'Computers and Industrial Relations: the AUEW Experience', *Industrial Relations Review and Report*, no. 10 (June 1971) pp. 3–7.
50 D. Zulauf, *Accounting Analysis and the Ability to Pay Wages*, unpublished Ph.D. thesis, University of Minnesota, 1965.

6 Some Issues for the Accountant

Although the indirect involvement of accountants (through the use of accounting information) in collective bargaining is not by any means a new phenomenon, recent legislative developments, allied to changing social attitudes on management-employee relationships, make it predictable that this involvement will increase in the future, particularly in the U.K. The purpose of this chapter is, therefore, to examine some of the conceptual and practical issues which the accountant can expect to meet in what may be, for the individual, an unfamiliar area of practice. To this end the chapter is divided along functional lines: financial accounting; management accounting and auditing, although the inter-relationships necessarily involved mean that much of the material should be of interest to most accountants whatever their main functional specialisation.

In this book we are not concerned with the undoubtedly important role of accountants in the management of trade unions. Accountants are, however, also involved in the collective bargaining function of unions, usually as members of research departments, in connection with the preparation of 'briefs' for labour negotiators and documentation supporting wage claims. In the future we may expect to see extensions of union interest in accounting information, particularly in the management accounting field as unions, employees and managements become more involved in the joint problem solving activities (integrative bargaining) which may be fostered by current trends towards 'industrial democracy'. Accountants may also be employed directly by the union side in the increased educational programme for union representatives which may be necessary if the hoped for benefits of increased information disclosure are to be realised.[1]

On the management side, on the other hand, accountants will necessarily continue to be involved in the preparation of accounting and economic information to be used by both sets of negotiators and should also become more directly concerned with the form in which such information is presented (e.g. in 'employment reports').[2] This should apply not only in the financial field – the presentation of information related to 'ability to pay' – but also in management accounting, through the need to provide 'labour force' data and detailed calculations of the effects of alternative bargaining outcomes on costs, employment, prices, investment alternatives etc.

On behalf of management and union sides jointly or separately, accountants may also be involved in an auditing capacity – to give an independent opinion on the 'truth and fairness' of any information which may be communicated over and above that covered in the general audit report, e.g. in an 'open book' situation. The function of the audit in such a case would be, as usual, to lend credibility to information which arises out of a basically management controlled system.

Issues which may arise out of these involvements by accountants in the collective bargaining field are the subjects of this chapter, the procedure of which is to discuss a series of what appear to us inadequately explored topics of concern in each of the three main accounting areas of specialisation. Before looking at functional issues, however, it is first necessary to deal with a conceptual problem which applies to accounting in general.

Insofar as accounting is a service function it may be said to exist primarily to meet the needs of the information *users*.[3] A vital question to ask, therefore, is: what information do management and labour negotiators 'need' in the context of collective bargaining? If this question can be answered, it leads immediately to another: *should* the information 'needs' of *labour* negotiators be met?

To a certain extent legislative developments may assist the accountant in dealing with this secondary question, by specifying or leading to the specification of the information to which labour negotiators are automatically 'entitled'. Otherwise, the issue may have to be referred to top management for decision, either directly or indirectly through the interpretation of a previously laid down managerial disclosure policy. Such questions of 'entitlement' are not the concern of this chapter.[4]

In any event, *identification* of negotiator's information needs still has to be carried out if social and managerial disclosure policies are to have a 'rational' foundation. But this gives rise to a conceptual dilemma well recognised by accounting theorists: should we, in identifying user needs, subscribe to the *user sovereignty*[5] or *educational*[6] view of the role of accounting?

The *user sovereignty* school of accounting theorists view the identification problem as one of determining what user needs actually *are* by means of empirical enquiry, e.g. through the use of questionnaires or indirect evidence such as trade union 'shopping lists' for information. This we will call the *positive* approach to the identification problem.

On the other hand, there is the *normative* approach, which considers that accounting information has an *educational* role. This view derives support from observations that potential users of accounting information may not be educated sufficiently in the discipline to 'know what is good for them', or alternatively, that they may be conditioned to accepting what is available and what they are familiar with, rather than 'what they really need'.[7]

The phrases in quotation marks make clear the nature of the normative approach: that it attempts to specify what information users *should* want as contrasted with what they actually *do* want. The methodology of this approach is to set up some kind of model of the way in which the users' decision processes would operate if 'efficient'[8] decisions are to be taken and to deduce from this what information the 'rational'[9] decision maker would need.

According to this view, therefore, information should be provided whether or not it is asked for and whether or not users are capable of using it immediately, but rather because it is believed that it *should be* relevant. An additional, implicit, assumption seems to be that providing such information will eventually educate users to make actual use of it to take 'efficient' decisions.

Quite apart from any doubts which may arise as to the validity of this last assumption, to implement the normative approach we should have to have models of the relevant decision processes (in this case decision models for collective bargaining) which are detailed enough for the contribution of specific kinds of information to the 'efficiency' of decisions to be identified. We have seen, in Chapter 4, that such models have yet to be developed.

On the other hand, the obvious limitations to the user sovereignty approach make it unsuitable as a complete substitute for the normative approach if we *are* concerned with what information should be provided to make the bargaining process more 'efficient', in some sense. Thus we are in a position where the normative approach alone is, currently, unworkable while the positive approach alone is, arguably, unsuitable.

In discussing the possible usefulness of various kinds of information below we shall, therefore, compromise by referring to the characteristics of the information both from the revealed preference (user sovereignty) or *positive*, and decision relevant (educational) or *normative*, points of view.[10]

FINANCIAL ACCOUNTING

For our purposes, we shall take it that the distinctive feature of the financial accounting function is that it results in the presentation of the 'final accounts' of an organisation. Throughout the rest of the chapter we shall also assume, unless otherwise indicated, that the bargaining unit is the entity for which accounts are produced (the 'organisation'). We shall, however, discuss the problems of aggregation and disaggregation which arise where this assumption does not hold.

The question which is addressed in this section is: what information relating to an organisation's overall financial results may be relevant to collective bargaining negotiations? From the observational evidence available,[11] i.e. from a 'positive' point of view, the short answer to this seems to be 'ability to pay'.[12] There is, however, a wide range of interpretations of what precisely is meant by ability to pay. Much of our analysis below is, therefore, concerned with the question of what may be an appropriate way to measure ability to pay, in theory and practice.

From a normative viewpoint, assuming that we are dealing with a bargaining situation which can be adequately characterised by the Walton and McKersie [25] 'model',[13] we may relate the concept of ability to pay to the desire by a negotiator to identify the position of his opponent's resistance point. It will be recalled that a negotiator's own target will probably be set on the basis of the best estimated position of the opponent's resistance point, i.e. a negotiator will preferably want to push the opponent into making the maximum possible concession. (See Figures 4.7 and 4.8).

If one assumes that management's resistance point will be based on some economic estimate of the maximum concession to labour the organisation could sustain then the possible relevance of *some* concept of ability to pay to estimate its position is clear. Of course, management's resistance points will actually be based on the maximum concession its *negotiators* would be willing to sustain. But it seems reasonable to assume that knowledge of the *organisation's* probable 'resistance point' (as determined by ability to pay) will enable a better prediction of the *negotiator's* resistance point to be made.

Thus, from labour's point of view a measure of ability to pay may be necessary as a basis for predicting the position of management's resistance point. The better this estimate is the less likely negotiations are to break down because of basic incompatibility between the negotiators' aspirations.[14]

One group of indicators of ability to pay which are currently used are those related to the profits of the organisation.[15] Even if we were to accept the positive point of view, however, there is some danger of confusion as to what this evidence really represents because of the tactical purposes which such information may serve for labour negotiators. In terms of the Walton and McKersie model these may be considered to be part of the process of attempting to influence management's perceptions of labour's valuations and/or risk perceptions, since they involve an apparent communication of information about labour's expectations and its commitment to them.[16] To serve this end there is obvious advantage to labour in making management's ability to pay appear as large as possible within credibility bounds. This may also explain the *selective* use of ability to pay information (and concepts) by labour, since the aim is presumably to influence management's perceptions unidirectionally. Management can, of course, respond by similarly selectively drawing attention to alternative ability to pay measures which are less favourable to labour's case. Such selective uses of financial information may, in practice, be beneficial insofar as they allow the parties' initially inconsistent aspirations and demands to be adjusted and reconciled without recourse to the actual implementation of bargaining 'threats'. Thus, for instance, the provision of 'fresh' information may make it possible for one of the parties to make a necessary concession without apparent loss of 'face'. It is important, therefore, to ensure that any accounting contribution to the collective bargaining framework does not impose unnecessary inflexibilities which might inhibit this adjustment process.

On the other hand, there seems to be a very real danger that *too much* flexibility in the choice and use of accounting information could mean that it is not taken seriously even when it may carry a 'real' message about management's resistance point.[17] In what follows, therefore, we propose to draw up a tentative analytical framework for evaluating the relevance of ability to pay indicators which may be acceptable to both sides in bargaining.

We shall see that this framework still leaves a great deal of room for diverse interpretations and predictions of organisational ability to pay, so that, in fact, the flexibility in the use of such information should be preserved. On the other hand, by creating such a framework some of the more obvious 'red herrings' may be eliminated, whilst arguments about ability to pay and its determinants could be channelled along more constructive (integrative) lines. In our discussion below, we shall look, therefore, at the use of ability to pay indicators from the point of view of their relevance to labour in estimating management's resistance point.[18]

To construct some kind of evaluative framework for ability to pay indicators it seems necessary first to set up some kind of definition of an 'ideal' measure of ability to pay. In fact, relatively few theoretical definitions of ability to pay have been offered,[19] and since these have not specifically been related to the problem we have identified (the estimation of resistance points) we propose to try to develop such a definition *a priori*.

It seems to us that the question of what may be the maximum net cost of meeting labour's claim which the organisation could bear (its 'ability to pay') is conceptually analogous to that of determining the maximum dividends the organisation could bear. We therefore begin our search for a definition of ability to pay by looking at a fairly recent approach to a solution of the latter problem.[20]

Revsine has described 'that portion of net operating flows that can be distributed as a dividend without reducing the level of future physical operations' as the 'distributable operating flow' of the firm [22, p. 34]. He then went on to show that this is effectively the same as the expected income component of economic income [22, pp. 96–7].

Since we are searching for decision relevant information an expected or *ex ante* measure seems appropriate for our purposes also. But what about *ex ante economic* income as a basis for ability to pay? This measure of income has been described as representing 'the maximum amount the owner of capital anticipates he can consume during the period without impairing his capital and future consumption' [17, p. 31]. It is based on a discounted cash flow measure of capital. As such it can be claimed to be normatively superior to alternative income measures[21] and, hence, is adopted here.

From the point of view of labour negotiators this concept of income could also be potentially acceptable in that it can be shown to imply the maintenance of future physical operations[22] which in turn could be related to the maintenance of future employment and/or total labour remuneration.[23]

But the most important quality required, as far as labour negotiators are concerned, may be predictive ability, i.e. will knowledge of economic income help them to predict where management's resistance point should be? From this point of view it can be argued that given the need for efficient resource allocation the break-even point of zero economic income should (normatively) be one of management's potential constraints. We tentatively suggest, therefore, that an 'ideal' definition of ability to pay which should be acceptable to both labour and management may be based on expected economic income, i.e. distributable operating flow. Remembering that this measure was used to define the maximum dividend payments possible, however, the maximum amount which is available to meet the increased organisational costs associated with labour's claim would seem to be: *distributable operating flow less the minimum required return to providers of capital*. This, then, is our proposed definition of 'ability to pay'.

In a perfectly competitive economy, and in the long run, this would result in ability to pay being measured as zero, since the distributable operating flow should be just sufficient to cover the risk appropriate rates of return for subscribers of capital. In the real world, however, ability to pay as we have defined it can be positive as a result, *inter alia*, of the existence of supernormal profits and imperfections in the capital market. Thus, there may exist some maximum level of 'slack' which *could* be available to meet the increased costs of labour's claim.

Whilst it is believed that this definition of ability to pay could be considered relevant by both management and labour, for reasons already stated there may still be disagreements about how it should be measured in practice, and it is to these we now turn.

If we accept the 'positive' evidence of Chapter 5 the use of some measure of profits as an ability to pay indicator is common experience in negotiations. It has also been observed that unions tend to use as 'gross' a measure of 'profits' as possible in their arguments, e.g. by adding back depreciation and interest charges. This in itself might be taken to imply an overwhelmingly tactical purpose for adopting such measures. Even if this was the primary motive, however, it would not preclude the possibly simultaneous acceptance of such measures as significant indicators by unions themselves in setting their own aspirations. In addition, as we shall see later, such 'gross' measures may serve purposes other than as indicators of ability to pay. Let us for the moment, however, assume that profit measurements (possibly grossed up in some way) are seriously considered to be acceptable indicators of ability to pay by labour negotiators and not merely an opportunity for bluffing.

First of all it is necessary to point out that *any* measure of profits derived from the published accounts of an organisation is unlikely to measure ability to pay precisely in the way that we have defined it.[24] On the other hand 'profits' *might* be an acceptable surrogate for our 'ideal' ability to pay concept.[25] We have therefore to provide for the possibility that the relevant question to ask may not be: does the proposed measure coincide with our definition; but rather, does it have the attributes to be an acceptable substitute?[26] Such a question will, in part, require an empirical answer which we do not attempt to provide here. What we can do, however, is to examine some *a priori* reasons why a proposed surrogate may not correspond with our 'ideal' conception and to consider whether these indicate that the principal-surrogate relationship is likely to be found to be a useful one if and when the appropriate empirical research into the question can be carried out.

The major advantage accounting profits can be said to carry as 'pragmatic-surrogates' is that they are 'objective'. On the other hand, labour negotiators have rejected accounting profits in the past precisely because of the discretionary (subjective) elements which may be involved in their calculation. Depreciation, for example, is considered to be a 'discretionary' item by virtue of management's apparent ability to change the size of the depreciation charge by adopting different depreciation methods, assumptions about asset lives and scrap values. As a result it is common to see 'profits' quoted by labour negotiators after adding back depreciation.

Such usage appears to incorporate the assumption that ability to pay can be calculated without taking account of the costs of fixed assets.[27] This is clearly not so from our definition since a provision for replacement of fixed assets is necessary for the maintenance of the economic value of the organisation.

Another aspect of 'capital costs' which is omitted by this usage is the dividends necessary to service the capital. The reluctance of labour negotiators to deduct dividends in arriving at ability to pay indicators may be related to a political belief in the irrelevance of shareholders. But the need to take account of an opportunity cost of capital exists regardless of the political structure of society. Of course, there is nothing to suggest that the actual dividends paid represent the opportunity cost of capital – but an estimate of the latter needs deducting in any case.[28]

Let us for the moment resort to the artificial assumption of a stationary (no growth and no price movements) state. Among other things this would involve the capital investment for a period being equal to the depreciation charge (in replacement cost terms). It would also involve a payment to suppliers of capital of the risk appropriate rate of return multiplied by the amount of capital each subscribes. Entries in the income statement could be expected to remain at the same level for ever, except, possibly, for 'extraordinary items' which were of a windfall nature.[29] The presence of profits implies a corporation tax liability which would presumably be reduced if labour costs were increased. It could not, however, be reduced below the tax charge on the profits required to maintain the minimum necessary dividends.

Thus, in a stationary state, as a first approximation, it is suggested that an appropriate measure of ability to pay might be: *Profits before tax and extraordinary items but after deducting the grossed up minimum dividends necessary to service the capital.*[30] Such a measure would, however, imply that the only 'slack' recurrent in the profit and loss account was that related to payments to shareholders. Suspicions that this may not be the case are not confined to trade unionists.[31] In our own non-stationary and imperfect economy there are, in fact, a multitude of reasons to suppose that accounting profits before tax but after grossed up dividends may not be equivalent to ability to pay. Some of these arise out of accounting conventions, as well as the concept of 'organisational slack'. The nature of the problems which arise because of the conventions adopted in financial accounting is probably too well known to the reader to require repetition at length here.[32] However, the discretion which is undoubtedly involved both in establishing the 'real level' of expenses and the choice of accounting representations of them may lead the user of accounting information to try to eliminate, for comparative purposes, obviously discretionary items such as depreciation from a quoted ability to pay indicator. To leave it at that, however, is a *non sequitur*, even for comparative purposes, since the precise circumstances of organisations (e.g. their holdings of fixed assets) vary, which means in turn that the 'real' values of the omitted items (e.g. depreciation) will vary. If an item is eliminated from ability to pay simply because of disagreement with its calculation, then the action required is the *replacement* of it by a better estimate of what its 'real' and 'necessary' level should be and not its omission. To perform this operation effectively, however, requires detailed knowledge of the circumstances of the organisation and its accounting policies. Ultimately, in accounting terms, this requires access to the 'building blocks' of the accounts to enable them to be reconstructed in a different manner. Taken to its logical conclusion this means that only a completely 'open book' management disclosure policy could satisfy labour negotiator's theoretical requirements for an ability to pay indicator on the lines of the one we have defined.[33] Whether or not such a disclosure policy prevails, however, 'profits before tax but after grossed up dividends' seems to qualify as a practical surrogate for ability to pay in a stationary state.[34] (We return to the difficulties introduced by non-stationary assumptions later.)

As already indicated (note 27) apart from their possible tactical usefulness, 'grossed up' profits may have an 'internal' significance for labour negotiators. That is, negotiators in 'valuing' the various possible outcomes of bargaining may be influenced by considerations of *equity*, either directly through their personal valuation functions or indirectly through the effects of a perception that 'equity' influences the attitudes of their 'principals' (the employees). To the extent that financial indicators may thus be significant in determining negotiators', and their principals', attitudes towards the relative equity of possible settlements, these indicators may in turn influence demands and bargaining outcomes. Consequently, the notion of the *divisible fund* of an organisation in which labour takes 'equitable' shares may perhaps give relevance to measurements much 'grosser' than those we have already discussed.

A concept which suggests itself as a possible measure of the 'divisible fund' is the organisation's *net output* or, perhaps more familiarly, its *value added*. Support has recently been given to the disclosure of this figure in published accounts: 'The simplest and most immediate way of putting profit into proper perspective *vis-à-vis* the whole enterprise as a collective effort by capital, management and employees is by presentation of a statement of value added (that is, sales income less materials and services purchased). Value added is the wealth the reporting entity has been able to create by its own and its employees' efforts'[1, p. 49]. A suggestion as to how value added information might be presented is shown in Table 6.1.[35] Although this proposal has been made in the context of disclosure to employees, there is reason to suppose that it would also be of interest to labour negotiators in the light of the discussion of the 'divisible fund' above.

The provision of such information to employees in general may, in fact, put pressure on labour negotiators to take account of it, since the implication is that their 'principals' may be being conditioned to evaluate questions of equity by means of such statements.[36]

The essential distinction between 'ability to pay' and the 'divisible fund' seems to relate to the question of equity. That is, the divisible fund must, in some sense, measure the total sum available to meet the claims of *all* 'contributors' to the organisation. If *relative* equity is then to be judged there must also be a breakdown showing the proportions of the fund going to each contributory group. It is from this point of view that we must examine the usefulness of the value added statement.

Firstly, it is necessary to question what we mean by 'contributors'. Fairly clearly we could include employees, creditors and shareholders without much objection, but what about the government and suppliers of raw materials and services? There are two possible ways of 'rationalising' the inclusion of payments to the government (taxes) in the divisible fund. Firstly, we may take the view that taxes represent the exchange value of the social goods provided by the government which benefit the organisation. Less tenuously, we can say that if, for instance, the whole of taxable profits were 'redistributed' to labour, then company tax would presumably be zero. Thus the tax charge should certainly be included in the divisible fund, whether or not we regard it as a necessary distribution to a specific 'contributor'.

TABLE 6.1 Statement of Value Added
X Ltd. 19XX

		£mn
	Sales	XX
Less:	Raw materials and services purchased	XX
	Value added (net output)	£XXX

Of which:

To pay employees:	
Wages, pensions and fringe benefits	X
To pay government:	
Taxes	X
To pay providers of capital:	
Loan interest	X
Dividends	X
To provide for maintenance and expansion:	
Depreciation	X
Retentions	X
Value added	£XXX

Shareholders, as contributors, benefit, directly or indirectly, from the payment of dividends and the retention of earnings (which, formally, belong to them). On the other hand it is not clear that the depreciation provision 'benefits' any such group specifically. To the extent that it measures the 'real cost' of using the services of fixed assets, it might be classified with the item 'raw materials and services purchased'. The essential difference between it and that grouping seems to be that its level is not directly fixed by market forces. But we have already stated that disagreements about the way in which an item should be computed do not warrant its exclusion from an otherwise appropriate category.

Thus, it seems to us that depreciation should be treated as being essentially of the same nature as the item 'raw materials and services purchased', at least from the point of view of measurement of the divisible fund. Taking the conventional view that suppliers (including suppliers of capital goods) are not contributors to the organisation, we can thus say that an appropriate measure of the divisible fund appears to be *Value Added–Depreciation*.[37]

Thus far, then, we have arrived at two suggestions for information which may be relevant to labour negotiators:

Ability to Pay = Profits before tax but after grossed up dividends

Divisible Fund = Value Added − Depreciation.

The latter needing to be accompanied by a breakdown of its constituents to allow for *relative* 'equity' considerations. We have also indicated that, because of the possible existence of organisational slack and disagreements about accounting policies, this information should, ideally, be supplemented by sufficient detail to 'rework' the calculations, if necessary.

In addition to possible disagreements about the appropriateness of the accounting practices adopted by the organisation, the fact that the world is imperfect and non-stationary gives rise to other conceptual difficulties which apply equally to ability to pay and the divisible fund. Perhaps the most obvious of these is that, since both measures are intended to be 'decision relevant', they should, strictly, be related to conditions expected to obtain in the future. As long as we have a stationary state past (historic) measures can be taken as perfect substitutes for future measures.[38] As soon as we move away from this assumption then past values are not directly relevant to the concepts we may wish to measure. This in turn implies the need to *forecast* the behaviour of our proposed surrogates.

One way in which this could be done would be for management to supply the forecasts direct, i.e. to give labour negotiators planned or budgeted information. The arguments about whether this is in management's interests are not relevant here.[39] Neither are we concerned, at this point, with the question of whether management's forecasts would be 'credible' to labour (although we shall have something to say about this when discussing the audit function later in this chapter). Rather, the more fundamental question of whether management's predictions are what labour negotiators *need* has to be faced.

The alternative to management providing direct *predictions* is for them to provide *predictive information*, i.e. information which labour can use to make their own predictions. The result may be two quite different estimates of the future value of a variable of interest. This difference does not merely arise because of the possibly conflicting views of negotiators about the effects of the various outcomes of negotiations, or even about what those outcomes might be. Rather it arises because *any* two sets of persons may come to different conclusions about what may happen in the future, because of different attitudes (optimism pessimism) and different assumptions about the impact of exogenous factors, even if they start with the same 'data base'.

From the point of view of the expected accuracy of the two estimates, it might be pointed out that management appears to be in the best position to evaluate the firm's future, by reason of its experience of the firm. Certainly, if management alone has access to the detailed information on which forecasts are based then they will start with a comparative advantage. But labour negotiators may also have a comparative advantage in their knowledge of other organisations in the same or related industries. [40] The result is that, given access to the *same* historic information there is nothing *a priori* to suggest that management is able to make better *forecasts* than labour representatives.

Thus it would appear that labour's information needs could be better satisfied by predictive information rather than predictions. Before we accept this view, however, it is necessary to consider the distinction between *forecasting* and *planning*.

If labour negotiators are given access to the bases of forecasts as well as their final versions, independent projections can be made by them by separately forecasting future levels of physical items (unit sales, production etc.) and applying forecast unit prices to these. There may, however, be a very important conceptual reason why the result will differ, and perhaps be inferior to, management's predictions. This is because financial aggregates such as ability to pay, value added etc. may be *planned* variables in their own right. For instance, if the achievement of a target rate of return is one of the current goals of the organisation, by working backwards from this management may 'plan' the values of the financial variables required, such as profits, value added etc. Such plans, when constraint information is applied, become management's overall predictions – which may be quite different to forecasts based on an assumption of passive response to external changes.

Faced by such difficulties, it is by no means clear that labour would benefit more from predictive information rather than predictions. If predictive information is given, however, it can be seen to require, ideally, [41] a detailed statement of planning objectives as well as the detailed building blocks of forecasts.

Thus, both predictions and predictive information should perhaps be provided – the first because it may be a better 'statement of intentions', and the second because it facilitates an independent check of management's forecasting abilities. If management is, however, neither convinced of the need to 'open the books' so wide nor willing or required to provide direct predictions, it may still be possible to improve the relevance of the organisation's financial reports to labour for the purposes of forecasting future ability to pay and the divisible fund. This could perhaps be done if, for instance, the classification of items in the organisation's profit and loss account were made more appropriate to the needs of external forecasters.

This problem is obviously analogous to that facing investors and potential investors in the organisation who have similar needs to forecast organisational earnings. In view of the possible needs to reconcile the 'rights' of labour *vis-à-vis* shareholders, therefore, there may be advantages if some new form of the profit and loss account could be found which was of improved relevance to both groups. One such statement has, in fact, been proposed in relation to investment decision making [8, pp. 121–2] and we have adapted it to produce Table 6.2.

It will be noticed that one significant feature is that, in Table 6.2, items are classified as to whether they are 'fixed' or 'variable' in relation to organisational activity. Whilst this is not a completely satisfactory basis for forecasting,[43] it does mean that future estimates of income, ability to pay and distributable surplus can be arrived at after taking account of at least one factor which may cause changes in them. Thus, a 'naïve'[44] estimate of future costs might, for instance, be calculated as follows:

$$\text{Future Costs} = \text{Present Variable Costs} \times \frac{\text{Future Sales}}{\text{Current Sales}} + \frac{\text{Present Fixed}}{\text{Costs}}$$

This does not, of course, take account of the fact that aggregates in the accounts are not composed of homogeneous items, so that different sectors of variable costs, for instance, may bear different relationships to activity measures. In addition, the effect of other factors on costs may be as important as that of activity. Nevertheless, the fixed/variable dichotomy does represent a potential improvement, for forecasting purposes, over the present system in which items in the accounts are totally uncategorised as to their possible behaviour patterns.

It will also be noted that we have recommended that the predictive information should be in replacement cost terms, rather than historic costs. To justify this, we rely on the analysis suggested by Revsine [22, chs. 4–6]. Firstly, he points out that current (replacement cost) operating profit is equivalent to distributable operating flow in a perfectly competitive economy, and that it may be used to approximate it in other circumstances [22, pp. 95–114]. From this we can deduce that *future* current operating profits may be used as a practical surrogate for *future* distributable operating flows, and can, therefore, be adjusted by an estimate of the minimum necessary dividends to give a surrogate for our 'ideal' ability to pay measure.

Secondly, Revsine suggests that in forecasting *future* distributable operating flows, *current and past* replacement cost information could have twofold relevance: (a) operating profits plus holding gains (replacement cost income) may be useful as a 'lead indicator'[22, ch. 4], while (b) operating profits may be useful for extrapolation purposes[22, ch. 5]. However, he points out the restrictive assumptions necessary for these variables to qualify *normatively* for such purposes, and the need for empirical research to confirm their practical relevance.

Briefly, in justifying replacement cost income as a lead indicator he contends that holding gains reflect possible increases in income in the future, although this will only happen if the rise in asset prices is a reflection of an increase in their 'user values'[45] [22, p. 114]. Alternatively, if operating profit alone is to be extrapolated, then there must be an assumption that current replacement cost margins will be maintained in the future – which may be true if the organisation is able and willing to pass on any future cost increases in absolute terms [22, p. 121].

Whether or not these assumptions hold, and even if they do not, whether replacement cost information is a good predictor of its own future values, is a matter for empirical research. Even without the benefit of the results of such research, however, we feel that replacement cost information is inherently more relevant for our purposes than historic costs.[46]

If we, then, accept Table 6.2 as a potentially useful basis for predicting ability to pay, it has the advantage that it can readily be adapted to show also the divisible fund. It would, however, imply an extension of current minimum disclosure practice. Nevertheless, if any significant improvement is to be made in the provision of predictive information, Table 6.2 seems to us to give an indication of its minimum necessary extent. It has the advantage, of course, that it might simultaneously improve the relevance of accounting information from the point of view of investors as well as labour negotiators.

Apart from accounting profits, a number of other indicators have been used by labour negotiators in actual bargaining situations.[47] Some of these have been labelled 'ability to pay' indicators and so merit consideration in this section.

A number of these measures are, however, quite clearly predictive aids to, rather than surrogates for, the organisation's ability to pay. Into this category seem to fall break-even charts and the numerous ratios which

TABLE 6.2 Profit and loss account for year ended 31 December 19XX
(In replacement cost terms)

				£
	Operations – Major:			
	Inflows: Sales (by product line)			XXX
	Less: Outflows:			
	(1) Responsive to sales or production volume and mix:			
	Materials		XX	
	Labour		XX	
	Other variable operating costs		XX	
			XX	
	± Inventory level adjustment		XX	
	Variable cost of goods sold		XX	
	Other variable costs (specify)		XX	
			XX	
	(2) Committed:			
*	Fixed operating costs (excluding depreciation)		XX	
	Interest		XX	
	Administrative expenses:			
	Labour	X		
	Materials	X		
	Other	X	XX	
			XX	
	(3) Discretionary:			
	Research and development (by programme)		XX	
	Advertising		XX	
	Directors emoluments		XX	
	Replacement of capacity		XX	
			XX	
	(4) Taxes		XX	XX
	Profits from major operations			XXX
	Operations – Minor:			
	Inflows: Interest and dividends (specify)		XX	
	Less: Outflows: investment expenses		XX	
	Profits from minor operations			XX
	Profits from operations			XXX
**	Realisable holding gains/losses (specify)			XX
	Replacement cost income			XXX
	Extraordinary profits/losses (specify)			XX
	Profits after extraordinary items			XXX
	Less: Distributions: dividends (by class)			XX
				XX
**	Retained: Holding gains/losses (revaluation reserves)		XX	
	For expansion		XX	XX

Notes
* adjusted for inventory level changes, where appropriate (adjustments should be shown).
** See note 42.

have been suggested. Even such ratios as future profitability (profit/capital employed) and % of labour costs in total costs[48] can be seen, in the light of our earlier definition, to represent only one facet of ability to pay, whilst more general ratio analysis of historic accounting results can serve no apparent purpose but to assist in the prediction of future results and, hence, 'ability to pay'. However, the use of one group of such indicators reflects an aspect of ability to pay which we have not yet discussed. These are the *liquidity* indicators.

As soon as we allow for uncertainty, the timing of cash flows, and hence liquidity, may become a critical determinant of ability to pay, since an, albeit temporary, adverse effect on liquidity could lead to the organisation's non-survival. To cater for this possibility, a supplementary statement similar to that in Table 6.2 may be produced, but in cash flow terms,[49] to serve as predictive information for the organisation's liquidity. A slightly less useful instrument for this purpose might, of course, be a conventional funds flow statement.

To summarise, in a non-stationary economy, in the presence of uncertainty, we maintain our belief in the potential relevance of the two measures of ability to pay and the divisible fund we arrived at earlier. However, in such conditions, clearly *ex post* versions of these measures are not directly relevant – their future values need to be predicted. If predictive information is to be provided for such purposes then, ideally, the predictor needs open access to the basis of management's forecasts and plans. As a second best solution, however, we suggest that statements such as Table 6.2, in both replacement cost accounting and cash flow terms may enable potentially more useful measures of ability to pay and the divisible fund to be derived.

Alternatively, management could, of course, publish its own direct predictions of both cash flows and accounting profits, from which ability to pay information could be inferred.

Whether predictive information or direct predictions are provided, however, problems may still arise as to the appropriateness of the results of the accounting entity in relation to the bargaining unit. So far, we have implicitly assumed that the bargaining unit is the same as the financial reporting entity. This will generally only be true for company, or group wide, bargaining. In the case of industry wide, or employers – federation bargaining situations, the basic reporting problem is one of aggregating the results of the individual organisation. This raises few problems of principle, except in relation to the need to standardise accounting practices between the underlying entities before aggregating their financial results if the latter are to be meaningful. The practical procedures involved in this have been well documented in relation to employer information sharing schemes already in existence, such as those run in the U.K. by the Centre for Interfirm Comparisons.[50] Provided that standard definitions can be arrived at, and differences reconciled, there seems no reason in principle why a statement such as that shown in Table 6.2 should not be prepared for the combined bargaining unit.[51]

More serious problems of principle occur when the bargaining unit is a sub-unit of a reporting entity, e.g. a factory in a multi-factory company. The problems raised here are those of disaggregation with which accountants who are concerned with the measurement of divisional performance should be familiar.[52] Briefly, these problems relate to the allocation of joint items and transfer pricing. Thus, for instance, there may be certain administrative costs which are incurred for the benefit of all factories in an organisation. If we are to present the results of one factory bargaining unit separately, presumably such costs should not be ignored and on the other hand, there seems little to be gained by management from 'over' allocating them for tactical reasons – such ploys are usually found out eventually and may then have a high cost in terms of the 'atmosphere' of future negotiations. Thus, some rational and credible basis has to be found for allocating the joint costs over the factories which benefit from them. The problem is that, in theory, there is no single method of allocation which can achieve this unequivocally[26, ch. 7]. In practice, of course, such allocations are performed as a matter of routine, e.g. in systems in which 'full costs' are calculated ('absorption costing'). Since such systems can never have full conceptual backing, however, there is always room for argument about financial reporting results which derive from them. Once again, ideally, this could be met by allowing access to sufficiently detailed information such that results based on different allocation assumptions could be compared.[53]

Whether or not the allocation 'problem' is resolved, there may still remain the question of the appropriateness of any transfer pricing methods used. To a certain extent this is similar to the allocation problem in that, where services are transferred between units of the organisation, a suitable transfer price for them might simultaneously provide a rational basis for allocating their associated costs (provided the transfer price was a cost based one). Another situation in which the transfer pricing problem may be critical is one in which some intermediate product is transferred from one bargaining unit to another. The result is that the price fixed for the product will affect the financial results of both units, in opposite directions.

Once again, if there was a theoretically 'correct' method of transfer pricing then there would be little problem, but in most cases there is not.[54] Thus, again there is room for dispute about whatever transfer pricing rule may be adopted for pragmatic reasons. Problems such as these obviously lay the financial results of sub-organisations open to challenge and suspicion, especially in relation to the subsidiaries of multi-national companies. The only satisfactory way to alleviate such suspicion, ultimately, seems to be to present sufficient information on the accounting practices and underlying 'building blocks' to enable the results to be reconstructed alternatively, if necessary. Failing this, a report on the 'fairness' of the practices adopted by someone who has access to the necessary detailed information *may* lend the sub-unit results credibility. Certainly, the impression from trade union sources is that sub-organisational financial information is sought after, 'warts and all'.

There are very many financial items other than ability to pay and distributable surplus measures which are of potential relevance to labour negotiators, at least if trade union shopping lists are to be taken as an indication.[55] Some of these (e.g. a breakdown of cost information in the Profit and Loss Account) would be covered if statements such as Table 6.2 were to become standard disclosure practice. Other items are of a more detailed nature and are covered in our next section, on management accounting. If the 'Corporate Report' [1] is an indication of future trends, however, the annual reports of companies may, sometime in the future, extend to include an 'Employment Report' [1, pp. 51–3] containing more of the information requested by labour negotiators. Again, much of the detail of this arises, presently, from the management, rather than financial, accounting system and so will be treated in the next section.

MANAGEMENT ACCOUNTING

Like financial accounting, management accounting information tends to be directly relevant to management negotiators and, hence, indirectly relevant to labour negotiators. For example, evaluations of strike costs, alternative outcomes and productivity deals (which are predominantly management accounting information) are directly relevant to management negotiators in decision making.

One difference between the discussion below and that related to financial accounting, however, is that with the latter it was possible effectively to ignore the kinds of specific 'issues' involved in bargaining, i.e. ability to pay, for instance, may be considered relevant whether negotiations are concerned with wage levels, fringe benefits, manning agreements or any other issue which might have an 'economic' impact on the organisation. On the other hand, since we shall be talking about much more detailed, possibly non-monetary, information below, it is theoretically necessary to relate the concept of its relevance to particular negotiating issues. Rather than refer specifically to each of the infinite variety of non-wage issues which may arise to justify the disclosure of a particular item, however, our approach below is to suggest some general classes of information which may be found useful to management and/or labour negotiators, leaving it to the reader to make adjustments for the actual scope of negotiations, as necessary. To begin with, though, we examine a possible use of information by management which applies whatever the negotiating content.

Bargaining implies the possibility of non-agreement. The result may be a work stoppage by labour, or some other conflict situation which imposes potential costs on management – e.g. a 'work to rule'. We have seen, in Chapter 4, that management's actions in collective bargaining may be affected by the estimated magnitude of these 'conflict costs'.[56] It is not necessary, in fact, to subscribe to a particular model of collective bargaining to see that these costs may be relevant to management decision making in negotiations. Since the information which relates to the calculation of conflict costs largely originates in the management accounting system, it seems relevant here to consider some of the measurement problems which may arise.

Strictly, the evaluation of conflict costs should be carried out in 'opportunity cost' terms, i.e. there should be a comparison between the forecast results of a non-conflict situation and a conflict situation in which the next best options are taken by the organisation. Since the results of a non-conflict situation imply agreement with labour, this side of the calculation involves evaluating, probably in terms of 'packages', the possible alternative outcomes of negotiations. This may obviously be a useful exercise in its own right, from the point of view of management negotiators. Let us for the moment, however, turn to the other part of the calculation – the evaluation of the possible results of a conflict.

As already indicated these have to be estimated assuming that management optimises its actions in the event of a conflict. It is this optimisation assumption that may give rise to the severest measurement problem. This is because the measurer has, essentially, to 'think himself into management's shoes' in a hypothetical situation. To illustrate some of the difficulties involved, consider the individual elements which may go to make up the costs of a conflict.

Firstly, there may be revenues lost, in terms of sales foregone or deferred. In the event that orders are deferred rather than lost, a prediction of the effects this may have on cash flows and any consequent 'time value of money' lost may have to be made, i.e.: if we suppose the effect is to defer a cash flow from Sales (S) by n periods, with the organisation's cost of capital equal to $i\%$ per period, then the incremental cost to the organisation of the deferral could be calculated to be $S[1-(1+i/100)^{-n}]$ in present value terms, where S, i and n may each give rise to serious estimation problems. Remember also that this cost has to be minimised by, for instance, buying in goods for resale, and that the probable effect of such cost minimisation policies on labour actions (picketing, 'blacking' etc) has also to be borne in mind.

Secondly, there is the impact of a conflict on the firm's input costs. Fairly obviously 'period' costs such as rent and rates may be unaffected, but other 'fixed' costs may in fact increase, for instance certain administrative costs may rise, e.g. for clerical work carried out in abnormal conditions. On the other hand, variable costs will almost certainly be affected – the effect on labour costs, for instance, being dependent on the type of conflict envisaged. If there is a 'go slow', labour cost/unit may actually increase, while materials costs may be affected by an abnormal amount of spoilage etc. In addition, all such items may have to be related to the estimated duration of the conflict if we are to work in present value terms.

Although only a few, general difficulties have been mentioned, it is obvious that the calculation of the expected results in the event of a conflict poses severe estimation problems. A further problem is that since we are dealing with forecasts, it may be necessary to give management not merely a single valued estimate but the whole range of possible results, with their associated probabilities, as in Figure 6.1 (where it is assumed that measurements are in NPV terms). A similar analysis needs to be carried out in respect of the financial results of all the feasible non-conflict (settlement) outcomes, with the same kinds of estimation difficulties applying.

Since for an opportunity cost calculation we need to compare the net effect of conflict versus non-conflict results, the above distribution of net present values of conflict outcomes needs to be compared in turn with the estimated results (in NPV terms) associated with each possible

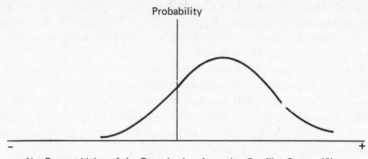

FIG. 6.1

agreement outcome. But these in themselves, since they are based on forecasts, will give rise to probabilistic distributions similar to Figure 6.1. We are thus theoretically faced with the necessity to amalgamate 2 probability distributions to get the combined distribution of opportunity costs associated with a particular settlement. This in itself can be done by simulation methods fairly straightforwardly, as long as the distributions are independent of one another. But, since external factors can simultaneously affect conflict and non-conflict results, the 2 sets of distributions are not likely to be independent.[57] In this case, care has to be taken to control the pairs of values which are to be combined.

Of course, management negotiators may not want information as sophisticated as that suggested above – indeed, they may not be able to understand it! But, as was suggested earlier for labour negotiators, the purpose here is to suggest what information *should* (ideally) be relevant to negotiators. In practice they may be satisfied with far less, but that is no excuse for the (management) accountant not to be aware of the conceptual problems involved in providing 'ideal' information, or, indeed, not trying to educate negotiators into the use of it.

A simpler approach, which may provide useful enough information for management negotiators in practice, is to display the effects of various bargaining outcomes on a break-even chart, as in Figure 6.2. This shows the new and existing relationships which may hold between costs, volume and profits. It can also be used to infer the maximum increase in variable labour costs which the organisation could sustain, i.e. that for which break even occurs at the expected sales volume. Thus, this type of diagram has been suggested as a useful visual indicator of one aspect of the organisation's ability to pay, which, therefore, may be presented to labour negotiators as such [9, pp. 553–4]. Obviously, in this connection it might be most effective where the union's claim could be shown as an increase in costs which were either completely variable or completely fixed in relation to sales, or production volume. In fact, much the same reservations as to its applicability for this purpose apply as have been pointed out in the context of its other possible uses.[58] The validity of break-even analysis in a multi-product organisation is, in particular, questionable, although as an instrument for emphasising the relationship between higher costs and output requirements it carries the possible advantage of easy understandability.

Information such as conflict costs, costings of the various possible agreements and break-even charts are all items which may be useful to negotiators. In a particular set of negotiations, it is also vital that management's negotiators are equipped with a detailed factual basis for evaluating *on the spot* any issues likely to be raised by labour negotiators, since the bargaining process frequently necessitates quick responses to changing demands or concessions by labour. It is suggested, for this purpose, that information of potential relevance to management negotiators should be prepared in advance and collected together in the form of a 'bargaining book'. What should be the precise

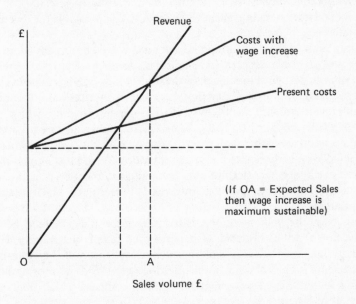

FIG. 6.2

contents of the bargaining book for a particular organisation can only be suggested by knowing the bargaining relationship and issues involved. In broad outline, however, 4 types of information have been suggested as being usefully included in the bargaining book:[59]

(a) External wage data − e.g. wages and salaries paid by other firms to particular groups of workers, and other organisations' wage settlements. The purpose of these data is obviously comparative.

(b) Internal wage data − details of basic rates, overtime, differentials, wages and salary structures etc., along with the number of employees involved in each case. This can serve, *inter alia*, as a basis for rapid costing of union demands or possible counter proposals.

(c) Productivity data − this might include information related to standards for the purposes of incentive payments, work study data, or simply the bases of performance reports in standard costing. Once again, it may serve the purpose of enabling the union's claims to be costed out roughly by negotiators. Such statistics as value added/employee are now being increasingly emphasised by unions, however, and thus should also be known to management's negotiators.

(d) Cost of living data and trends in 'real' take home pay − since these have been emphasised by unions in supporting wage claims, it is incumbent on management to have such data available for its own reference.

Sources of such information and the ways in which it might be used have already been covered in Chapter 5. At this stage it is merely necessary to point out that much of the information will originate in the management accounting function, so that it is necessary for the management accountant to ensure that the information which is gathered for this purpose is the best available and that any possible limitations on uses other than that for which it may have originally been prepared are clearly pointed out to negotiators. Clearly this implies the need for management accountants to familiarise themselves with the functions, and hence possible information needs, of management negotiators.

Much of the content of the bargaining book may, in fact, be a derivative of what information it is believed labour negotiators will actually use, or what they will consider relevant. It will therefore be necessary to look, *inter alia*, at the question of the kinds of information falling within the management accounting compass which may be relevant to labour.

From the evidence of Chapter 5, it appears that much of this may be summarised as 'labour force' data. We have also seen in Chapter 5 the types of information which might fall under this heading, as evidenced by their appearance in union shopping lists and documentation supporting wage claims.

What is clear is that management will require guidance, in formulating a disclosure policy on such items, not only as to the possible entitlement of labour negotiators to such information, but also on its possible relevance. By being the group most familiar with what kinds of information of this type are actually available, and their limitations, management accountants may have an important future role in this aspect of industrial relations. What we have not felt it useful to do here is specify exactly what information of the 'labour force' type may prove to be relevant in a particular set of negotiations, since that would depend primarily on what both sets of negotiators, consciously or unconsciously, believe to be relevant to the bargaining issues, which may vary even *during* negotiations.

Even if labour negotiators are provided with the type of information they consider relevant, however, it may still not be acceptable to them, and hence have no effect on their decisions, because it lacks *credibility*. The credibility of information is the concern of the audit function.

AUDITING

It can be maintained that the primary function of the auditor is to lend credibility to the information on which he reports.[60] The need for an audit function arises because the system from which information is derived is not independent of one of the parties who are interested in it – management. Thus, for example, if a company's accounting results are regarded as a report on the stewardship of management there arises the possibility that the group who are judged by such results may have the incentive *and opportunity* to manipulate them. The result is that the accounting information may lack *credibility* for its potential users, with the result that the information may not be used by them in decision making. Where it is considered that such information *should* be used then a way must be found to make the information more credible for the intended users.

One possible solution to this problem would be to let the users check the veracity of the information themselves by giving them full access to the system generating it. In most situations this solution is not practical. Reasons for this include the fact that most intended users would have neither the resources nor skills requisite to carry out the necessary checks. Rather, the task is delegated to a person, or persons (the auditors) who can act effectively on their behalf. Since such persons are intended to identify any 'bias' in the information introduced, consciously or unconsciously, by management's control over the information system, it is vital that they be recognised as independent of management by the information user. The perceived *independence* of the auditor may therefore be an important prerequisite for the use of information which is normatively relevant.

It might be objected that, in the case of collective bargaining information there is no necessary role for the auditor. This might be claimed, for instance, where a company 'opens the books' to labour representatives so that they are able to perform their own credibility checks. But, in such a situation the practical argument for an independent auditor remains – the users may have neither the skills nor resources to carry out an effective audit function themselves.

Alternatively, it might be pointed out that the scope of an organisation's statutory audit should cover the information concerned. Such an argument neglects the importance of the limited responsibility of a statutory auditor – to report on the 'truth and fairness' of the published accounts – which means that there is no guarantee that published information would be considered to be 'true and fair' by the auditor if the suitability of its use in collective bargaining was the subject of his report. The statutory auditor reports on the truth and fairness of the accounting results in their entirety and his report in normal form cannot therefore lend credibility to individual pieces of information, even if extracted from the accounts or, at the least, covered by his statutorily determined investigations.

Whether we are talking about information culled from the annual accounts or additional disclosures, then, the need for an independent audit function may arise. This is not to say that all accounting information communicated in collective bargaining will necessarily have to be separately audited. Whether an auditor is formally involved or not will presumably depend, in any particular situation, on factors such as the importance labour negotiators attach to the information, the 'atmosphere' of industrial relations, etc. This said, there will undoubtedly be situations in the future in which auditors will be called upon to report specifically on information communicated in collective bargaining. It is therefore necessary to consider the question of the perceived independence of the auditor in this relatively novel situation.

Whether an auditor is *actually* independent is a matter of fact. This can be stated since independence *in fact* is an attitude of mind allied to the skills and experience necessary to render an unbiased opinion based on audit work carried out in line with the average standards of the profession.[61] But to render information credible, it is not independence *in fact* which is important but independence as *perceived* by the information user.

Some social, psychological and economic factors which tend to weaken the perceived independence of auditors from management have been analysed by several authors [16, ch. 4], [20, ch. 8]. A number of suggestions for tackling this problem have also been put forward,[62] although mainly in the context of auditor independence as perceived by investors and creditors. Some of these suggestions have recently been implemented in the U.K. – e.g. the new ethics code of the Institute of Chartered Accountants in England and Wales may require disposals of shares in client companies and restrictions in the possible economic dependence of a professional firm on income from any one client [14,sec. E]. Such changes cannot, however, completely remove the causes of the identification of auditors, both as a profession and as individuals, with management and the 'business ethic'. That is auditors, *qua* auditors and accountants, *must* be involved with managements on a professional and social basis as an inevitable consequence of their work. As long as such relationships can be seen to exist, it may be useless in practice for auditors to protest that they are, in fact, independent, since it is other groups' perceptions of that independence which count. Unfortunately, perceptions of the auditor as a tool of management are particularly prone to arise in relation to collective bargaining information because of the entrenched social and political attitudes of many labour negotiators. This is a vicious circle out of which it is difficult to see a way. One radical suggestion[63] is for the effective 'nationalisation' of the audit profession, i.e. to have some central auditor-employment agency which levies charges on organisations for audit work and which assigns the necessary staff. The disadvantages of such a scheme have been thoroughly discussed in relation to statutory audit work and do not require repetition here. Rather, the suggestion is included as an illustration of the kinds of drastic remedies which some people believe to be necessary if perceptions of auditor independence are to be improved (and remember these suggestions were made in relation to a potentially far more sympathetic relationship – investor/management).

If auditors are to play a more significant role in the future in lending credibility to information used in collective bargaining or employee relationships generally, then the issue of their perceived independence of management will require more consideration. 'We must get away from the idea that accountants are the tools of management'[64] is a sentiment with which all auditors will probably agree. What seems to be needed at present is a greater discussion as to how the necessary shift in attitudes can be best achieved. Our intention here is merely to try to encourage such discussion to take account of collective bargaining, as well as investment needs.

Let us suppose that the issue of auditor independence can be resolved satisfactorily and this leads, as we believe it will, to a much greater involvement by auditors in the 'vetting' of information of potential use in collective bargaining, either on an *ad hoc* (investigations) or systematic (part of an information agreement ?) basis. What kinds of issues are likely to arise for the auditor?

One which occurs immediately is in connection with the possibility that management may provide predictions (rather than predictive information) to labour negotiators. Understandably, in the past auditors have been reluctant to take responsibility for checking the veracity of forecast information, perhaps on the grounds of the possibility of liability arising if the forecasts are not achieved. But the fact remains that such 'opting out' occurs in relation to the situation in which there may be most need for the auditor's services. This applies whether the forecast information is intended for use by investors or labour negotiators.

In fact, involvement with reporting on forecast information has already occurred both in relation to the contents of prospectuses and documents circulated in connection with proposed takeovers and mergers.[65] It is clear, from such experience, that the auditor can report on the acceptability of the accounting bases and calculations and also, perhaps, on the 'reasonableness' of the forecasting model and assumptions used, without necessarily taking responsibility for the achievement of the forecasts. All this seems to involve is an extension of the conventional audit approach to deal with a new set of 'facts'.[66]

A second possible extension of the auditor's duties, implied by what we have written earlier, is that, where the bargaining unit is not coincident with the normal accounting entity, then the auditor might be called upon to report on information relating specifically to the bargaining unit. This raises particular difficulties, as we have already noted, in relation to sub-organisational reporting.

Thus, the auditor may, for instance, be asked to report on the appropriateness of transfer prices and allocation methods for common costs. Insofar as such duties already arise in relation to intergroup transactions for the purposes of consolidation this merely seems to raise an old problem in a new guise.

SUMMARY OF THE CHAPTER

In this chapter we have raised a number of issues which we feel to be worthy of further analytical and empirical research. Our efforts have not been directed towards providing 'the' answers to problems raised, although quite clearly we have indicated on a number of points in what direction we think that answers might most usefully be sought. Some problem areas identified were:

(1) Financial Accounting – the measurement of:
 a) 'ability to pay'; and
 b) the 'divisible fund'
(2) Management Accounting:
 a) the evaluation of conflict costs and the effects of bargaining outcomes; and
 b) the contents of the 'bargaining book'
(3) Auditing – the problems of:
 a) independence: and
 b) forecast and 'segmental' information.

Whilst this is by no means an exhaustive list, it is, we feel, sufficient to demonstrate that collective bargaining affects, potentially, almost the whole spectrum of accounting theory and practice. To that extent we hope that this chapter will serve the purpose of encouraging all accountants, whatever their specialisation, to take an interest in developing the theory and practice of the use of information in collective bargaining.

NOTES

1 For some U.K. evidence on the need for education of trade unionists in the use of financial information, see for example [18].
2 See [1, pp. 51–3 and Appendix 3].
3 'Accounting [is] the process of identifying, measuring and communicating economic information to permit informed judgments and decisions by users of the information' [2, p. 1].
4 Rather, see Chapter 1 for an outline of the statutory provisions and proposals relating to 'entitlement', and Chapters 2 and 4 for considerations relating to the need for a voluntary disclosure policy.

5 This apposite label is suggested in [6] although the concept has much earlier origins – see, e.g. [22, pp. 49–53].

6 See [23, pp. 106–7] and [22, pp. 53–6].

7 For a more extensive critique of the 'positive' (user sovereignty) approach – see [22, Appendix to Chapter 2].

8 We are not concerned here with the specification of the efficiency criteria which may be appropriate for this purpose, as long as they *can* be specified, e.g. in terms of organisation or societal objectives.

9 'Rational' in the sense of seeking to make 'efficient' decisions.

10 The dichotomy is not, in any case, as complete as it seems. The normative, model building, approach can only be useful if, ultimately, its assumptions about user behaviour and objectives correspond with real world conditions – something which requires 'positive' confirmation.

11 See Chapter 5.

12 This is not to imply that ability to pay is necessarily thought of as a determining factor in settlements. There are, however, situations in which inability to pay has been claimed to be an effective constraint on settlements, and to that extent ability to pay can be considered to be 'positively' relevant.

13 There could be doubts about whether Walton and McKersie's 'theory' is normative or positive in itself, but the concept of resistance points may also be derived, for instance, from the net contract ophelimity calculations of Pen's model (see Chapter 4 and [21, ch. 4]) – which is certainly normative in character.

14 This is not to say that it is desirable for labour to be *certain* about the position of management's resistance point, since this would probably provoke an adamant demand for a settlement at that level. Fortunately for management, as we shall see later, the provision of ability to pay information can never be sufficient to eliminate entirely labour's doubts about the 'correctness' of its own perceptions in this respect.

15 See Chapter 5.

16 Apart from such tactical uses (which have been termed 'persuasion'), another purpose (termed 'rationalisation') may be to influence third parties, such as the general public, governments and potential arbitrators who may have an indirect effect on outcomes. For a discussion of such uses, see [19, p. 117].

17 This danger may arise through the frequently observed ability of the two parties to select accounting measures which, on the face of it, appear to be contradictory. The result may be a 'neutralisation' of whatever message such information may be actually capable of providing. This, in turn, could be one explanation for the relatively limited significance negotiators attach to financial information as a determinant of bargaining outcomes in practice (see Chapter 5).

18 If it proves possible to develop a particular measure of ability to pay which is perceived as relevant by both sides in bargaining in relation to this particular information need, then it can be argued that it should also be effective as a persuasive tool and thus be relevant for tactical uses too.

19 Zulauf [28, pp. 136–7] provides a comparative table of 6 suggested definitions of ability to pay, of which his own 'theoretical definition' appears to be analytically the most well developed. It is: 'The maximum amount of total wages a firm *could* pay in a specific period consistent with the long run retention of invested assets and other productive factors in the firm' [28, p. 137]. This definition is obviously fairly close to our own, although Zulauf, in fact, emphasises the achievement of a particular rate of return, rather than the maintenance of physical capacity, as the feature essential to its measurement.

20 Readers who may find our analysis below insufficiently rigorous are referred to Revsine [22, chs. 4–6], who deals, *inter alia*, with the necessary assumptions and caveats in much greater detail than we have space for here. It is important to note, in this connection, that we feel that, in practice, the establishment of *some* consensus

definitional framework for ability to pay may be more important than its precise specification – which is why we feel it constructive at this point to put forward tentative suggestions, based on what the reader may feel to be unduly 'heroic' assumptions.

21 For a concise discussion of the properties and relative advantages of alternative measures of income and capital, including economic income, see [17, *passim*].

22 See [22, pp. 97–9].

23 There has been much theoretical controversy as to whether maximisation of employment or the total remuneration of its members are or should be union goals. Here, however, we take the view that either or both could be effective constraints as far as union negotiators are concerned, depending on the attitudes of union members and their interaction with the union negotiator's personal goals. See [3].

24 Perhaps the most obvious reason for this is the essential futurity of the concept as compared to the *ex post* nature of accounting results.

25 For a discussion of the relationship between 'surrogates' and 'principals', see [13, ch. 1].

26 Given the futurity of the concept, there are two inter-related aspects to this question. Firstly, what measurement rule for ability to pay, if its future value were known, would 'best' reflect the 'ideal' concept as far as the decision maker is concerned. Secondly, what is the 'best', presently available, measure to use in predicting the future measurement concept decided upon. For a discussion of the theoretical and practical difficulties involved in establishing such measures, see [4].

27 There may be an alternative explanation – that 'grossed up' profits may be being used as a measure of the 'divisible fund' (see later).

28 In a stationary state it could be argued that dividends need not be paid since no further equity finance would be necessary, i.e. shareholders would be 'imprisoned'. In fact, such a situation could not persevere in practice since, perceiving this probability shareholders would presumably require some enforceable commitment from the organisation to pay dividends *before* they subscribed the initial capital. More realistically, in a dynamic economy, dividends have, in any case, to be paid in order to provide for the possibility of raising more external capital for foreseen and unforeseen purposes.

29 Even though underlying economic relationships may produce a stationary state, there may be stochastic factors at work which affect organisational results on a random basis but which do not have any lasting effects.

30 Hereinafter referred to as 'profits before tax but after grossed up dividends'. Notice at this stage we are basically trying to identify an acceptable *a priori* surrogate for ability to pay regardless of whether it is a good predictor of its own future values (see note 26). On the other hand, extraordinary items are clearly not predictable and we have therefore anticipated events by eliminating them at this stage.

31 See for example [27] for a discussion of the existence and effects of 'organisational slack'.

32 If necessary, refer, for example, to [5, ch. 1.].

33 On the other hand, access to 'too much' information could, conceivably lead to *information overload* [22, pp. 13–19] implying that 'opening the books' might not after all be an 'ideal' solution.

34 As long as suitable adjustments are made to suit varying assumptions about, e.g., the nature of organisational slack and appropriate accounting policies. This in turn implies that management and unions may arrive at very different estimates of the 'profits before tax but after grossed up dividends' which are relevant to each of them.

35 Adapted from M. Renshall, *Accountants Weekly*, 25 July 1975, p. 15.

36 The mechanism by which labour negotiators' attitudes may be shaped by those of their principals' is discussed by Walton and McKersie under the heading of 'intra-organisational bargaining' [25, chs. 8 and 9].

37 Since we do not deal separately with predictive ability relative to the divisible fund it is

worth pointing out at this stage that, for similar reasons to those stated later with respect to ability to pay, we feel both value added and depreciation should here be measured in replacement cost terms.

38 In a non-stationary state we need to distinguish between the 'stream' of future measurements and its present value equivalent. Irregularities in flows can always be eliminated by using an 'equivalent annuity' but in an uncertain world this may result in the loss of crucial information (e.g. about liquidity implications). An implicit assumption here, therefore, is that the need is for estimates of the *stream* of future measurements.

39 Rather, see Chapter 2.

40 This does not imply that unions need to break any confidences in using such information. They do not need to make reasons for their beliefs explicit, just as management may not wish (or be able) to reveal the basis for its beliefs.

41 Subject to the possibility of information overload (see note 33).

42 Whereas *all* realisable holding gains should be included in Replacement Cost Income, not all of them need necessarily be retained in order to maintain physical operating capacity. Thus, a difference between the two double starred items might arise when holding gains have been made on assets held for purely speculative purposes (see, e.g. [15, pp. 21–3]) – since these may not need to be retained in order to maintain the expected flow of income from operations.

43 Because, *inter alia*, it does not take account of management's planning intentions.

44 'Naïve' in the technical, forecasting sense of an estimate derived purely from its own past values, see [7, ch. 2].

45 i.e. their net present values to the organisation.

46 Notice that we have preferred replacement cost, rather than 'current cost' information because of its potentially better predictive ability (see [15, p. 222, note 2]).

47 See Chapter 5.

48 The % of labour costs in total costs may, for instance, when considered along with the price elasticity of demand for the organisation's products, be useful for predicting the feasibility of passing on increased labour costs in prices – one determinant of future ability to pay.

49 The progenitor of Table 6.2 [8, pp. 121–2] was, in fact, in cash flow terms, but in this form is not, we believe, such a useful instrument for predicting ability to pay in general.

50 For an illustration of a published system similar to that used by the Centre for Interfirm Comparisons see Business Ratios (Dunn and Bradstreet, published 1966–70) especially no. 1, Autumn 1966, pp. 20–32.

51 However, using aggregate information to measure ability to pay implies a comparison of labour's demands with the results of the 'average' organisation. Some organisations could thus find themselves 'unable to pay' labour costs which are negotiated on an industry wide basis, see, e.g. [9, pp. 542–3]. A result may be that managerial resistance points in industry wide bargaining may be set on the basis of a somewhat lower ability to pay criterion than our analysis above suggests.

52 For an analysis of such problems, see [24].

53 This presumes that unions have both the resources and incentive to rework such calculations – neither of which assumption may be true at the moment, but both of which might be affected by actual experience with greater information disclosure.

54 See [24, chs. 3 and 4].

55 See Chapter 5.

56 See, for example, the Pen model (pp. 89–93 above), in which it is necessary to evaluate U_{lc} and U_{mc}, which probably depend in turn on estimating conflict costs in monetary terms.

57 For an illustration of simulation and the combination of probability distributions (although in a capital budgeting context), see [11]. Note that statistical dependence is implied because we are comparing *total* NPVs with and without conflict. We do not

work with *incremental* NPVs because the pattern of labour costs may be different for the 2 situations, even *after* the conflict period.
58 See for example [10].
59 See Chapter 5 for a more detailed discussion.
60 See [16, pp. 30–31].
61 For a fundamental analysis of the concept of auditor independence see [20, ch. 8].
62 For a summary of these, see [16, pp. 81–4].
63 See [16, p. 82].
64 K. Sharp, outgoing president of the Institute of Chartered Accountants in England and Wales, reported in *Accountants Weekly*, 23/30 May 1975, p. 11.
65 See Chapter 3 of *Published Profit Forecasts*, the Accountants International Study Group, 1974.
66 For a discussion of the theoretical constraints on auditing forecast information, see [12].

REFERENCES

1 Accounting Standards Steering Committee, *The Corporate Report* (London: author, 1975).
2 American Accounting Association, *A Statement of Basic Accounting Theory* (Evanston, Ill.: author, 1966).
3 W. N. Atherton, *Theory of Union Bargaining Goals* (Princeton, N.J.: Princeton University Press, 1973).
4 W. H. Beaver, J. W. Kennelly and W. M. Voss, 'Predictive Ability as a Criterion for the Evaluation of Accounting Data', *Accounting Review*, 43 (1968) pp. 675–83.
5 H. Bierman, *Financial Accounting Theory* (New York: Macmillan, 1965).
6 R. Castillo-Enriquez, *A Consideration of 'Predictive Ability' as a Criterion for Selecting Accounting Information in the Light of the Objectives of Accounting Reporting*, unpublished M.A. dissertation, University of Lancaster, 1975.
7 R. K. Chisholm and G. R. Whitaker, *Forecasting Methods* (Homewood, Ill.: Irwin, 1971).
8 Committee on External Reporting, 'An Evaluation of External Reporting Practices: A Report of the 1966–68 Committee on External Reporting', *Supplement to Accounting Review*, 44 (1969) pp. 79–123.
9 E. Dale, 'The Accountant's Part in Labor Relations', in *Handbook of Modern Accounting Theory*, M. Backer, ed. (Englewood Cliffs, N.J.: Prentice-Hall, 1955).
10 J. Dean, 'Methods and Potentialities of Break Even Analysis', reprinted in *Studies in Cost Analysis*, D. Solomons, ed. (London: Sweet and Maxwell, 1968), pp. 195–229.
11 D. B. Hertz, 'Risk Analysis in Capital Investment', *Harvard Business Review*, 42 (1964) pp. 95–106.
12 Y. Ijiri, 'On Budgeting Principles and Budget-Audit Standards', *Accounting Review*, 43 (1968) pp. 662–7.
13 Y. Ijiri, *The Foundations of Accounting Measurement* (Englewood Cliffs, N.J.: Prentice-Hall, 1967).
14 Institute of Chartered Accountants in England and Wales, *Members Handbook* (London: author, updated continuously).
15 Inflation Accounting Committee, *Inflation Accounting* (London: HMSO, 1975).
16 T. A. Lee, *Company Auditing: Concepts and Practices* (Edinburgh: The Accountants Publishing Company, 1972).
17 T. A. Lee, *Income and Value Measurement: Theory and Practice* (London: Nelson, 1974).

18 D. Lyall, 'Opening the Books to the Workers', *Accountancy*, 86 (Jan 1975) pp. 42–4.
19 K. T. Maunders and B. J. Foley, 'Accounting Information, Employees and Collective Bargaining', *Journal of Business Finance and Accounting*, 1 (1974) pp. 109–27.
20 R. K. Mautz and H. A. Sharaf, *The Philosophy of Auditing* (Sarasota, Fla.: American Accounting Association, 1961).
21 J. Pen, trans. by T. S. Preston, *The Wage Rate under Collective Bargaining* (Cambridge, Mass.: Harvard University Press, 1959).
22 L. Revsine, *Replacement Cost Accounting* (Englewood Cliffs, N.J.: Prentice-Hall, 1973).
23 R. R. Sterling, 'A Statement of Basic Accounting Theory: A Review Article', *Journal of Accounting Research*, 5 (1967) pp. 95–112.
24 C. R. Tomkins, *Financial Planning in Divisionalised Companies* (London: Accountancy Age Books, 1973).
25 R. E. Walton and R. B. McKersie, *A Behavioral Theory of Labor Negotiations* (New York: McGraw Hill, 1965).
26 P. J. D. Wiles, *Price Cost and Output*, 2nd ed. (Oxford: Basil Blackwell, 1961).
27 O. E. Williamson, *The Economics of Discretionary Behavior* (Englewood Cliffs, N. J.: Prentice-Hall, 1964).
28 D. J. Zulauf, *Accounting Analysis and the Ability to Pay Wages*, unpublished Ph.D. thesis, University of Minnesota, 1965.

7 Conclusions and Implications for the Future

The disclosure of information in collective bargaining is a subject about which much discussion has been generated at a practical level, especially in relation to proposals for making such disclosure mandatory. Apart from bringing together the strands of these practical arguments this book has included a survey of the theoretical material which the authors feel could serve as a framework for analysis of the issues involved.

We have not attempted to build the fully articulated multi-variable model of decision making in collective bargaining which would be logically necessary for predicting the precise relationship between information inputs and bargaining outcomes in any particular circumstances.[1] To that extent the book does not provide specific guidance for those who have to be decision makers in this field. Nevertheless, by drawing together apparently disparate practical and theoretical arguments we hope at least to have assisted the decision maker to identify the general nature and sources of the relevant costs and benefits of information disclosure. We have left the evaluation of the relative importance of these costs and benefits to the decision maker in the light of his own particular circumstances. Even given the generality of our approach, however, certain fairly specific conclusions have been suggested by the analysis.

Firstly, in the case of an organisation, it has been suggested that information disclosure needs to be evaluated in terms of the *continuing* relationship between management and labour negotiators. Thus, if a piece of information is considered to be relevant by management then it will probably need to be disclosed on a *systematic* basis, since the *ad hoc* production of information only when it is favourable to management is not likely to encourage labour negotiators to treat it seriously.

Secondly, and relating to the first point, it is suggested that such systematic information disclosure should be the subject of a *policy* decision, to be taken at top management level. This is necessary because, as we have seen, the effects of disclosure can only be properly evaluated on an organisation-wide and long term basis. There is a particular danger of sub-optimisation where functional managers are left to take disclosure decisions, since they are, understandably, likely to focus on the short run, tactical effects of providing information. This is not to deny that, in appropriate circumstances, such tactical effects may not be over-ridingly important. But we have argued here that explicit consideration needs to be given to the effects of information disclosure on the organisation's total activities and relationships – and this can only be done adequately at top management level.

Our belief is that, given full consideration of the effects of disclosure, organisations should move voluntarily, as a matter of self interest, towards more 'open' management-labour communication systems. This in itself implies that the interpretation of what is 'good industrial relations practice' may shift over time so as to require increased disclosure from those not already providing it.[2]

Additional reasons for believing that U.K. legislators in particular will require increased disclosure in future are as follows:
(a) by direct analogy with legislative positions elsewhere (*vide* the situation in the U.S.A. – Chapter 1);
(b) by indirect analogy – given the pressures for extending industrial democracy (cf. the position in other E.E.C. countries – Chapter 1 again); and
(c) by extrapolation, on the basis of legislators' apparent commitment to the principle of a more 'open' society, given the nascent state of statutory disclosure in collective bargaining.

We need, perhaps, to elaborate on (c). From the 'right' of the political spectrum, the Conservative Government's White Paper on 'Company Law Reform' of 1973 included the following statement of principle:

Disclosure of information is an essential part of the working of a free and fair economic system. Obviously there are limits – imposed, for example, by the need to preserve commercial confidentiality in a competitive situation. *But the bias must always be towards disclosure, with the burden of proof thrown on those who defend secrecy.* The more people can see what is actually happening, the less likely they are to harbour general suspicions – and the less opportunity there is for concealing improper or even criminal activities. Openness in company affairs is the first principle in securing responsible behaviour [3, p. 7] [Italics added].

Since the White Paper was partly concerned with the accountability of company managements to employees we may assume that this statement is intended to cover disclosure of company information to employees (and, *de facto*, to their negotiating representatives). As such, although it is very carefully qualified, the quotation implies a willingness to *impose* a 'liberal' disclosure policy on companies, if necessary. This is, of course, in line with previously expressed Conservative beliefs in freedom of competition, for which freedom of information can be claimed to be one necessary constituent.

On the left of the political spectrum, on the other hand, there is also a commitment to increased disclosure, although for different ideological reasons. The Conservative White Paper was, in fact, followed by a 'Green Paper' from the Labour Party – 'The Community and the Company: Reform of Company Law', in 1974 [7]. This proposed a considerable extension of disclosure. Whilst it was considered that:

> it is not critical whether [the disclosure requirements] are included in company law or industrial relations legislation . . . it would be sensible to include mainly Control Questions and Financial Details in the former and Manpower, Development and Related Plans in the latter. Some forms of disclosure will be required from the company in its capacity as a corporate organisation; others in its function as an employer. With reference to the latter it is essential that legislation should ensure that disclosure is made through recognised trade union machinery at both plant and higher levels [7, p. 29].

Whether information is to be channelled through employees or goes to trade unions direct, the implication is that future legislation is likely to tend to increase the information available to labour negotiators in the U.K. at least. It therefore seems useful to explore some of the possible implications of an increase in disclosure from the point of view of: (1) government policy, (2) management, (3) unions, (4) the accounting profession and (5) academic accounting.

(1) GOVERNMENT POLICY

From the point of view of current social priorities perhaps the most important issue is whether an increase in disclosure is likely to be inflationary. In Chapter 3 we examined some of the evidence for a relationship between wage or earnings changes and company financial results. The hypothesis that the two are linked appears, on the whole, to be 'not proven'.

Even if the two were found to be statistically dependent to use such evidence to make deductions about the effects of increased disclosure on inflation involves two additional assumptions: (1) that increased *information* on financial results leads to changes in labour payments and (2) that increases in labour payments lead to increases in prices. The second assumption is the familiar 'cost push' thesis and itself is difficult to substantiate. However, the first assumption seems positively 'heroic' if it is supposed to be founded on an analogy with a financial results–change in labour payments relationship. The kinds of financial results which have been linked empirically with wages/earnings change, e.g. profits, profitability, liquidity indicators etc., are already available to labour negotiators, so such relationships cannot, on the face of it, assist in predicting the possible impact of *new* types of information.

There is, in fact, no empirical evidence bearing directly upon the relationship between information inputs and labour costs and prices at a macro-economic level. It is therefore necessary to try to reason deductively from 'micro' to 'macro' levels at the risk of committing some 'fallacy of composition'. Taking the popular practitioner's view, for instance, it is possible to argue that the disclosure of information must be inflationary since it strengthens the 'power' of labour negotiators thus giving an upward bias to wage claims and settlements. Research into negotiating behaviour is ambivalent on this point however, both from theoretical and empirical points of view (see Chapter 4) – it is not clear that a more informed negotiator will necessarily gain disproportionately from the bargaining process. One possible explanation for the ambivalence is that 'factual' information may have no *systematic* effect on either claims or outcomes since such information may cause labour's expectations to be revised *downwards* as well as upwards.

Even if disclosure of information *could* be shown to be inflationary in the short term, the social and private costs might be swamped by longer term benefits associated with an increase in joint problem solving (or industrial democracy).

As a final point, note that the above analysis presupposes that we are talking about a situation in which wages and earnings are set in 'free' collective bargaining. If bargaining outcomes are to be constrained under some form of 'incomes policy', as in the U.K. at present, then it may be possible to obtain some of the potential benefits of increased information without, for the period of the policy at least, too much risk of inflationary results.

(2) MANAGEMENT

The possible effects of increased disclosure on labour's claims and settlements will obviously be of concern to management. As already indicated, even the *directional* effects of new information are not unequivocally predictable according to theory or past evidence.

In any event, it is necessary to stress that it is not information *per se* that will affect negotiators' aspirations and actions but their *interpretations* of that information. Fairly clearly the notion that knowledge of 'the facts' will somehow eliminate conflict is overly simplistic. Two parties could use the same set of data to support totally differing arguments – and this is doubly the case where those data are to be used as a basis for prediction. A more relevant question is, therefore: will increased information reduce the scope for disagreement? One view appears to be – not necessarily. For instance, it has been questioned whether 'the provision of greater quantities of information, whether shared or not, may serve not to diminish but to reveal and emphasise the basic conflicts of interest that are inherent in the collective bargaining situation' [1, p. 10]. This seems, however, to be too pessimistic a view, based on a short run view of industrial relations. It appears to derive from observations of the following kind: 'Indeed we can envisage the circumstances where the provision of yet more information, far from resolving a conflict situation, may even aggravate it. Certainly such information as might reveal, if well analysed, the strike vulnerability of a firm (e.g. the order-book, cash flow, and capacity situation), if disclosed, let alone discussed, could shift bargaining power to an extent that there would no longer be the room for compromise, on which the whole process depends' [1, p. 10].

But this is merely stating that sometimes the effects of information provision may make the outcome worse for management. Even given such a situation, the analysis is not complete. That is, if such information is discovered *after* settlement (and sooner or later such 'facts' seem to get back to union members), then the *perceived* value of the outcome to the labour negotiators will be reduced, resulting in a possible hardening of attitudes in future negotiations.

In any case we have argued that the best way to gain union acceptance of the relevance of certain types of information is to disclose it on a systematic basis. The information referred to above, which was interpreted as favouring the union, could then also presumably be claimed to be relevant when the maintenance of employment is at stake.

The disclosure of information on a systematic basis does of course conflict with its use as an *ad hoc* tactical instrument by management, although fresh interpretations and presentations of information can still be used tactically to support arguments and positions.

What is being given up by a voluntary disclosure policy, therefore, is the possibility of 'concealing' information which might otherwise be considered to be relevant to negotiations. What is gained in return? Possibly:

(a) the more convincing use of 'relevant' information when it is favourable to management;

(b) a reduction in negotiating time and effort spent on issues which might be more easily resolved if the relevant information *was* disclosed; and

(c) a contribution to the establishment of trust in the long run, with the possibility that this will lead to a more positive attitude to joint problem solving activities.

These effects have to be weighed against any adverse shifts in particular bargaining outcomes due to disclosure.

One possible way of obtaining a reduction in bargaining time and effort may be to obtain agreement in advance on what definitions of certain types of information will be accepted as relevant by both parties. Our discussion of 'ability to pay' in Chapter 6 may be of some use in this respect.

With a measure such as ability to pay the important point to realise, however, is that it is not intended to *determine* what the settlement should be, but rather to make possible a more 'rational' framework for arguments about the impact of any particular settlement on the organisation and its employees. In this respect there may be distinct advantages for management, as well as unions, if information relevant to *future* ability to pay is provided. This is because the measurement of future ability to pay, as we have seen, implies that a view needs to be taken of the organisation's minimum financial requirements and their employment consequences. Whether or not management and labour can agree on an appropriate benchmark for these, their very discussion may necessarily involve the union side in explicitly taking a longer term view of factors affecting the organisation's performance.

This is, of course, one possible argument in favour of the type of 'budgetary disclosure' provisions in the U.K. Industry Act [6, sec. 30 (3)(c)]. That information on ability to pay may be seen by the unions to be relevant in such a context is indicated in the suggestion for a draft planning agreement put forward by the A.S.T.M.S., which includes the following sample clause: 'It has been agreed between the relevant trade

unions and the company that employees' remuneration will be negotiated in a free collective bargaining atmosphere but that negotiations
take some account of the Surplus Revenue position of the company'
[2, p. 32].

Of course, it may be counter-argued that the implicit involvement of
unions in organisational planning constitutes a reduction in management's freedom of action. Whether or not *some* reduction in managerial
prerogatives in this direction could be desirable is a moot point.
However, it may be questioned whether there would, in fact, be an
effective reduction. More information being given to the unions may
indeed widen the range of issues which are subject to bargaining, but
once agreement on these issues is reached the result should be a
reduction in one general source of uncertainty, with a consequent
improvement in management's forecasting and planning environment.
Some alternative choices of action may indeed be eliminated but,
equally, others may be added as a result of the stimulation of joint
problem solving activities. Overall, this may imply an extension of the
potentially *effective* scope of managerial decision making and control,
rather than its reduction.

Efficient management in a more 'open' information context may, of
course, require certain organisational adjustments. Where information
is communicated to employees in general, resources may have to be
directed into explaining the meaning of that information. Where
information is provided to labour negotiators at a plant or company
level there may be an effective extension of bargaining since 'issues' may
arise more frequently as a result of the information. The scope for
disputes based on 'red herrings' or misinterpretation of the information
may then need to be contained by providing facilities for more joint
consultation in connection with the information. Insofar as 'real' issues
are highlighted, however, there may be benefits in being able to deal with
them at an earlier stage and lower level than otherwise.

Such points suggest that management may have a primary interest in
communicating information to employees and their plant or company
level representatives. Since bargaining on minimum wage rates usually
takes place between management representatives and the unions at a
higher level, however, there is an argument that an equally free
communication system should operate between management and the
union hierarchy, if only as an instrument for encouraging mutual trust in
such bargaining. A further practical argument for such direct communication is that the union could probably obtain the information
indirectly in any case, and to appear to 'favour' plant or company level

representatives may have particularly adverse effects on union attitudes in the light of their internal political structures.

To summarise, for the 'typical' organisation, the wider provision of information will have certain predictable implications – greater joint consultation is likely to become necessary and 'bargaining' may be of a more continuous nature. In addition, in respect of the content and presentation of information, there will be a greater need for co-operation and mutual education between the industrial relations and information specialists in the organisation.

(3) UNIONS

At first sight the prospect of obtaining more information relevant to bargaining would appear to be 'pure jam' as far as the unions are concerned. In addition, if the process goes so far as to require all potentially relevant information to be disclosed, we have seen in Chapter 6 that organisations may ultimately need to 'open the books'–an outcome much advocated by certain unionists.

In fact certain implications need to be considered before judging a situation of having relatively unrestricted access to organisational information on demand to be one of pure gain for the union. In the first place there will be problems and costs of adjustment: expertise will need to be developed in handling the information. This in turn probably means a need for greater resources in union research and education. The source of the necessary resources is a particular problem for smaller unions. One possible solution would be some form of co-operation between unions in such fields.

Insofar as certain problems, such as education and the collation of information, are common to all unions then there is an obvious argument for centralised services operated, e.g., in the U.K., through the T.U.C. Since union education and, as we have argued, the use of information by unions, may be socially desirable, there is also an argument that such centralised services have a prima facie case for government financial support. In the meantime, however, whilst some unions are proceeding with educational programmes and the development of research facilities to deal with increased information there are clearly going to be cases in which management offers to 'open the books' are not taken up with alacrity.

One reason for this, apart from a lack of the requisite skills, may be a suspicion that such offers are only made in order to demonstrate 'inability to pay'. Whilst this may often have been true in the past, unions may gather from this book that managements should in the future, out of self interest, begin to provide information on a systematic basis whether or not it favours their own case. The lesson is clear – the results of an investigation could now strengthen *either* the unions' *or* the managements' case.

A further reason for reluctance to take up offers of information may be a feeling that to get involved in financial arguments would essentially mean a step towards accepting management's views on the objectives of the organisation. That is, unionists may feel that there is a danger of being 'conditioned' by information. Whilst it is undeniable that the purpose of providing information is to change attitudes and beliefs, it is also true that 'facts' can serve more than one objective. The same set of data could often be interpreted in totally different ways by people with different aims. Thus, to resist the offer of information which *could* be turned to one's own advantage smacks of 'don't confuse me with the facts – my mind's already made up'. It is true, of course, that some minimum sophistication in the use of information is necessary to check the validity of arguments and the possibility of alternative in-terpretations, but such skills develop partly out of experience.

In relation to information of the 'labour force' type, which is often most obviously relevant to bargaining issues, initial problems are likely to be of the 'information overload' type, and negotiators' education may thus need to take the form of providing 'data handling' skills, e.g. training in the use of averages and other descriptive statistics. Organis-ational financial information, on the other hand, is already likely to be in summary form and skills may need to be built up both in interpreting and reconstructing it. In the short term, however, where financial information is felt to be critically relevant, it may be necessary to obtain the assistance of independent accountants to deal with it.

Research staff, as well as negotiators, will probably need to be trained in the use of financial information. Whilst some union research departments already collect such information to provide services to negotiators, there may be an obvious advantage if some form of common 'data bank' on companies can be built up on which small as well as large unions can draw.

A particular problem exists at present with respect to obtaining information on multi-national companies' operations. Some improve-ment in this respect may come about as a result of changes in company law, but as far as overseas operations are concerned some form of international information sharing scheme amongst unions might have to be the answer.[3]

One further potential problem with respect to information provision is its possible effects on the structure of unions. In writing about the effects on management it was pointed out that management may have a primary interest in providing information directly to employees or plant or company level representatives. As also pointed out this may tend to increase the number of issues which are raised, and perhaps settled, at such levels. To some extent this may bring about a downwards shift in decision making, and perhaps power, within unions. Whether this is good or bad in itself is a moot point but it points up the need for a greater educational effort with respect to shop stewards, both as regards information usage and general bargaining skills.

When non-confidential information is provided at a plant or company level it is important that it is available for use by negotiators elsewhere for comparative purposes. Whilst information sharing at shop-steward level may be valuable it is likely to be carried out on an *ad hoc* basis. Thus, unions also need to make provision for such information to be collected centrally in order that case histories can be built up and systematic sources of comparative data established. In some cases in the past there has been difficulty in obtaining information from shop stewards for what has been perceived as union hierarchical purposes. The education programme for shop stewards already underway in many unions may help to resolve this difficulty. It may be the case, however, that some unions will need to give more recognition to the importance of shop stewards and their needs. In this way it can then be demonstrated that useful information can only be provided downwards by headquarters if it is fed upwards to them in the first place.

(4) THE ACCOUNTING PROFESSION

Much of what has been said above carries implications for accountants. Fairly clearly, as specialists in the measurement and communication of economic information, any potential expansion in information disclosure creates opportunities, as well as challenges, for professional accountants.

In relation to unions it has been made clear above that increased educational and research facilities will be needed to deal with the increased information. Accountants may be involved in both of these fields, as educators and by being directly employed in research on behalf of unions. In cases where summarised information is provided, there may also be a need for an independent accountant to 'audit' the information if it is to be rendered credible for bargaining purposes. [4] Problems related to the perceived independence of accountants for these purposes were discussed in Chapter 6.

On the management side of negotiations also, there is likely to be a need for advice from accountants, both inside and outside the organisation, on questions related to the content and effective presentation of information in an industrial relations context.

Overall, then, it is relatively easy to predict an increase in the opportunities for accountants to become involved in the field of industrial relations. Whether these opportunities are taken up depends, *inter alia*, on the willingness of accountants to adapt their skills to the needs of a novel set of information users. The revolution in accounting thought in recent years should have made it plain to all that it is accounting which must adapt to new users rather than the reverse. It is to be hoped that this book will help accountants to identify some of the directions in which adaptation may be necessary.

(5) ACADEMIC ACCOUNTING

As has been made plain in the introduction to the book and this chapter we do not claim to have made any kind of an analytical break-through herein. Instead, what we hope to have achieved is a kind of 'ground clearing' operation which may benefit future researchers in the field (including ourselves).

Many of the problems which such researchers will have to face have been well documented in relation to other user groups. One measure of this book's usefulness may therefore be the degree to which we have succeeded in pointing out that there are research-worthy problems which are peculiar to the collective bargaining context.

What remains to be done, if detailed, would read like a complete statement of the necessary methodology in a new field of research.

NOTES

1 For a taste of the difficulties involved in constructing and using such a model, see [5]. A further complication in the case of collective bargaining is that it is a dynamic *interdependent* decision making process.

2 This is deducible from the wording of the Employment Protection Act – [4, sec. 17 (1) (b)].

3 The need for information on multi-nationals now seems to have been recognised as an international union problem – for instance the International Confederation of Free Trade Unions at its 11th World Congress in Mexico recently agreed on an international disclosure charter for multi-national companies (see 'World Workers Have Another Try at Uniting' – *Sunday Times*, 19th Oct, 1975).

4 In a recent survey of U.K. trade unionists' views it was found that 'There was an overwhelming feeling that company financial information should be certified by an auditor before being issued' and 'Some 85 per cent of the respondents felt that the professional accountant would be acceptable [as auditor], provided he was appointed by the trade union' [8, p. 15].

REFERENCES

1 D. Alexander, 'The Information Explosion and Collective Bargaining', *Industrial Relations Review and Report*, no. 9 (June 1971) pp. 5–10.

2 Association of Scientific Technical and Managerial Staffs, *The Crisis in British Economic Planning and a Draft Planning Agreement: A Discussion Paper from ASTMS* (London: author, 1975).

3 Department of Trade and Industry, *Company Law Reform* (London: HMSO, 1973).

4 Employment Protection Act 1975 (London: HMSO, 1975).

5 G. A. Feltham, *Information Evaluation*, Studies in Accounting Research no. 5 (Sarasota, Fla: American Accounting Association, 1972).

6 Industry Act 1975 (London: HMSO, 1975).

7 Labour Party, *The Community and the Company: Reform of Company Law* (London: author, 1974).

8 D. Lyall and R. Perks, 'How to Present Financial Information to Employees', *Accountants Weekly* (16 Jan 1976) pp. 15–16.

Index